THE CHALLENGE OF DIVERSITY

Walter Johnson

BLACK
ROSE
BOOKS

Montreal/New York/London

Black Rose Books No. II339

National Library of Canada Cataloguing in Publication Data

The challenge of diversity / Walter Johnson. Johnson, Walter, 1947-

Includes bibliographical references and index.

ISBN: 1-55164-273-5 (bound)   ISBN: 1-55164-272-7 (pbk.)

(alternative ISBNs 9781551642734 [bound]   9781551642727 [pbk.])

1. Canada--Ethnic relations. 2. Canada--Race relations. 3. United States-- Ethnic relations. 4. United States--Race relations. 5. Multiculturalism-- Canada. 6. Multiculturalism--United States. I. Title.

E49.J63 2005   305.8'00971   C2005-902390-2

Statistics Canada information is used with the permission of the Minister of Industry, as Minister responsible for Statistics Canada. Information on the availability of the wide range of data from Statistics Canada can be obtained from Statistics Canada's Regional Offices, its World Wide Web site at http://www.statcan.ca, and its toll-free number 1-800-263-1136.

Statistics for Chapter 5, with permission from the *Toronto Star*.

Pages 256 and 257 constitute an extension of this copyright page.

Cover design: Associés libres

BLACK ROSE BOOKS

C.P. 1258	2250 Military Road	99 Wallis Road
Succ. Place du Parc	Tonawanda, NY	London, E9 5LN
Montréal, H2X 4A7	14150	England
Canada	USA	UK

To order books:

In Canada: (phone) 1-800-565-9523 (fax) 1-800-221-9985
email: utpbooks@utpress.utoronto.ca

In United States: (phone) 1-800-283-3572 (fax) 1-651-917-6406

In the UK & Europe: (phone) 44 (0)20 8986-4854 (fax) 44 (0)20 8533-5821
email: order@centralbooks.com

Our Web Site address: http://www.web.net/blackrosebooks

A publication of the Institute of Policy Alternatives of Montréal (IPAM)

Printed in Canada

The Canada Council | Le Conseil des Arts
for the Arts | du Canada

THE CHALLENGE OF DIVERSITY

CONTENTS

ILLUSTRATIONS

This book is dedicated to the memory of *Our Generation* editors
C. George Benello
Abe Limonchik
Dan Daniels
Bert Young
and the artist/teacher Clifton Ruggles

All were deeply committed to the task of
intercultural bridge building
and the cause of social justice.

PREFACE

Discriminatory practices and legislation were socially sanctioned and entrenched in the legal system in Canada at the beginning of the 20th Century. In the intervening period, the country has experienced a human rights revolution with a dramatic improvement in the level of tolerance and understanding and a much broader recognition of the rights of other people, the benefits of diversity, and the need to recognize and even compensate for past injustices. These changes took place because of the dedication and social activism of countless number of courageous individuals and groups who challenged the established norms of society. Legislation such as the *Charter of Rights and Freedoms* is really only the "icing on the cake" for the efforts of such people. Chapter One of the book documents the extent to which inequality for women, religious and ethnic minorities, and recently arrived immigrants was a fact of life in Canada for much of the 20th Century.

Chapter Two outlines the physical and cognitive differences that exist among human populations and the attempts to explain these differences over time. At the beginning of the 20th century the explanations offered were essentially pseudo-scientific rationalizations for widespread social and ethnic inequality. The intervening years have seen a dramatic shift in emphasis from the differences that exist among human populations to the essential similarities. In the scientific field, for example, the work of the human genome project has served to undermine many biologically based explanations for inequality and reinforced the importance of social and cultural factors in explaining the differences that do exist. Chapter Two also contains some of the most recent census data on emerging demographic trends in Canada and the United States.

Chapter Three, Four and Five of the text deal with some of the challenges posed by the increasing ethnocultural diversity of Canadian society through an examination of immigration history, the current debate over immigration policy, and the "hot button" issues of multiculturalism, racism, employment equity legislation, and racial profiling. Opposing viewpoints on many of these issues are presented as a way of encouraging critical thinking. Chapter Five includes an in-depth analysis of the controversial *Toronto Star* series on racial profiling and the ensuing debate.

Chapter Six deals with the growing religious and cultural diversity in Canada and how it is related to changes in immigration and refugee policies. Key components of the four fastest growing religious affiliations in Canada are reviewed. Underlying tensions between the cultural traditions of long-established residents and newcomers are examined through recent debates and controversies over the wearing of Hijabs (head scarves) by Muslim women in schools, the possession of Kirpans (ceremonial daggers) by orthodox Sikhs, and changes to police uniform requirements which permit the wearing of turbans. Other more intractable challenges posed by such cultural practices as female circumcision are also discussed in the context of Canada's constitutional commitment to multiculturalism.

Within some communities the tension between religious tradition and the secular nature of Canadian society has manifested itself in increasing generational conflict, the rise of street gangs, and controversies over the changing role of women. This chapter also describes some of the major issues that have arisen in the past decade as many cultural communities attempt to cope with these challenges.

Heightened public security concerns in the wake of the terror attacks on the World Trade Center on September 11, 2001 have focused intense scrutiny on immigrants and refugees from countries torn by religious and ethnic divisions. This chapter concludes by outlining the historical roots of some of these conflicts and how the turmoil in their countries of origin continues to plague many new immigrants once they have arrived in Canada.

Chapter Seven documents the effects of government policy on aboriginal populations since the birth of Canada. The evolution of policy, which lurched from initial cooperation and partnership to paternalism and attempted assimilation, and eventually to the idea of cultural autonomy, is examined critically with an emphasis on the *Indian Act* and its consequences. A variety of viewpoints are presented on current controversies over aboriginal self-government, land claims, the legacy of residential schools, the role of aboriginal women, and differential treatment of aboriginal offenders in the criminal justice system. New data on comparable health indicators and some of the most recent Canadian census information on the aboriginal population are included in this chapter.

Chapter Eight reviews recent data from Corrections Canada and the United States Department of Justice to illustrate how social and ethnic inequality affects the likelihood of being incarcerated in the two countries. While the rate of prison construction in the United States has steadily increased over the past twenty years, Canadians have been moving towards the idea that alternatives to imprisonment may be more effective in reducing the likelihood of recidivism and actually preventing crime in the first place.

Chapter Nine describes how French-speaking Quebecois, a linguistic minority on the North American continent, struggled to maintain their language and culture in the face of overwhelming pressures to assimilate from the dominant English speaking majority. The strategies used to achieve this goal are evaluated critically and related to the ongoing constitutional debates that have dominated the political agenda in Canada for the past forty years. The chapter concludes with some of the most recent census data on language trends both in Quebec and the rest of Canada.

Chapter Ten outlines the dimensions of economic inequality in Canada and the criteria by which inequality is measured. The most recent census data is used to assess the relative social mobility of identifiable groups in Canada such as the young, recently arrived immigrants, the aboriginal population, and people of colour. The role of education in promoting social mobility is examined critically. Controversies over the measurement of unemployment, the definition of poverty, and the efficacy of programs designed to reduce inequality, are presented and evaluated. Opposing viewpoints on such issues as the relative merits of social programs, "family values" and the proper role of government are broadly outlined as a way of illustrating the nature and content of many public policy debates in Canada.

Walter Johnson

ACKNOWLEDGEMENTS

In acknowledging those who made this book possible, first and foremost are Lucia Kowaluk and Dimitri Roussopoulos, two colleagues and friends from the *Our Generation* editorial board, who have been unfailing in their support and encouragement of my work for over thirty years. Many thanks also to the talented Linda Barton, Black Rose Books Managing Editor, who adroitly and expeditiously supervised the production of this book for publication.

Although I take complete responsibility for the contents of this book, there are a number of people I would like to thank for their valuable insights and suggestions. I am indebted to colleagues and friends in the Department of Anthropology and Sociology at John Abbott College who give true meaning to the idea of academic collegiality. They are Sharon Rozen-Aspler (Chairperson), Katherine Allen, Jose Benmoyal, Richard Element, Richard Gilbert, Wendy Hadd, Edwin Holland, Marcia Kovitz, Jacque Lavoie (retired), Raymond Lieu, Roger Maclean, John Pestana, Steve Soroka, Margaret Waller, and our late, much beloved colleague and friend, the incomparable Bert Young.

A special thanks to Stephane Blackman, a former student and now Sergeant with the Deux Montagnes Regional Police Force, who, for many years, has demonstrated his commitment to public service, and community-based policing, by sharing his experiences as a police officer with my students.

Others who have provided inspiration, encouragement, or assistance at different stages of the project include Marjorie Hambides Stubbs (John Abbott Nursing), Dr. Duncan G. Sinclair, Francoise Dykler, Jessica Mosher and Patti Altridge.

To the thousands of students who have taken my courses over the past twenty years in Humanities, Social Science, Police Technology, Nursing, Dental Hygiene, Correctional Intervention, and Documentation Technology, I wish to acknowledge my gratitude for the privilege of both teaching them and learning from them.

Finally, to my partner Donna Johnson and our family, Kelly Johnson, Ryan Johnson, Edmund Idziak, and Eliane Rouben, my heartfelt thanks for their patience and encouragement while I was working on this book.

Chapter One
THE HUMAN RIGHTS REVOLUTION IN CANADA

Over the past one hundred years Canada has experienced nothing less than a human rights revolution. At the beginning of the 20th Century women and visible minorities still did not yet have the right to vote, marriage between blacks and whites was taboo, and homosexuality was illegal. The aboriginal population was marginalized and believed to be a culture in decline. Restrictive covenants prevented the sale of land or rental of apartments to "non-gentiles" and other minority groups. Immigration from non-European areas of the world was actively discouraged except in cases where the demands of the labour market left no other option.

The Canadian population was predominantly white, French or English speaking and of European origin. In keeping with the social Darwinist ethos of this era (see Chapter Two: Perspectives on Human Diversity), non-European immigrants and people of colour were viewed as "inferior races" that would "corrupt the morals" and undermine the standard of living of the white, Canadian-born population. Popular protest against the presence of Chinese immigrants, many who had been brought over to help complete the construction of the Canadian Pacific Railway, led to the creation of laws restricting Asian immigration.

In 1885, under the *Chinese Immigration Act*, the first head tax of $50 was imposed on any Chinese person wishing to immigrate to Canada. The tax was increased to $100 in 1900 and $500 by 1903. By a federal Order in Council, all Asian immigrants had to be in possession of $200 in order to get into Canada in 1908. In that same year, Chinese, Japanese, and other Asian or Indian persons were denied the right to vote in any municipal election in the province of British Columbia. The following year the province of Saskatchewan denied Chinese-Canadians the right to vote in provincial elections. Being denied the right to vote also automatically excluded the targeted groups from holding a liquor license, practicing law or becoming pharmacists.

In 1910, under the *Immigration Act (S.C 1910 c.27, s.38)*, the Governor in Council required that all Indian immigrants to Canada come by "continuous journey from a through ticket purchased in that country or prepared in Canada." The effect of the legislation was to prevent immigrants from India coming to Canada because there was no way that such immigrants could make the journey without stopping in a third country.

At the beginning of World War I, in 1914, the Supreme Court of Canada upheld a Saskatchewan law that prohibited Chinese businesses from hiring white women (*Quong-Wing v. R—1914*). In that same year the province of Ontario passed the *Act to Amend Factories, Shops and Office Buildings (S.O 1914, c.40)*, which prohibited "Oriental" persons from employing white females. The anti-Asian sentiment reached its zenith in 1923 when the *Chinese Immigration Act (S.C. 1923 c.38 S.5*—sometimes referred to as the Chinese Exclusion Act), made it impossible for Chinese people to immigrate to Canada unless they were students coming to Canada to study at university, or Chinese children born in Canada who were returning to Canada.

As late as 1938 the *Dominion Elections Act* prevented Canadians of Japanese, Chinese, or Indian (from India) origin from voting in federal elections because they were not permitted to vote in provincial elections. The only exceptions were military veterans who had served in the Great War of 1914-1918 (*Dominion Elections Act S.C. 1938, c.46-s. 14(2) (i)—*).

No Room At The Inn

Unlike the United States and South Africa there were no laws specifically targeting the black population in Canada. However, the prevailing prejudices of the time were reflected in the routine denial of access to services and accommodations that whites took for granted. For example, on January 26, 1918, a black man bought a ticket for an orchestra seat at Lowe's Theatre in Montreal, Quebec. When he tried to take his seat the ushers in the theatre told him that "coloured" people weren't allowed to sit in the "orchestra" section. He was then directed to the "mezzanine" area, which permitted the presence of "Negroes." The man objected to this discrimination and decided to take his case to court. The Quebec Court of Appeals ruled that the theatre had the right to establish the "seating rules" even if they were discriminatory (*Lowe's Montreal Theatre Ltd. V Reynolds [1919] 30 Que. C.B.R. 459*).

On July 20, 1923, a black man entered a restaurant in London, Ontario and was immediately confronted by the owner who told him that "coloured" people were not welcome in the establishment. The man decided to sue the restaurant in the belief that every Canadian citizen had the right to be served regardless of skin colour. The case went to court in 1924 and the judge decided that the restaurant owner had the right to refuse a customer, even if the refusal was racially motivated, because there were no laws that prevented him from doing so (*Franklin v. Evans [1924], 55O.L.R. 349*).

On July 11, 1936, a black man and a few of his friends wanted to have a few drinks at the Montreal Forum tavern (one-time home to the Montreal Canadian's hockey dynasty). He was informed by one of the waiters that the "house rules" did not permit serving a "Negro." The man sued the tavern for $200 in damages and was awarded $25 in damages by the judge who first heard the case on the grounds that "no licensee for a restaurant may refuse without reasonable cause, to give food to travelers" (*s.33, Quebec License Act*). However, on appeal, a higher court overturned the decision on the grounds that as a private business the proprietors of the tavern could do what they wanted in order to protect their commercial interests. The case went all the way to the Supreme Court of Canada, which ruled that the general principle of the law in Quebec was complete freedom of business. As long as a merchant did not break the law, he or she was free to refuse any member of the public on any grounds (*Christie v. York [1940] S.C. R. 139*). The Supreme Court went one step further in this case. In the decision it added that businesses could set rules unless they violated laws or ran "contrary to good morals or public order." In the mindset of the Supreme Court justices of that era they did not deem the Montreal Forum's "no service to coloureds" house rule to be "contrary to good morals or public order."

As late as 1940, a black man in British Columbia was informed that he was no longer welcome at his favourite bar in a Vancouver hotel because the new owner did not want to serve "Negroes." The man took the hotel owner to court claiming discrimination because the previous owner had never barred him from the premises. Once again a lower court ruling in favour of the plaintiff was overturned by a higher court on the grounds that the owner's right to refuse service took precedence over the individual's right to fair and equitable treatment (*Rogers v. Clarence Hotel Co. [1940] 3 D.L.R. 583 (B.C.C.A)*.

Grandmother Was Not A Person

By 1900 women had won the right to vote in municipal elections in the provinces of New Brunswick, Nova Scotia, Ontario, and Prince Edward Island but were still not allowed to exercise this right in federal or provincial elections. In many provinces they could not make legal contracts or go into business for themselves. When they married they lost their right to hold property and any assets they might have were automatically assumed to be the property of their husbands. Divorce laws were highly restrictive and punitive.

Women won the right to vote in federal elections in 1920 but as late as 1928 there was a debate in Canada as to whether or not a woman was a "qualified person." The debate arose over whether or not a woman could be appointed to the Canadian Senate. Many legal scholars at the time believed that the constitution—*the British North America Act (BNA)*—implied that women were not "qualified persons," and therefore could not run for or hold public office. Nellie McClung, and four other famous Canadian suffragettes, petitioned the Canadian government to ask the Supreme Court of Canada to determine if women were to be considered as "qualified persons." The government eventually brought the case before the five male justices of the Supreme Court. They decided unanimously that a review of the relevant legislation (written in the social context of 1867 when women did not hold public office) indicated that women were not to be considered as "qualified persons" (*Edwards v AG for Canada [The "Persons" Case] [1928] S.C.R. 276*).

An appeal was launched and one year later the British Privy Council overturned the decision of the Supreme Court of Canada and allowed women to be appointed to the Canadian senate (*Edwards v. AG for Canada [The Persons" Case] [1930] A.C. 124*). The decision represented a recognition that the interpretation of laws and legislation, particularly legislation passed in an earlier era, had to take into consideration the evolving social context, in this case the belated acknowledgement that women too were "persons" deserving of the same rights and opportunities as other "persons" known as men.

Human Rights In The Post-War Era

The end of World War II marked a dramatic leap forward in the human rights revolution in Canada. By 1948, Canadians of Asian origin were finally granted the right to vote (*S.14 [2] [1] of The Dominion Elections Act S.C. 1948 c.46*). Aboriginal Canadians could vote in provincial elections but would wait for another twelve years for the right to vote in federal elections. Most provinces had passed *Married Women's Property Acts* that granted married women the same legal capacity as men when it came to the ownership of property and assets after marriage. (An important laggard in this regard was the province of Quebec where legal and property rights were not fully accorded to women until 1964, although they still had to wait until 1971 for the right to serve on a jury.) Women had won the right to vote in federal elections in 1920 but had to wait to1940 for the same right in Quebec provincial elections (*An Act Granting to Women the Right to Vote to be Eligible as Candidates, S.Q 1940, c.7*).

In 1944, Ontario enacted the *Racial Discrimination Act*. The Act prohibited the publication or display, on lands, premises, by newspaper or radio, of any notice, sign, symbol, or other representation indicating racial discrimination. The Act was used a year later to challenge a deed that prohibited selling land to Jews, Orientals, and Blacks. However, the Supreme Court upheld the right of the land-owner to discriminate because putting a restriction in the deed and then register-ing it in the Registry Office did not qualify as "publishing" according to the terms of the *Racial Discrimination Act (McDougall and Waddell [1945] 2 D.LR.244*).

The technicality that permitted this type of discrimination to continue did not sit well with either the judges in this case or, increasingly, with a more sensi-tized general public as the horrors associated with the conflict in Europe became more apparent. Later the same year, a restrictive covenant restraining the sale of land to Jews was struck down as contrary to public policy and contrary to pre-vailing opinion (*Re Drummond Wren [1945] O.R.778*). In many provinces, restric-tive covenants that had prevented the sale of land or rental of apartments to minority groups were challenged in the courts and prohibited. By 1950, both Ontario and Manitoba would amend their laws to prohibit restrictive covenants based on colour, race and creed.

Employment Practices And Social Programs

In 1945 the province of British Columbia prohibited discrimination based on col-our, creed, race or political affiliation in the administration of its social assistance programs (*B.C Social Assistance Act S.B.C. 1945, c.62, s.8*). A decade earlier, during the Great Depression, the province, in order to get federal support for unemploy-ment relief money, made it illegal to refuse to employ someone because of their race, political or religious view (*Unemployment Relief Act S.B. C. 1932, c.58*). One year later it amended the *Unemployment Relief Act* further to prevent discrimina-tion on the basis of political affiliation, race or religious belief when allocating farmland (*S.B.C. 1933, c.71*).

In 1947, the provincial government of Saskatchewan, under the leadership of Premier Tommy Douglas, introduced the landmark *Saskatchewan Bill of Rights*, Canada's first general law prohibiting discrimination with respect to ac-commodation, employment, occupation, education, skin colour, religion or eth-nic and national origins. In the same year Saskatchewan pioneered the first publicly funded hospital insurance program in North America. It provided access to hospital care for the entire population, rich or poor, without direct out of pocket payment for services rendered.

Throughout the 1950s discriminatory employment barriers and practices were reduced because of the enactment of fair employment and fair employment practices legislation. The groundbreaking legislation that set the pattern for many other provinces was the *Ontario Fair Employment Practices Act (1951 [S.]. 1951, c.24)*, which established employee complaint procedures and fines for employers in non-compliance with the law. In the same year the Ontario legislature also brought in the *Female Employee's Fair Remuneration Act*, which attempted to reduce the income disparities between males and females doing the same type of jobs. The federal government enacted its own *Fair Employment Practices Act* two years later in 1953 to deal with discrimination in the civil service. Within the decade most other Canadian provinces enacted similar legislation. Ontario also pioneered the *Fair Accommodation Practices Act* in 1954, which declared that "no one can deny to any person or class of persons the accommodation, services, or facilities usually available to members of the public." As a general principle, in its provincial *Bill of Rights* in 1947, Saskatchewan had already prohibited discrimination with respect to accommodation.

The Universal Declaration Of Human Rights

The human rights revolution gained momentum worldwide in the wake of the atrocities and violations of human dignity that had occurred before and during World War II. Something had to be done to prevent the deliberate attempts by governments to exterminate entire population groups such as had occurred in Nazi Germany. At the newly formed United Nations on December 10, 1948, representatives from around the world unanimously passed *Resolution 217 A (111)*, the *Universal Declaration of Human Rights (UDHR)*. It marked the first comprehensive agreement among the nations of the world as to the specific rights and freedoms of all human beings. It was a document that was later to serve as a model for Canada's own *Charter of Rights and Freedoms*. A Canadian, John Humphrey, was instrumental in creating the original draft of the UDHR.

According to the *Universal Declaration of Human Rights* "everyone is entitled to fundamental rights, without regard to distinction of any kind, such as race, colour, sex, language, religion, political or other opinion, national or social origin, property, birth, or other status" (*Article 1*).

In principle, the UDHR guarantees such rights as equality before the law and equal protection of the law, without discrimination, freedom of opinion and expression, and the freedom of peaceful assembly and association.

The *Canadian Bill Of Rights*

By the late 1950s Canada was poised for its next significant step towards the advancement of human rights. In the immediate post-war era many Canadians were still fearful that the economy might sink back into the type of depression that had plagued the 1930s. As these fears abated and the economy experienced sustained growth, issues of equality and social justice moved to the top of the national agenda.

In 1957, the Liberal government under Prime Minister Louis St. Laurent was defeated at the polls and replaced by the Progressive Conservative Party led by John George Diefenbaker. Diefenbaker, known affectionately by his supporters as "Dief the Chief," was a strong-willed, charismatic man with a finely honed sense of social justice. He had made his reputation in western Canada as a populist and crusading lawyer who often took on unpopular cases and won. Diefenbaker was determined that Canada should have a bill of rights that would be a practical application of the United Nations *Universal Declaration of Human Rights.* The problem was that such a bill, to be effective, would require amending the *British North America Act (BNA)* of 1967, which was, in essence, the Canadian Constitution at that time. Attempts to reach an agreement among the provinces posed enormous problems because under the *BNA* there were clear divisions of power and responsibility between federal and provincial jurisdictions. Faced with seemingly insurmountable hurdles related to issues of language, religion, property rights and the interpretation of laws, Diefenbaker became frustrated by jurisdictional squabbles and unilaterally pushed through the *Canadian Bill of Rights* on July 1, 1960.

The *Canadian Bill of Rights* outlined the following human rights and fundamental freedoms, namely (a) "the right of the individual to life, liberty, security of the person and enjoyment of property, and the right not to be deprived thereof except by due process of law (b) the right of the individual to equality before the law and the protection of the law (c) freedom of religion (d) freedom of speech (e) freedom of assembly and association (f) freedom of the press." These rights were to apply "without discrimination by reason of race, national origin, colour, religion or sex" (*Article 1, Canadian Bill of Rights*).

The *Bill of Rights* was an important milestone but its effect was limited by the fact that it applied only to rights that already existed and could only be applied to federal laws. The consent of the provinces had not been obtained to extend its jurisdiction, which would have required an amendment to the *BNA*. Another 22 years would pass before the rights and freedoms contained in the *Bill of Rights* would be enshrined in the Canadian Constitution.

John Diefenbaker was also the first Prime Minister to appoint a female, Ellen Fairclough, to a cabinet position in federal government. As Minister of Immigration, Fairclough amended the Immigration Act regulations in 1962 to effectively remove barriers to immigration based on ethnicity or country of origin, thus ending the de facto "colour bar" that had existed in immigration policy since 1910.

Human Rights Codes

The 1960s were marked by the development of provincial human rights codes. As with the fair employment practices legislation, Ontario pioneered the first comprehensive human rights code in Canada in 1962. It prohibited discrimination on the basis of skin colour, creed, nationality, ancestry or place of origin. However, unlike previous legislation such as the *Bill of Rights*, the *Saskatchewan Bill of Rights*, or the United Nations *Universal Declaration of Human Rights*, the *Ontario Human Rights Code* established an independent *Human Rights Commission* with the power to ensure actual compliance with the law through a variety of penalties and sanctions for violators. By 1970 eight other provinces (Nova Scotia, Alberta, New Brunswick, Prince Edward Island, Newfoundland, British Columbia, and Manitoba) had enacted similar legislation.

The Quebec Difference

Quebec in the 1960s was undergoing a profound social and political metamorphosis (see Chapter Nine). A strong movement for political independence from the rest of Canada had arisen in the wake of the "Quiet Revolution" (an attempt to modernize Quebec's social and economic structure in the early 1960s). The goal was to advance the economic interests of Quebec while also protecting the continued existence of a distinct French language and culture. This meant the creation of laws and regulations that reflected the unique Quebec reality. In this context, the Liberal government of Robert Bourassa, introduced and passed the Quebec *Charter of Human Rights and Freedoms* in 1975. Like the *Canadian Bill of Rights* or the *Saskatchewan Bill of Rights* before it, the new legislation outlined the political rights and freedoms to which all citizens were entitled but added anti-discrimination and equal pay provisions that had been incorporated in other provincial human rights codes.

The *Canadian Human Rights Act*

In 1977, the federal government passed the *Canadian Human Rights Act* after which discrimination based on "race, national or ethnic origin, colour, religion, age, sex, marital status, disability or conviction for an offence for which a pardon has been granted" was prohibited. The Act was amended in 1996 to include a prohibition on discrimination based on "sexual orientation." This change came about as the result of an incident involving an officer in the Canadian Armed Forces. Because he had revealed his homosexuality his superiors told him that he would longer be eligible for career advancement.

Since the *Canadian Human Rights Act* contained no explicit reference to protection from discrimination based on "sexual orientation," the officer took his case to the courts. He argued that the Armed Forces were violating the equality rights guaranteed to Canadians under *Section 15 (1)* of the *Canadian Charter of Rights and Freedoms*. Although *Section 15 (1)* makes no specific reference to "sexual orientation," the Courts agreed that discrimination could occur on this basis and amended the existing legislation.

Like the provincial human rights codes that preceded it, the *Canadian Human Rights Act* outlined an extensive range of prohibited discriminatory practices related to employment, the provision of goods, services, facilities and accommodation, and forms of hate speech. It also resulted in the establishment of a *Human Rights Commission* with the power to investigate any complaints received as well as the right to initiate complaints against violators of the Act.

The Canadian *Charter Of Rights And Freedoms*

Perhaps the most important milestone in the human rights revolution in Canada was the passing of the Canadian *Charter of Rights and Freedoms* in 1982. The driving force behind its implementation was a man with a passionate commitment both to social justice and individual rights, Pierre Elliot Trudeau. Trudeau had spent a good part of his youth fighting against the authoritarian government of Premier Maurice Duplessis in the province of Quebec. Duplessis had used the power of the state to suppress freedom of expression and other basic civil liberties for workers, trade unions, socialists, political opponents, and religious groups like the Jehovah's Witnesses. As a witness to these abuses of power Trudeau developed a strong belief in the need for a *Charter* to protect citizens from discriminatory laws and violations of human rights and freedoms.

The problem with the old *Bill of Rights*, pioneered by John Diefenbaker, was that it had no constitutional force and only applied to federal legislation. Trudeau knew that if the new legislation was to be effective, it had to be entrenched in the Canadian Constitution, thereby applying to both the federal government and the provinces. In other words, the Supreme Law of the country. As part of the Canadian Constitution the new *Charter* would protect the fundamental rights of individuals, regardless of skin colour, national origins, religious or political beliefs, and which no government, federal or provincial, could arbitrarily eliminate. Under the *Charter*, the type of discriminatory laws, regulations, and practices that targeted particular religious and ethnic groups at the beginning of the 20th Century would not occur.

However, Trudeau did not stop there. In addition to the basic human rights such as freedom of belief and expression, freedom of association, legal rights, mobility rights, and equality rights, Trudeau wanted to incorporate language rights, which guaranteed the recognition of two official languages in Canada, French and English, and the right to learn and use either of the two official languages.

As a result of intense lobbying by women's groups, Aboriginals, cultural communities, and the disabled, the *Charter of Rights and Freedoms* would also include a provision that would ensure that all rights in the *Charter* are guaranteed equally to both sexes (*Section 28*), a recognition and affirmation of the rights of Aboriginal peoples (*Section 35*), and a provision that encourages the maintenance and enhancement of Canada's multicultural heritage (*Section 27*).

The Effects Of The *Charter Of Rights And Freedoms*

One of the major effects of the entrenchment of the *Charter of Rights and Freedoms* in the Canadian Constitution was an increase in what is sometimes described as "judicial activism," meaning that the courts were to play a bigger role in shaping social and public policy. When people, individuals or groups, feel that their *Charter* rights have been violated, they can now challenge the government in courts. However, *Section 1* of the *Charter* "guarantees the rights and freedoms set out in it subject only to such *reasonable limits prescribed by law as can be demonstrably justified in a free and democratic society*" (italics mine). This means that governments can defend their actions, even a violation of the *Charter* guarantees, under certain conditions. It is therefore left to the Courts to decide if the government has committed a justifiable or unjustifiable *Charter* violation. The Courts also have the power to strike down a law, and "read down" or "read in" changes to make a law comply with the *Charter*.

Judicial Activism

The newfound power of the courts found expression in a series of judgments throughout the 1980s and 1990s. For example, in 1987, a women's right's group in Quebec complained to the *Human Rights Commission* that Canadian National Railway (CNR) had violated a section, (*s.10*), of the *Canadian Human Rights Act* by making no attempts to recruit women for technical jobs or manual labour jobs in the CNR yards. A human rights tribunal agreed that the company had done little to encourage female employment and ordered it to establish an employment equity program. The company refused and took the case to the Supreme Court of Canada, which upheld the decision of the human rights tribunal to impose an employment equity program as a necessary step if discriminatory hiring and promotion practices were to be overcome.

Sexual Harassment And Sexual Orientation

In 1989 the Supreme Court of Canada decided that "sexual harassment" was a form of sex discrimination in a case that involved a restaurant where female waitresses were continually subjected to verbal abuse and unwanted, inappropriate physical touching by a fellow male employee. When they complained to the owner of the restaurant they were fired. The women filed a complaint with the *Manitoba Human Rights Commission* and the case eventually ended up in the Supreme Court. The Court decided that sexual harassment was a form of "sex" discrimination because only the women at the restaurant were subjected to this type of unwanted attention. In keeping with the equality provision of *Section 15 (1)* of the *Charter*, the Court decided that the women were being treated differently than men only because they were women and that constituted a form of discrimination (*Janzen v Platy Enterprises [1989] 1S.C. R.1252*).

Three years later the Supreme Court ruled that, although not explicitly defined as a prohibited ground for discrimination under *Section 15 (1)* of the *Charter*, discrimination on the basis of sexual orientation was a violation of the *Charter of Rights and Freedoms* in the case of an army officer (previously mentioned) who was considered ineligible for career advancement because of his public revelation that he was homosexual (*Haig v. Canada [1991]. 86 D.L.R. 617, Ont. C.A*).

The prohibition of discrimination based on sexual orientation was reinforced by a Supreme Court judgement in the case of two women who had lived together for a long period of time and then separated. One of the women had depended on the other for financial support. When they broke up the financially dependent partner made a claim for support from her former partner under a section (*s29*) of the *Ontario Family Law Act*. She was refused on the grounds that her "spouse" had to be a member of the opposite sex. When the case went to the Courts both the Ontario Court of Appeal and the Supreme Court of Canada judged that the woman's application for "spousal support" was justified because *section 29* of the *Family Law Act* violated the equality provision, *Section 15 (1)*, of the *Charter of Rights and Freedoms* by discriminating against a group (homosexuals) on the basis of their sexual orientation *(M. v. H [1996] 31 O.R. [3d] 417)*. After this decision the wording of the Ontario *Family Law Act* was changed so that the term "spouse" could refer to same-sex partners.

In 1994, a soldier was discharged from the Canadian Armed Forces when it was discovered he was both homosexual and HIV (Human Immuno-deficiency Virus) positive. At the time of his discharge the soldier felt healthy and had no difficulty carrying out his duties. He appealed the army's decision claiming discrimination. The Federal Court of Canada agreed that discrimination against a person just because they are HIV positive should not be permitted *(Thwaites v. Canada [Armed Forces] [1994] F.C.38)*.

Applications Of The *Charter*
Since the implementation of the *Charter of Rights and Freedoms* in 1982 a variety of individuals and groups have used its provisions to challenge age discrimination in the workplace and mandatory retirement requirements, restrictions on religious freedom, the right of union's to use member's dues for political purposes, the lack of penitentiary inmates right to vote, the right of Canada's government to allow cruise missile testing in Canadian airspace, the language of signs in Quebec, the funding of religious schools, the language of schools, the right of Quebec to separate, the right of tobacco companies to advertise, the regulations of the *Indian Act*, the regulations of the federal *Immigration Act*, the right to an abortion, and a host of other issues. Increasingly, the resolution of the controversies surrounding the aforementioned issues, and others like them, are determined by the Courts rather than through the political process and representative institutions like the Canadian Parliament. This has led to criticism of the effects of the *Charter* on aspects of Canadian democracy.

The *Charter* And Its Critics
Calgary constitutional law professor Ted Morton decries what he calls the "Court Party," a "coalition of interest groups that regularly appear in our courtrooms using *Charter* litigation to pursue policy demands that elected governments rejected." According to Morton, they include "feminists, civil libertarians, gay rights activists, aboriginals, francophones outside of Quebec, anglophones

inside Quebec, environmentalists, immigration advocacy groups, prisoners' rights groups, visible minorities, and so on" (*Toronto Star*, April 16, 2002).

Morton's views are echoed by many on the right-wing of the political spectrum who are alarmed by what they perceive as the growing influence of "special interest" groups on the legal system. In their view the *Charter* has served to promote "group rights" over the "rights of the individual."

However, critics on the political Left, such as Osgoode Hall law professor Michael Mandel, argue that the *Charter* "has weighed in on the side of power and in both crude and subtle ways has undermined popular movements as varied as the anti-nuclear movements, the labour movement, the nationalist movement in Quebec, the aboriginal people's movement, and the women's movement" (*Toronto Star*, April 16, 2002).

In Mandel's view, the transfer of power from elected officials to unelected judges has had the effect of reinforcing the status quo and existing economic power and, in important ways, has made the existing inequalities in Canadian society worse. According to Mandel, "we have more people behind bars now than we did in 1981, even though violent crime has gone down. In terms of freedom and equality, we were better off before the *Charter*."

Supreme Court Justice Beverly McLachlin sees the role of the Courts in interpreting the provisions of the *Charter* as a balancing act; a role that was clearly indicated at the outset in *Section 1* of the document whereby the rights and freedoms outlined can be curtailed by *"reasonable limits."* According to McLachlin, "this puts the balancing of the collective interests versus individual rights at the center of every issue. I don't think you can avoid making those kinds of balancing policy decisions anytime you have rights entrenched in a constitution. The United States has an absolutist kind of 'congress shall make no law' approach, absolute terms. But nevertheless the courts have had to find a balance of collective interests because absolute freedom of expression, for example, is simply not possible in a democracy. Our *Section one* means that we bring that kind of balancing out into the opening and we acknowledge it, which I think is a very good approach" (*Toronto Star*, April 16, 2002). This, in McLachlin's view, leaves the judges with no other option but to assume the responsibility of reviewing policy, regardless of the concerns of the critics.

Freedom Of Expression And Religion And The Origins Of The *Charter*

The *Canadian Charter of Rights and Freedoms* owes its existence, in no small measure, to several cases involving freedom of expression and religion in the 1940s in the province of Quebec.

In 1937, the *Union Nationale* Party ruled Quebec. It was a conservative political party that depended upon strong support from the tradition-minded Roman Catholic Church and the business community. In keeping with the views of his core constituency, the leader of the party, and Premier, Maurice Duplessis, held very negative opinions about the influence of such groups as the Communists, anarchists, trade unionists, and certain religious groups like the Jehovah's Witnesses. In an attempt to counter their influence the Duplessis government passed a piece of legislation that became known as the "Padlock Law" (*The Act Respecting Communist Propaganda—consolidated as R.S.Q. 1941 c.52*).

The law gave the government the power to close down any house or establishment for a year which "printed, published or distributed any newspaper, periodical, pamphlet, circular, document or writing, propagating Communism or Bolshevism." Although the legislation did not specifically target Jehovah's Witnesses, the discretion granted the Attorney General of Quebec enabled him to use it to cast a broad net and harass not only Communists but also any groups in disagreement with Duplessis or his government.

The Jehovah's Witnesses, in particular, represented a problem for the government. They had made it a practice to attack the Roman Catholic Church in a very intemperate and offensive manner. When World War II broke out in 1939, Witnesses refused to serve in the military believing that all participants in the war were "Satan's Instruments." In July of1940, under pressure from the Roman Catholic Church hierarchy, the Quebec Justice Minister, Ernest Lapointe, was persuaded to ban the Jehovah's Witnesses, as an illegal organization (the ban was repealed in 1943). Throughout the war, Witnesses were harassed and even imprisoned for their refusal to serve in the forces or support the war effort. In spite of the legislation and the repressive tactics of the Duplessis government, their numbers actually grew from about 3000 before the war to 10-15,000 by the end of the conflict six years later.

The hostility of the provincial government towards the Witnesses continued in the post-war era as the proselytizing efforts of the group intensified. One incident involved a farmer, and Jehovah's Witness, named Aime Boucher who was convicted of the crime of *"seditious libel"* (conduct or speech inciting rebellion against the authority of the state) for circulating a religious tract alleging that many of his fellow Witnesses had been harassed, mistreated and wrongly imprisoned by the Quebec government because of their faith. Boucher was found guilty of the charge by a trial jury in Quebec, a decision later upheld by the Appeal Court of the Queen's Bench. However, when the case reached the Supreme Court of Canada in 1950, a majority of the Justices decided that Boucher had simply circulated his pamphlet to criticize the actions of the Quebec government and the Courts and did not intend to incite violence or rebellion against the state. Put simply, it was a legitimate exercise of the freedom of expression to protest against the Quebec government's mistreatment of a religious minority.

Two years later, another Jehovah's Witness, Laurier Saumur, was arrested for distributing leaflets protesting the government's treatment of Jehovah's Witnesses in Quebec City. Quebec did have a statute protecting free speech but the Jehovah's Witnesses were not a popular group. In the pamphlets circulated by Saumur, Roman Catholicism, as a religion, was attacked and denounced. Most Quebec residents at the time were devoutly Roman Catholic and deeply resented the type of religious proselytizing associated with the Witnesses. In addition, Premier Duplessis had made opposition to this religion a personal crusade.

A municipal bylaw (*Bylaw 184*) prohibited the distribution of "any book, pamphlet, booklet, circular, or tract without having previously obtained a written permission from the Chief of Police," in Quebec City. According to the authorities, the purpose of such a bylaw was to manage the streets and maintain public order. Saumur had tried to obtain permission to circulate his pamphlets but was refused and decided to engage in an act of *civil disobedience*. When the case eventually reached the Supreme Court of Canada, important constitutional issues, as well as the right to freedom of religious expression, were raised. For example, under the *British North America Act* (*BNA*), civil rights, including religious freedom, were thought to be under provincial jurisdiction. The Justices ruled by a close 5–4 margin that the purpose of *Bylaw 184* had nothing to do with the maintenance of public order but was designed instead to censor religious expression. The majority also disagreed that religious freedom was a civil right under provincial jurisdiction. The dissenting Justices defended the right of Quebec City to pass such a bylaw, interpreted the *BNA* as supporting the provincial jurisdiction in these matters, and maintained that the right of freedom of religious expression was not absolute.

Duplessis Versus Roncarelli

The final and most important case also involved Jehovah's Witnesses and had a profound effect not only in extending the freedom of expression but also in its influence on the constitutional vision of a future Prime Minister of Canada, Pierre Elliot Trudeau.

The case involved Frank Roncarelli, a Montreal restaurant owner and Jehovah's Witness, who posted security bonds (based on the value of his property) as bail for his fellow Witnesses when they were jailed for distributing religious pamphlets. Given the prevailing political atmosphere at the time the local authorities deeply resented Roncarelli's ability to help his beleaguered co-religionists. In an effort to prevent bail from being granted to jailed Witnesses, they insisted that Roncarelli provide cash instead of security bonds, which made it virtually impossible to continue with his activities. Shortly thereafter, Roncarelli's license to sell liquor at the restaurant his family had owned and operated for many years was revoked, for no apparent reason, eventually forcing Roncarelli out of business. Roncarelli realized his license had been revoked because of the financial support he had provided his fellow Witnesses. He filed a civil action against Maurice Duplessis demanding damages for the loss of his business.

At the first trial, evidence presented indicated that Montreal's Chief Prosecutor, who was overwhelmed by cases involving Jehovah's Witnesses, had complained to the Chairmen of the provincial Liquor Licensing Board. The Chairman took the complaints to the Attorney General and premier Duplessis, who advised him to revoke Roncarelli's license. The purpose was to discourage anyone who had the temerity to support the activities of the Witnesses.

Roncarelli won the case and was awarded $8,123.53 in damages. However, the Quebec Court of Appeal later overturned the judgement on the grounds that the liquor license had been revoked before the Chairman of the Liquor Board had consulted with Duplessis.

The case ended up in the Supreme Court of Canada in 1959, twelve years after the initial trial. A majority of the Justices decided Roncarelli's license had been revoked because of his support of the Witnesses. In their view, this represented an abuse of power by the premier, Maurice Duplessis. They ordered him to pay Roncarelli $33,123.53 in damages. Although Roncarelli never again re-opened his restaurant this ruling represented a final body blow to the repressive Duplessis regime.

The "Padlock Law" Struck Down

Two years earlier, in 1957, the notorious "Padlock Law" had been struck down on the grounds that it was beyond the province's jurisdiction and limited the right to free expression. The Quebec provincial courts had sided with the Duplessis government but when the case eventually reached the Supreme Court of Canada eight of nine justices decided that the law did, indeed, go beyond the province's jurisdiction by interfering with the *Criminal Code of Canada*, a federal responsibility.

The judges also determined that the law had the effect of limiting freedom of expression. According to Justice Ivan Rand, "the object of the legislation here (the Padlock Law) as expressed by the title, is admittedly to prevent the propagation of communism and bolshevism, but it could just as properly have been the suppression of any other political, economic or social doctrine or theory" (*Switzman v. Elbing [1957] S.C. R. 285*).

The Supreme Court decisions concerning the "Padlock Law" and Roncarelli extended and refined the principle of freedom of expression in Canadian society. Both cases highlighted the absence of constitutional guarantees of civil liberties. Only a constitutional bill of rights would apply to both federal and provincial levels of government and ensure that such discriminatory legislation, and the type of legislation targeting minorities at the beginning of the Twentieth Century, could not be enacted. The *Canadian Charter of Rights and Freedoms* was created to achieve this end.

In both the case of Roncarelli and the "Padlock Law" the lawyer who had upheld the human rights of the individual against the state was Frank R. Scott. Scott was a McGill University constitutional law professor, poet and social activist. He had been one of the authors of the "Regina Manifesto," the founding document of the Cooperative Commonwealth Federation (CCF), the forerunner of the contemporary New Democratic Party (NDP). Scott had a profound influence on the constitutional thinking of a young law student, Pierre Elliot Trudeau. Trudeau had heard Scott speak at the University of Montreal in 1943 and was impressed by his commitment to the principles of individual rights and social justice. The expression "Just Society," which has come to be associated with the Trudeau era, was taken from an essay published by Scott in1939. Scott's later victories in getting the "Padlock Law" struck down, and in the Roncarelli decision, greatly reinforced Trudeau's belief in the need for a *Charter* to protect citizens from the unfettered power of the state.

On April 16, 1982, the day before the signing of the new Canadian Constitution with the *Charter of Rights and Freedoms*, Prime Minister Trudeau introduced Frank Scott to the Queen by saying, "Madame, if we have a *Charter of Rights* in this country, we owe it to this one man. Canada owes a lot to him and I, for one, am in his debt" (*Toronto Star*, April 13, 2002).

Chapter Two
PERSPECTIVES ON HUMAN DIVERSITY

Discussions about "race" are often highly charged emotionally because there is little common agreement about the exact meaning of the term. For most people the idea of "race" refers mainly to perceived differences in skin colour, the shape of faces, and hair texture. However, these are very superficial observable characteristics that represent only a small proportion of the enormous range of biological variations that exist within human populations. Despite this fact, attempts have been made to use these superficial differences as the basis for classifying the human species into distinct categories called "races." One of the first attempts was by a Swedish naturalist, Carl von Linne, better known as Linnaeus, who published a book in 1734 called *Systema Naturae*. In it, he created four geographic racial subdivisions: black Africans, white Europeans, yellow Asians, and red Americans. Not surprisingly, these divisions now represent the popular understanding of race based on observable characteristics.

Linnaeus did not attempt to rank any group as higher or lower than another but he did assign character traits that were alleged to be associated with each race. Later in the 19th century, some "social scientists" argued that white-skinned people belonged to a distinct race labeled "caucasoid," dark skinned people belonged to a distinct race labeled "negroid" and yellow skinned people belonged to a distinct race labeled "mongoloid." Some even argued that these "races" represented a series of evolutionary stages, with particular races judged as "more advanced" than others in terms of intelligence and behavioural characteristics. This type of thinking led to a kind of '"biological determinism" whereby unfair and sometimes destructive generalizations about people are made based on their alleged genetic make-up. At its extreme this resulted in "*racism*," the idea that races differ in the possession of certain important abilities and social traits, and thus justifies the ranking of people as inferior or superior with some entitled to special rights and privileges that are denied to others. Slavery in the United States and the Apartheid system in South Africa are examples of how this type of thinking played out in society.

Biology And Ideology

At the beginning of the 20th century the idea that certain abilities and social traits were associated with specific groups and could be passed on genetically resulted in a popular pseudo-science known as *eugenics*, which aimed to improve the human species by "selective breeding" or controlled reproduction to eliminate traits that were deemed to be undesirable. Many countries, including Canada, introduced eugenic measures such as forced sterilization of unwed mothers, habitual criminals, the mentally handicapped, and the children of "racially mixed" parents, to prevent "the degeneration of the race."

In Sweden, between 1935 and 1976, some 60,000 people were sterilized, including the children of racially mixed parents, and people with "Gypsy features." The policy was also extended to include unwed mothers with large numbers of children. The Danes had eugenics laws in force from 1929-1967. The idea was popular in the United States as well where 22 states had laws providing for the sterilization of the "unfit" by 1918. At least 60,000 Americans were sterilized against their will between the early 1900s and the 1970s for official reasons ranging from mental handicap to promiscuity. Survivors of the experience who recently sought compensation in states like North Carolina say they faced a host of complications, from physical and emotional problems to public stigma and discrimination (*Newsweek*, June 2, 2003, p.12).

Eugenics Popularity Across The Political Spectrum

Eugenics was popular right across the political spectrum. It was introduced in Sweden by Social Democrats who also pioneered the idea of the "Welfare State." In Great Britain, leading socialists such as Sidney and Beatrice Webb, and the famous playwright, George Bernard Shaw, were all proponents of eugenics as a necessary step in attaining "human perfectibility," along with scientific planning and government intervention in the economics sphere. At its worst, eugenics led to the genocidal, race based policies of Adolf Hitler, who used this theory to justify the elimination of Gypsies and Jews in Germany. He believed in the idea that there had once been a "pure" German race known as the "Aryans," which over the years had been "contaminated" by "race mixing." Under Hitler's 1933 eugenics law thousands of men, women, and children were also forcibly sterilized or killed if they were physically deformed, or suffered from schizo-phrenia, epilepsy, Huntingdon's disease, blindness or deafness.

Origins Of Eugenicist Thinking

Although the worst excesses of eugenics are associated with Hitler, the theory was deeply rooted in Western society. It did not originate in Germany but in the Britain of the 1880s, advocated by Francis Galton, a cousin of Charles Darwin and a lead-ing member of the scientific establishment of the time. Galton believed that society was being weakened by the failure of natural selection to weed out its unfit and inferior members. For "social progress" to occur, it was necessary to purge "unde-sirable genes," which could only be accomplished by restricting the poor, the men-tally ill, immigrants, and non-whites from propagating (Shipman, Pat [1994] *The Evolution of Racism: Human Differences and the Use and Abuse of Science*, New York, Simon and Shuster, p.21).

Galton's solution was government regulation of such things as marriage and family size. His ideas were popular among the upper classes where concerns about immigration and widespread criminality were essentially a rhetorical cover for unspoken fears about the threat of an increasingly restive and assertive working class.

Eugenics In The Modern Era

Eugenicist thinking survived the Hitler period and continued to have vocal sup-porters after World War II. William Shockley, a Stanford University professor, and the co-inventor of the transistor, wanted to pay people with "below normal intelligence" not to have children. The co-discoverer of DNA (deoxyribonucleic acid), Francis Crick, wanted to put chemicals in drinking water to sterilize the entire population, and then provide an antidote to a selected number of people who were "eugenically desirable." Eugenicist policies are now rarely articulated explicitly but still find resonance in debates over birth control and pre-natal ge-netic testing. India experimented with compulsory sterilization in the late 1970s focusing on "backward elements" in the society. After a public uproar, the state resorted to using money and consumer goods as a way of bribing poor men to get vasectomies. Coercive sterilization was also a component of the original "one child policy" in China.

In the United States, sterilization is much more common as a form of birth control for poor black and aboriginal women than it is for white women. Because early advocates of birth control, such as Margaret Sanger in the United States, and Marie Stopes in Great Britain, were prominently associated with the eugenics movement of their era, some activists in minority communities view the motivations of population control advocates with suspicion, warning of a "hidden agenda" of "black genocide."

The Sickle Cell Testing Controversy

In the early 1970s the federal government in the United States funded a screening program for sickle cell anemia, an inherited blood disorder that is found primarily in people of equatorial African origin but also, less commonly, among people of Mediterranean origin. In sickle cell anemia, the red blood cells are abnormal, resulting in a chronic, very severe form of anemia (reduced oxygen carrying capacity of the blood). Victims suffer fatigue, headaches, shortness of breath upon exertion, and susceptibility to a variety of potentially life threatening infections. Until about 30 years ago, it usually proved fatal in childhood but improving treatment methods have enabled sufferers to survive into adulthood.

At first the genetic testing program proved popular because carriers of the defective sickle cell gene could be easily identified from just one drop of blood through an inexpensive test. Some church ministers conducted tests on their congregations and even the militant Black Panthers became involved offering the tests door to door in the black communities. However, because of a lack of education about the meaning of the tests many healthy "carriers" of the defective gene were led to believe they were sick. This lack of understanding was not confined to the recipients of the test. In the early 1970s a screening program in the State of Massachusetts required, by law, that African-American children at risk for the "diseases" of "sickle cell anemia" and "sickle cell trait" be tested before entering school. The children carrying a single defective gene associated with the sickle cell trait were thought to be "diseased" even though there was no outward manifestation of the disease. This was based upon a misunderstanding about the nature of the disease (a sickle cell carrier—with one normal and one abnormal gene—will be healthy. But if someone with the gene marries another carrier, their offspring will have a one in four chance of inheriting two defective copies of the same gene and being born with sickle cell anemia).

Even though the mass testing started out with the best of intentions, it ended up doing more harm than good by becoming a vehicle for the expression of long-standing prejudices. "Ignorance about the nature of the disease led to insurance companies denying black carriers (of the "trait") coverage on the grounds that they had a "pre-existing medical condition" or that their children were bad "risks." The U.S Air Force Academy rejected black applicants who were carriers. Some commercial airlines refused to hire carriers as flight attendants because of the erroneous belief that such individuals were particularly likely to faint at high altitudes" (*Scientific American*, June, 1994, p.92).

Adding fuel to the fire was a solution proposed on network television by some prominent scientists that blacks carrying the defective gene forgo having children so they wouldn't pass it on to future generations (1 out of every 12 African-Americans is a carrier of this defective gene, which provides a survival advantage against falciparum malaria in equatorial Africa). Many in the black community saw it as a eugenicist attempt to limit the growth of the African-American population. As a consequence of this experience, many American blacks now prefer not to be screened for the sickle cell trait, fearing that they may be labeled as "diseased" and thereby denied employment or insurance coverage.

Social Darwinism

Eugenics flourished at the beginning of the 20th century, which was the heyday of "*laissez-faire capitalism*," an economic arrangement based on the idea that governments should not intervene in the workings of the marketplace through excessive rules, regulations and legislation. Public policy was, therefore, dominated by an individualistic, "survival of the fittest" mentality that has often been described as *social Darwinism*. It was associated with a self-taught philosopher, and editor of *The Economist* magazine in London, England, named Herbert Spencer. This "philosophy" or, more correctly, ideology justified the inequalities that existed between the rich and the poor, and between peoples of different colour, by arguing that the differences were the result of evolutionary processes. It was believed, for example, that the rich were rich because they were smarter, stronger, or more cunning than the poor, and therefore were better adapted to succeed whereas the poor lacked these attributes and were therefore "unfit." Anything done to help these "unfit" poor people would weaken or undermine the ability of the species to survive, hence "*survival of the fittest*." The same rationale was used to avoid doing anything about inequalities between the "races" or ethnic groups. Theoretically, these ideas attempted to apply the ideas of the British naturalist Charles Darwin (*The Origin of Species*—a book first published in

1859) on species differentiation to explain the social differences that existed in society. This misrepresentation of Darwin's ideas on "natural selection" permitted the rich to ignore the plight of the poor, recently arrived immigrants, and people of darker colour, and enjoy their own affluence and high social standing without a guilty conscience.

Problems With The Concept Of "Race"

People use the term "race" as if it meant something clear-cut and specific. The idea is that there is such a thing as a "pure black" or "pure white" race which once existed separately from the other. But researchers now believe that "pure races" never existed. Humans have always migrated and interbred with new groups (sometimes referred to as *miscegenation*). Because of this fact, racial characteristics, to the extent to which they exist, occur in gradations, from one population to another, without clear defining boundaries. For example, if you were to walk from Europe to Africa, where would you put the line that separates the "Caucasian race" from the "Negroid race?" The lines that do exist are a consequence of historical and political factors.

Furthermore, the current available research suggests strongly that the human species has a common origin in Africa. One recent confirmation of this was a study published in the Proceedings of the National Academy of Sciences in the U.S which showed that the population of modern China owes its genetic origins to Africa, undercutting a long held belief that modern humans may have originated independently in China (*Montreal Gazette*, Saturday, October 10, 1998).

The science of genetics offers no clear-cut differences between the "races." Racial differences are superficial rather than fundamental according to the findings of the Human Genome Project completed in April 2003. According to J. Craig Venter, one of the key researchers on the project, "at the genetic level, we are all virtual genetic twins. Race is a social concept, not a scientific one" (*New York Times*, August 22, 2000).

A 1972 Harvard University study examined 17 genetic markers in 168 separate populations. It concluded there were more *differences within one race than between one and another* (Lewontin, Richard, [1972] "The Apportionment of Human Diversity," *Evolutionary Biology* #6, p.381-398). For example, if you consider a particular feature deemed to be associated with one race such as skin colour, nose shape, hair texture, bone size, body hair, etc., you soon find that a person of one "race" can be more like a person of another "race" than their own.

In the case of skin colour, millions of people on the Indian sub-continent, classified by some anthropologists as members of the "Caucasoid" or "white" race,
have darker skin than most "black" Americans. Similarly, many "Negroid" or
"black" people living in sub-Saharan Africa have skin no darker than many people from the Mediterranean such as the Greeks, Italians, or Spaniards. Hair texture is another supposedly defining feature associated with skin colour. The
aborigines of Australia are often confused with sub-Saharan black Africans but
their hair colour is often long, wavy and blond as children. The same problems
arise if you try to classify people into a "race" by height. For example, within a
few hundred miles of each other in Africa are two tribes, the Mbuti pygmies of
the Democratic Republic of the Congo, the world's shortest people with an average height of 4 foot 1 inch, and the Tutsi of Rwanda, the world's tallest people
with an average height of 6 foot 1 inch. Each of these groups is closer in size to
other ethnic groups thousands of miles away. The ethnic group that comes closest to the Tutsi would be the very light-skinned Scandinavian peoples who also
happen to be very tall. Both Kenyans and the Congolese would be classified as being of the "Negroid" race but they have completely different body types, the
Kenyans being tall and thin whereas the Congolese are stocky and well muscled.

Blood Groups
But the variation within groups is greater than merely superficial characteristics
such as skin colour and nose shape. Among the human species there are four
major blood types: A, B, O and AB. if you are a Type O, your blood is more
closely related to that of any other Type O person—*regardless of race*—than it is
to a Type B or Type A of your own "race." This fact often comes as a shock to
many racists who need an emergency blood transfusion and the only available
donor is a person of a different skin colour. The same is true for organ trans-
plants where the closest genetic match for a donated kidney might be a person of
another "race." While in skin colour Europeans and Chinese are closer to each
other than either is to Africans, the distribution of blood groups indicate that Europeans and Africans are closer to each other than either is to the Chinese.

Blood groups were once thought to be clear genetic markers that could be
associated with particular races. Some population groups do share almost 100%
prevalence of a blood type. For example, the Indian population of Peru is virtually 100% Type O. Roughly 79% of the aboriginal population of North America
is Type A. Asiatic populations are characterized by a greater frequency of Type A

and B. Type B is more commonly found in western Africa and in Northern India. Approximately 49% of the black population of the United States is Type O compared to 45% of the white population (www.aboblood.com). A high prevalence of a particular blood type reflects the degree to which a particular population marries and reproduces within the group over an extended period of time. The distribution of blood types becomes more uniform as population groups intermingle. The idea that particular blood types were unique to "pure races" was popular with some racists until it was discovered that our closest living relatives, the chimpanzees, have the same blood groups as humans!

Population Variations

The problem associated with "race" classification can be illustrated by the example of earwax, which comes in two kinds. One is wet and sticky, and the other is dry and crumbly. Africans and Europeans have the same kind—wet and sticky—while Asians tend to have the dry and crumbly kind. If our intent is to divide the human species into categories called "races" it is just as reasonable, and a lot less provocative, to do it on the basis of earwax rather than on more visible characteristics like skin colour. We could do the same thing with body odour, which varies depending upon the number of apocrine (sweat) glands in the human body. Some Asian populations have virtually no apocrine glands whereas European and African populations have many. The point is that people ignore all the unseen genetic variability that doesn't fit the visible pattern of skin colour, nose shape and hair texture to erroneously conclude that a biological category called "race" exists. The variations in genetic makeup that account for racial differences only make up about 0.01% of our genes. The differences that exist are trivial in the biological sense as illustrated by the fact that all peoples of the human species can intermarry and have healthy children. The categories of "race" exist mainly as a consequence of a misunderstanding about how human beings evolved or to justify certain forms of social differentiation.

According to Dr. Douglas C. Wallace, a professor of molecular genetics at Emory School of Medicine in Atlanta, Georgia, "the criteria that people use for race are based entirely on external features that we (humans) are programmed to recognize. And the reason we're programmed to recognize them is that it's vitally important to our species that each of us be able to distinguish one individual from the next. Our whole social structure is based on visual clues, and we've been programmed to recognize them, and to recognize individuals. Unfortunately for social harmony, the human brain is exquisitely attuned to differencing in packaging details, prompting people to exaggerate the significance of what has come to be called race" (*New York Times*, August 22, 2000).

Biological Explanations That Account For Variation In Human Populations

The differences that exist among distinct groups of people are mainly a consequence of three factors known as *natural selection, sexual selection*, and *reproductive isolation*, concepts associated with the British naturalist Charles Darwin and his discoveries about evolution first published in 1859.

Natural selection can be understood simply by comparing two birds, one red and one green, living in a green forest and threatened by the same predator. The green bird is more likely to survive and pass on its genes because its colour makes it harder for the predator to detect. The same principle applies to humans. Features that enable people to live longer, and most important for evolution, have more children, are the most likely to be passed on. Eventually, those who possess such features will outnumber those who don't. For example, darker skin in sunny climates provides some protection from sunburn and skin cancer. However, in northern climates, there is less sunshine and darker skin might not be as useful since it makes it harder for the body to absorb adequate amounts of vitamin D from the sun, leading to a disease called rickets (poorly developed bones). In this case, lighter skin would provide a survival advantage, particularly if rickets deformed the pelvic bones of darker skinned women making it more difficult for them to have children. Eventually natural selection would favour lighter skinned people in northern climates.

The shorter arms, legs and torsos of some arctic peoples may also be an adaptation to reduce heat loss in cold climates whereas the longer, lankier bodies of some African populations may provide a survival advantage in the tropics to avoid overheating. Similarly, people in colder climates tend to have longer, beak-shaped noses in comparison to the broader nostrils of people living in the hot, humid tropics. In theory, this trait might provide a greater survival advantage by allowing more time to warm and humidify the cold air before reaching the temperature sensitive lung tissue. Characteristics such as skin colour, hair form, eyes, and bone traits tend to coincide with climatic zones suggesting that variations in human populations are often adaptations to environmental forces. For example, darker skinned peoples tend to have more pigmentation in the iris of the eye whereas lighter skinned people have less. The less pigmented the iris the more sensitive it is to colours at the red end of the colour spectrum, which might enable someone with such a feature to see better in situations illuminated with reddish light. Cold northern climates required people to live in caves illuminated by firelight. Longer twilights also favoured people with better night vision. Over time the sensitivity of the eye to various wavelengths of light might encourage such an adaptation to enhance the chances of survival.

Sexual Selection

Sexual selection is different in that it is not an environmental advantage that causes certain genes to be passed on but the choices of prospective mates. For example, if the beauty standard of a society stresses large lips, the people possessing that desired trait are more likely to attract partners, have children, and pass on the genetic trait responsible for large lips to succeeding generations. The physical traits that are deemed desirable vary considerably from one culture to the next thereby accounting for the distinctive features associated with particular human groups.

A focus on large-breasted women created a multi-million dollar empire for the founder of Playboy magazine in North America. However, large breasts are not a universal beauty standard and in some cultures are considered to be dysfunctional. Even in North America, the ideal body type has evolved for both women and men over the years. Female models and film stars are now thinner and more athletic, and the males are leaner but more muscled, than their counterparts of forty years ago.

Reproductive Isolation

Reproductive isolation refers to the fact that through migration human populations become isolated from others for long periods of time. During that period genetic mutations may occur in one group that do not occur in another group. As long as the two isolated groups don't interbreed, a particular trait can become associated exclusively with one group such as blood type, or a particular genetic defect. This also helps account for such things as different languages. Although reproductive isolation is essential to produce the differences that exist among human populations, the evidence suggests that no group of humans has stayed isolated for more than a few thousand years. Cross-mingling of populations may, in fact, be beneficial in the sense than too much inbreeding could lead to the proliferation of undesirable traits. The fact that few populations have a 100% prevalence of any particular trait (blood type, etc.) suggests that genetic blending has always been a part of human history. Therefore, it is questionable to seize on a few traits and claim they define a distinct biological category.

Environmental Suppressors

Some differences among human populations can be explained by factors such as diet, geographical location, climate, pre-natal exposure to viruses, drugs or toxins, child-rearing practices, and cultural norms regarding family size. For example, Asian populations, on average, are shorter than European or African populations. Many people automatically assume that there is a genetic basis for this difference. However, children and grandchildren of Asian parents, who were born and raised in North America, are often significantly taller than their parents or Asian born relatives. Since it is impossible for genetic change to occur that quickly, some other factors must account for this dramatic change in height within one generation. In this case, low protein diets may have suppressed the developmental potential (sometimes referred to as *genotype*) of large groups of people in the same geographical areas.

Disease And Population Groups

The fact that certain diseases and medical conditions are often disproportionately associated with particular ethnic groups causes discomfort and concern among people who fear that these differences will be exploited for nefarious social or political purposes. While these fears can be legitimate (see the case study on mass screening for sickle cell anemia), the explanations for the differences that exist are the same as for any other patterned biological variations in the human species, no more and no less. They are heredity, environment, dietary practices, cultural factors, and prolonged periods of reproductive isolation. For example, children around the world are born with the ability to digest milk because their bodies produce lactase, an enzyme that helps to metabolize (break down) lactose (milk sugar) and allow it to be safely absorbed by the body. However, about 80 to 90% of the Asian, African, and the North American Indian populations lose this ability when they reach adulthood and can become very sick after consuming milk products. About 90% of Europeans continue to produce the lactase enzyme into adulthood and therefore have no trouble digesting milk.

Many other conditions and diseases are found among particular populations. They can be broken down into two categories; purely genetic diseases, which people develop if they inherit certain genes, or susceptibility diseases, which occur because of dietary or lifestyle choices.

Tay Sachs disease, an inherited neurological disorder that usually kills its victims in the first few years of life, is almost entirely confined to the Askenazic Jewish population, whose origins are in eastern or central Europe. About one in 25 white Americans carries the gene for cystic fibrosis (CF), a disease which results in a thick, sticky mucus in the lungs that can cause death by age thirty because of severe respiratory infections. Like sickle cell anemia, a CF carrier—with one normal and one abnormal gene—will be healthy. However, if someone with the gene has children with another carrier, their offspring will have a one-in-four chance of inheriting two defective copies of the gene and being born with CF.

Roughly 10% of the population of lowland Greece is affected by a condition called Favism, a disorder characterized by an extreme sensitivity to the broad bean fava. If an affected person eats these beans, a chemical in the bean causes rapid destruction of his or her red blood cells, leading to a severe form of anemia. It is caused by an inherited defect in a chemical pathway within a person's red blood cells that helps to protect the cells from injury. Thalassemia, another inherited blood disorder, is most prevalent in Mediterranean countries (Italy, Greece), the Middle East, and Southeast Asia. A bone disorder known as Paget's disease is found most frequently among people of English descent.

Susceptibility diseases, like certain cancers, heart disease, type 2 diabetes, typically occur later in life and are associated with diet, consumption of alcohol, lifestyle, and cultural factors. There is significant variation by ethnicity and culture to these types of diseases as well. For example, there are higher rates of emphysema (a lung disorder causing breathlessness), and respiratory problems of all kinds (including lung cancer) among cultures where smoking is an accepted social norm as in China or among many of the aboriginal populations in North America. There is a higher prevalence of conditions like high blood pressure (hypertension) in the black population of the United States. High blood pressure increases the likelihood of a potentially deadly stroke. There is a strong association between high stress levels and high blood pressure. Many black Americans live in poor, highly stressful, urban neighbourhoods that lack adequate medical facilities and care. It is not surprising that a variety of health problems associated with stress, unrelated to any genetic predisposition, would emerge in such an environment.

IQ Debates

IQ tests have generated controversy since their introduction about a hundred years ago. From the beginning of testing, certain ethnic groups have scored, on average, higher or lower against the national average. For example, at the beginning of the last century recently arrived immigrants from rural areas of central, eastern, and southern Europe were given IQ tests (in English). They tended to score, on average, about 15 points lower on IQ tests than the American-born. Opponents of immigration at the time used this information to label the newcomers as being "feeble minded," and of "inferior stock" in an attempt to block the flow of people from countries they deemed "undesirable." However, later studies consistently showed that children reared in rural areas *in the United States* score about fifteen points lower on average than children reared in urban areas. Other environmental factors such as family size and birth order also affected average IQ scores. For example, children raised in large families score lower on IQ scores, on average, than children from smaller families. Later born children have lower average IQ scores than first- born children.

The "Bell Curve" Controversy

About a hundred years after the debate over the lower average IQ scores of immigrants, another controversy arose with the publication of a book (*The Bell Curve: Intelligence and Class Structure in American Life*, by Richard Herrnstein and Charles Murray, New York, Free Press, 1994) which presented data claiming that "African-Americans" tended to score, on average, 15 points lower than "white" Americans on IQ tests. Some prominent "social scientists" in the United States used this information to imply that spending money on improving educational opportunities for disadvantaged minority groups is wasted because of a "genetic" disadvantage. In both the case of immigrants at the turn of the century, and contemporary black Americans, the results of a purportedly "scientific" and "objective" test were used for insidious political purposes.

Studies do show that there is a significant hereditary influence on what is called "intelligence" as there is a significant hereditary influence on height. Even when raised in drastically different environments, "identical twins" (who are the most genetically alike) tend to be most similar in characteristics such as height, and score virtually the same on IQ tests. IQ scores of biological parents and their children also tend to be quite similar, which is not the case of foster parents and their adopted children.

There is little dispute over hereditary influences among individuals in terms of a wide range of physical and cognitive attributes. The controversy arises when the genes assumed to be associated with a particular attribute such as "intelligence" are also assumed to be associated with an entirely different attribute such as skin colour, or height. It seems highly unlikely that this concordance of genes exists. Furthermore, there are few debates over the average IQ scores between short people and tall people but raging debates over differences in the average scores of populations with different skin tones. There is also no general agreement on the traits that actually constitute "intelligence," other than what is measured in IQ tests themselves. For example, it is difficult to quantify human qualities such as judgement, empathy, or emotional maturity but the lack of such qualities are severely dysfunctional for anyone in a social setting. Does intelligence include creativity and musical talent? IQ tests measure a specific type of *performance* based on a person's past experience, their motivation at a particular time, and some measure of their innate ability. As such they do serve a useful purpose in predicting, for example, a person's likely academic success, where the same type of variables are being measured. However, it is doubtful that IQ tests are a reliable measure of any broader definition of "innate intelligence" as a genetic disposition.

Differences in IQ scores (assuming it's possible to devise a culturally unbiased test) among ethnic groups exist for the same reason as other "patterned variations" in the human species. They are reproductive isolation, family size, diet, prenatal and post-natal nutrition, child rearing practices, social status, climate, geographical isolation, and most importantly, cultural orientations. Average IQ's of children from an isolated area in the mountains of Tennessee increased by ten points within a few years after they were first exposed to the "modern world" in the 1930s (*Newsweek*, October 24, 1994, p.53).

Genetics cannot explain the dramatic changes in IQ scores that can occur within one generation. For example, in Holland, the average score on IQ tests for young eighteen year old men increased by twenty points between 1952 and 1982 (*Psychological Review*, Vol.108, No.2, April, 2001, p.346-369). During World War I, Jewish soldiers were tested by the American government and scored so low that a prominent academician at the time claimed that the test results would surely "disprove the popular belief that the Jew is highly intelligent" (Brigham, Carl [1923] *A Study of American Intelligence*, Princeton University Press, p.190). Now, over eighty years later, Jews, as an identifiable group, score on average, above the American national average on IQ scores. Similarly, recently arrived Italian and Polish immigrants at the turn of the last century, who scored about fifteen points lower than the American national average at the time now score at, or above, the American national average of 100. Black Americans raised in affluent surroundings score at, or above, the national average.

IQ Scores And Economic Status

As different groups improve their economic status, IQ scores rise, regardless of skin colour or national origins. For example, the average IQ in Japan rose by about seven points in one generation since the end of World War II. Since the Japanese population is one of the most ethnically homogeneous (very little inter-marriage with other ethnic groups) in the world, this rapid improvement cannot be explained by genetic factors. However, the economic status of the Japanese population, as a whole, has also increased dramatically in the same period. Money can buy better diets, improved living conditions, and exposure to more educational and cultural opportunities. In fact, since the 1930s, there has been a slow but steady increase in average IQ scores of about three points per decade, or over 18 points in the last sixty years (*Psychological Review*, Vol.108, No.2, April 2001, p.346–369).

Research has demonstrated quite persuasively that changes (up or down) in average intergroup IQ differences are better explained by changes in social status rather than genetics.

Forensic Anthropology—A New Dimension To The "Race" Debate

Forensic anthropologists can attain a high degree of accuracy in assessing a person's ancestry through an examination of bones. Using measuring tools called calipers with adjustable pieces that slide or spread apart to measure length or thickness they take hundreds of measurements from a skeleton to assess its likely origin. The measurements include the length, width and projection of the nasal bones, the shape of the skull and brow, the form of the chin, femur traits, and the way bones have fused together. The measurements are then compared to the indexes made from thousands of measurements of major population groups, which can then determine where a person's ancestors came from. Law enforcement agencies increasingly use the services of forensic anthropologists for skeletal identification. As a consequence, since the early 1990s, U.S National and regional anthropology organizations have insisted that both traditional and new methods of measurement be tested quantitatively to assess for accuracy in legal cases. It is estimated that a combination of the available tests can determine skin colour from an examination of small bones with an accuracy level in the range of 90% (Gill, George W. [1998]) "Craniofacial Criteria in the Skeletal Attribution of Race," in *Forensic Osteology: Advances in the Identification of Human Remains*, edited by Kathleen J. Reichs, pp.293-317, Springfield: Charles C. Thomas Publisher, Ltd.).

The degree of accuracy of the tests has raised an important question for scientists in this field. Is forensic physical anthropology forced to use traditional "racial categories" (Black, White) in order to present information that can be understood by law enforcement officials, judges, and juries? George W. Gill, one of the most prominent forensic anthropologists in the United States, believes it is necessary to use these outmoded categories because "as long as society perceives human variation in terms of discrete races (sometimes even social races) then the forensic anthropologist must be prepared to articulate results or analysis in those terms" (Gill [1998] p.295). Researchers in criminal cases, for example, must present results that determine a *probable* race, sex, build, etc., and therefore, in Gill's view, don't have the luxury of scientific objectivity on the "race" issue. Physical anthropologists are "providing information on ancestry that is comprehensible to law enforcement and the rest of the society in which we must all operate. Therefore, it would seem likely that whatever the rest of biological science may choose to do about race in the future, forensic physical anthropologists will likely continue to articulate results of their analysis within the framework of the traditional race concept, at least as long as society does it itself" (Gill-1998, p.294). Gill's rationale for maintaining these distinctions in this field are based on the assumption that it is human nature to categorize and compartmentalize what we perceive as differences between classes of objects and organisms, and this is likely to continue until, through either greater interbreeding or genetic blending, the perceived differences become less important.

However, notwithstanding Gill's concerns, it is important to remember that human differences are a continuum with gradual changes rather than a few sharply defined biological groups. Traits that show a person is related to a larger population group are not the same as a biological category called "race." *The determination of race in forensic anthropology is essentially a probability game in much the same way as in all statistical procedures.* When several characteristics are examined there is a high probability of accuracy in correlating skeletal remains with skin colour but that doesn't validate the existence of distinct racial groups. However, until public perceptions change with respect to racial categories, forensic anthropologists will have little choice but to use these categories in order to provide useful and comprehensible information in criminal investigation and prosecution.

Genetic Blending And Recent Trends

There is a long history of so-called "race-mixing." For example, about 80% of "black" Americans have at least one white ancestor somewhere in their genealogical history. DNA evidence recently proved that Thomas Jefferson, one of the most famous of American Presidents, had at least one child with Sally Hemmings, a black slave who lived on his plantation. About 40% of French speaking Quebecois have at least one aboriginal ancestor somewhere in their genealogical tree. In South Africa, there is a whole group of people, once classified as the "Coloureds" under the old Apartheid regime, who descend from the mixing of Europeans, Indonesians, and the original "black" inhabitants. The people of northern India are descendants of intermarriages between white invaders and the original darker skinned population. The "Mestizos" of Central America and South America are a hybrid of the indigenous population and their European (mainly Spanish) conquerors.

The degree of genetic blending is illustrated by an interview golf star Tiger Woods did with Oprah Winfrey a couple of years ago. When Winfrey asked Woods about his importance as a "black" star in a sport dominated by "whites," Woods shocked everyone by saying that he didn't see himself as "Black" but as "Cablinasian." He told Winfrey that this was a name he had made up because his father had one white, one Native American, and two black grandparents, and his mother was half Chinese, half Thai. He saw himself as a mix of Caucasian, black, Indian, and Asian—hence the term "Cablinasian."

Recent trends have accelerated this genetic blending. For example, some 60% of Asian born Americans in their 20s marry somebody of another "race," and about two-thirds of the North American "Indian" population under the age of twenty-five do the same. In Great Britain, about 30% of the people of West Indian origin are married or in long-term relationships with "white" partners. In the United States, even the huge "taboo" about "Black" men marrying "White" women is increasingly broken. For example, in the 1940s and 1950s, less than 2% of black men married white women but in the past fifteen years this figure has soared to 10%. This change is particularly noticeable in the American armed forces where white women are seven times more likely to marry black American males than white women in civilian life (American Census, 1996-2000, Social Trends, United Kingdom, Census, Social Trends, 1996-2000).

Figure 2.1: Couples (Married and Common-Law) by Visible Minority Status, Canada, Montreal, Toronto, and Vancouver, 2001 and 1991

	Number	% of all couples	Number	% of all couples	% change 1991–2001
Canada					
All couples	**7,059,835**	**100.0**	**6,402,090**	**100.0**	**10.3**
Total intermarried couples	**217,490**	**3.1**	**167,515**	**2.6**	**29.8**
Two different visible minority groups	27,950	0.1	16,995	0.3	64.5
One visible minority and one non-visible minority	189,540	2.7	150,520	2.3	25.9
Montreal concensus metropolitian area					
All couples	**766,065**	**100.0**	**731,030**	**100.0**	**4.8**
Total intermarried couples	**24,565**	**3.2**	**22,080**	**3.0**	**11.3**
Two different visible minority groups	2,215	0.3	1,645	0.2	34.7
One visible minority and one non-visible minority	22,350	2.9	20,435	2.8	9.4
Toronto concensus metropolitian area					
All couples	**1,070,960**	**100.0**	**888,250**	**100.0**	**20.6**
Total intermarried couples	**63,205**	**5.9**	**45,395**	**5.1**	**39.2**
Two different visible minority groups	13,805	1.3	8,445	1.0	63.5
One visible minority and one non-visible minority	49,400	4.6	36,950	4.2	33.7
Vancouver concensus metropolitian area					
All couples	**453,395**	**100.0**	**366,400**	**100.0**	**23.7**
Total intermarried couples	**31,940**	**7.0**	**20,515**	**5.6**	**55.7**
Two different visible minority groups	5,020	1.1	2,295	0.6	118.7
One visible minority and one non-visible minority	26,920	5.9	18,220	5.0	47.7

Census Trends In Canada

The trend towards "racially mixed" populations is even stronger in Canada as is evident by a walk down any major street in Toronto, Vancouver, or even Montreal. The 2001 Canadian census revealed that there were 217,500 mixed unions (marriages and common-law unions) involving a visible minority person with a non-visible minority person or a person from a different visible minority group (*"Visible minorities"* are defined by the *Canadian Employment Equity Act* as "persons other than Aboriginal persons, who are non-Caucasian in race or non-white in colour"). Mixed couples are more likely to be found in certain Census Metropolitan Areas (CMA). For example, the proportion of mixed couples was higher in Vancouver (see figure 2.1), where they accounted for 7% of all couples, and Toronto, where they accounted for 6% of all couples (Statistics Canada, Census of Canada, 2001).

"Visible Minorities" In Canada

Almost 4 million people identified themselves as "visible minorities" in the 2001 Canadian census, representing about 13.4 % of the total population (see figure 2.2). This proportion of the total Canadian population has risen steadily over the past twenty years. In 1981, 1.6 million people or 4.7 % of the total population were identified as visible minorities, rising to 3.2 million or 11.2% of the total population by 1996. The visible minority population is growing much faster than the total population. Between 1996 and 2001, the total population of Canada increased by 4% but the visible minority population rose 25% or roughly six times faster than the overall population growth. The total population of Canada increased 6% between 1991 and1996, while the visible minority population rose 27%. Three out of every ten individuals who were identified as "visible minorities" were born in Canada, mainly blacks and persons of Japanese descent, both groups which have a long history in the country (Statistics Canada, Census of Canada, 2001).

People of Chinese descent are the largest visible minority group in Canada, now surpassing 1 million, according to the 2001 census (see figure 2.3). A total of 1,029,400 individuals identified themselves as Chinese, up from 860,100 in 1996. They accounted for 3.5% of the total Canadian population and 26% of the visible minority population. The second largest visible minority group in Canada are people of South Asian ancestry, that is to say people from India, Bangladesh, Sri Lanka, and Pakistan. A total of 917,100 people identified themselves as South

Asians in the 2001 census, up from 670,600 in 1996. South Asians accounted for 3.1% of Canada's total population and 23% of the visible minority population. Blacks are the third largest visible minority population with 662,200 persons in 2001, up 15% from 573,900 in 1996, and now representing 2.2% of Canada's total population and 17% of the visible minority population (Statistics Canada, Census of Canada, 2001).

Figure 2.2: Proportion of Visible Minorities, Canada, 1981–2001

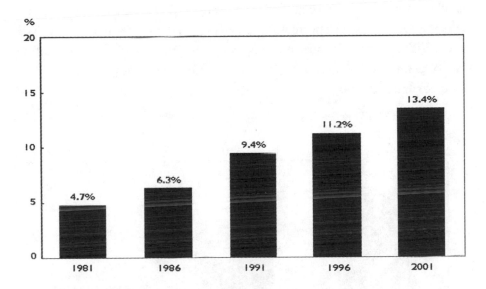

Figure 2.3: Visible Minority Groups, Canada, 1991 and 2001

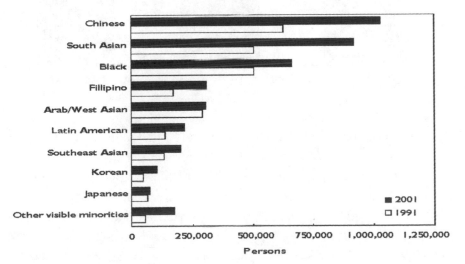

Foreign Born Population Of Canada

In Canada, 18.4% of the population is foreign born (Census of Canada, 2001), with most recent immigrants drawn from the darker skinned populations of South Asia, Southeast Asia, the Middle East, and Central and South America (see figure 2.4). The only country with a larger foreign-born population is Australia at 22% in 2001. This trend will continue because the lighter skinned European populations are increasingly prosperous and therefore less likely to immigrate to Canada. Seventy-three percent of all immigrants who arrived in Canada during the 1990s were "visible minorities," up from 68% in the 1980s and 52% from the 1970s. Visible minorities now make up roughly 43% of Toronto's population. Twenty percent of Canada's residents will be visible minorities by 2016, according to current projections.

Figure 2.4: Proportion of Foreign-Born, Selected Countries

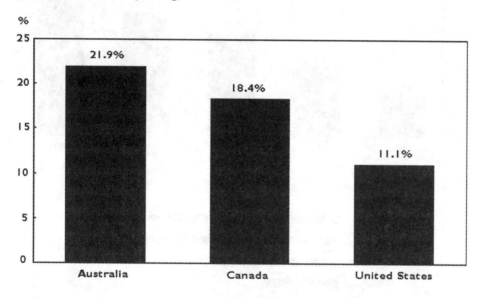

Urban Trends

In the major urban centers like Toronto, Vancouver, and Montreal the trends are even more pronounced. More than 73% of all immigrants who arrived between 1991 and 2001 were living in these three cities. In the Toronto Census Metropolitan Area (CMA), more than 445,000 immigrants arrived in the five-year census period between 1996 and 2001. They represented a 2% addition to the overall population of the city. Almost 44% of the entire current population in the Toronto CMA was born outside of Canada. This represents one of the largest foreign-born populations of any city in the world, even more than the city of Miami in the United States where 40% of residents are foreign born because of a large influx of Haitian and Cuban immigrants and refugees (see figure 2.5). The second most favoured destination for newcomers to Canada is Vancouver receiving 324,800 immigrants in the 1990s or 18% of the total for Canada. The foreign-born now total roughly 38% of the population of the city of Vancouver.

Between 1991 and 2001, 58% of the 1.8 million immigrants who arrived in Canada came from Asia, including the Middle East; 20% from Europe; 11% from the Caribbean, Central and South America; 8% from Africa, and 3% from the United States.

Figure 2.5: Foreign-Born as a Proportion of Total Population in Selected International Metropolitain Areas

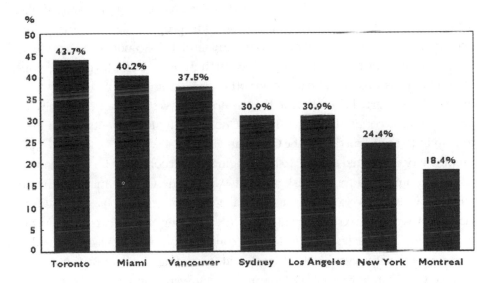

Multiple Ethnic Ancestries And Intermarriage

According to Statistics Canada, intermarriage has most likely led to an increase in the number of people reporting multiple ethnic ancestries on the Canadian census surveys. In 2001, 11.3 million people in Canada, representing 38% of the total Canadian population reported multiple ethnic origins, up from 10.2 million, or 36% in 1996. In 1991, 7.8 million people reported multiple ancestries, and 7 million in 1986 (Statistics Canada, Census of Canada, 2001).

Chapter Three
FROM "WHITE CANADA"
TO THE MULTICULTURAL MOSAIC

In the years since Confederation (1867), some 15 million immigrants have come to Canada, almost a third before World War I. At the outset, immigration policies were designed to maintain a "white Canada." Potential immigrants were ranked into categories with "preferred" status granted to people emigrating from Great Britain, the United States, France, Germany and the Scandinavian countries. When recruitment efforts did not produce enough of the most favoured groups, preferred status was extended to include other "white" immigrants—Poles, Ukrainians—if they agreed to migrate to the less desirable western prairie lands. By the 1880s it was necessary to recruit the first "non- white" immigrants, the Chinese, to help in the construction of the Canadian Pacific Railway (CPR). About 15,000 Chinese workers (often referred to disparagingly as "coolies" by the local population) were imported for the task at hand. The young Chinese men (women or families were not welcome) were often assigned dangerous jobs, which Canadian-born workers were reluctant to do (dynamiting, etc.). As a consequence, many were killed or disabled during the construction of the railroad. One dead Chinese worker for every mile of track laid, according to Pierre Berton, the acclaimed Canadian author of *The Last Spike*. They were also resented by many of the Canadian-born that saw their willingness to work long and hard for starvation wages as a threat to the white working man's standard of living. Newspaper editorialists and aspiring politicians capitalized on this fear of the *"Yellow Peril"* by agitating for restrictions on any further Chinese immigration. Chinese men were often characterized as "opium addicts" out to seduce white women. This fear intensified when the completion of the CPR released a flood of Chinese labourers to compete directly with white workers.

Although anti-Chinese organizations had existed as early as 1873, legislation to directly restrict further Chinese immigration was not enacted until 1885, which, not surprisingly, coincided with the completion of the railroad. In that year, a "head tax" of $50 was imposed on any Chinese wishing to enter the country. The idea was that this fee, an enormous amount of money at the time, would discourage further Chinese immigration. It didn't. Consequently, the fee was increased to $100 in 1900 and finally $500 in 1903, equivalent to one year's salary for the average Canadian production worker at the time. Some Chinese still managed to raise the money so on July 1, 1923, referred to thereafter as "Humiliation Day" by those affected, the government enacted the *Chinese Immigration Act*, sometimes called the Chinese Exclusion Act, which completely prohibited further Chinese immigration until the act was repealed in 1947. Chinese who were already in Canada experienced prejudice and discrimination in housing and employment up until the end of the World War II. In many provinces, they were not allowed to vote. In 1936, elderly "Oriental" persons were denied access to the province of British Columbia's homes for the aged. Laws were passed which prevented white women from working for Chinese employers. Even after the Chinese Exclusion Act was repealed the only category of immigration open to the Chinese, until 1962, was sponsored relatives of Chinese Canadians.

The federal government recently offered medals and certificates to head-tax payers and their survivors but would not refund the $23 million it collected during the period the tax was assessed. Four hundred survivors and four thousand of their descendants launched a class action suit asking for $1.2 billion in compensation (today's equivalent of the $23 million collected) for the head tax. An Ontario Superior Court judge struck down the lawsuit in June of 2002. The survivors intend to appeal the decision to the Supreme Court of Canada.

Japanese And "The Yellow Peril"

Japanese immigrants, mostly young men, arrived in Canada somewhat later than the Chinese. A favoured destination was British Columbia where many found employment in the fishery, the cannery industry, logging camps and on the railroad. Many later moved into farming in the Fraser Valley where they experienced great success. The Japanese experienced the same type of prejudice and discrimination as the Chinese, and for the same reasons. They were excluded by law from most of the professions and denied the right to vote in 1895. A white mob rampaged through the Japanese area of Vancouver in 1907 in an attempt to expel the "heathen Japanese." Earlier in the year white workers had learned that the Grand Trunk Pacific Railway had planned to import thousands of Japanese workers to work on the completion of their line. After the riot occurred, the Canadian and Japanese governments agreed to restrict further Japanese immigration to Canada to no more than 400 people a year under the terms of a *Gentleman's Agreement*. In 1928, the Agreement was revised to restrict Japanese immigration to Canada to 150 people annually. Canadians of Japanese origin were prevented from entering the civil service, the professions and teaching right up until 1967.

Internment Of Canadians Of Japanese Origin

The experience of Canadian-born residents of Japanese origin during World War II is one of the great tragedies of Canadian history. In 1941, many Canadians were shocked by the surprise raid on the American naval base at Pearl Harbour, and expected a Japanese invasion of Canada. This added a new dimension to the old fears about the "Yellow Peril." This time the peril was the alleged threat of subversion of the Canadian war effort by Canadians of Japanese origins. In 1941, they were fingerprinted, photographed, and required to carry registration cards. From 1942 until 1946, they were harassed, ejected from their homes, thrown into jail, or deported. Personal property was seized; houses were sold off at prices well below market value, or stolen outright. The Custodian of Enemy Property used the proceeds of these sales to pay for the costs of internment. Three months after the Japanese attack on Pearl Harbour, the Canadian government ordered the removal of all people of Japanese origin residing within 100 miles of the Pacific Coast. They were given 24 hours notice to vacate their homes, then sent to relocation or "internment camps" in the British Columbia interior for the duration of the war. Sometimes families were separated. The *"Internment"* (forced detention) of about 26,000 Canadians of Japanese origin was carried out under the *"War Measures Act,"* which permitted the federal government to suspend their civil liberties, including the right to due process (the same piece of legislation was used by the federal government to suspend the civil liberties of Quebecois during the October Crisis of 1970). After the war, restrictions were placed on where Japanese Canadians could live and neither their land nor personal property was returned to them. Many were re-settled east of the Canadian Rockies. The Canadian government attempted to deport about 10,000 of them to Japan under a "repatriation scheme." The policy was challenged and the case was brought before the Supreme Court of Canada, which sided with the government decision, but public protests caused Prime Minister Mackenzie King to end the deportations in 1947. By that time, however, about 4000 Japanese-Canadians had already been forced to leave, even though more than half had been born in Canada. They were finally granted the right to vote in 1949 but it was not until 1984 that the Canadian government issued an apology for these injustices. In 1988, the government allocated $300 million in compensation to Japanese Canadians and their descendants for their losses during and after the war.

Today, Canadians of Japanese origin are overrepresented in universities, the business world and the arts in comparison to their proportion of the total population. They have a higher than average income in comparison to most other "white" ethnic groups. As their success has increased, the level of prejudice and hostility towards them has rapidly declined. One of the most well known Canadians, nationally and internationally, is Dr. David Suzuki, a geneticist and television host, who spent several years of his early life in an internment camp in British Columbia.

Early South Asian Immigration

South Asian immigration to Canada began at the end of the 19th century when soldiers of the British army in India (mainly Sikhs) visited Canada to attend Queen Victoria's Diamond Jubilee celebrations in 1897. They received a warm welcome from their fellow soldiers of the British Empire and mistakenly assumed that they would be well received as immigrants to Canada. This perception was incorrect. When they returned to take up residence in 1899/1900 Canada was in the midst of an economic recession. The Canadian-born resented the presence of these dark-skinned "foreigners" competing with them for scarce jobs. Many Sikhs had found work in British Columbia's lumber mills and logging camps. They became targets of racist organizations like the Asiatic Exclusion League, which agitated to deny them their right to vote. The campaign succeeded in1908 and their right to vote was not regained again until 1947.

Restrictions On South Asian Immigration

By 1907 there were about 5000 immigrants from India in Canada. With popular feeling leading to numerous incidents of assault, harassment and even open riot, the federal government acted to limit immigration. With both Canada and India sharing bonds to Great Britain, it was an action that had to be accomplished subtly.

In January 1908, a "*Continuous Journey Stipulation*" (later incorporated into the *Immigration Act of 1910*) was made law in Canada. It specified that immigrants coming to Canada "otherwise than by continuous journey from countries of which they were natives or citizens, and upon through tickets purchased in that country, may be refused entry." At that time, the Canadian Pacific Railway was the only company that could provide transportation from India to Canada. The company was ordered by the Canadian government not to sell any "through tickets" for boat passage between India and Canada, thus serving the purpose of excluding South Asians without explicitly discriminating against them. The effect on South Asian immigration patterns was dramatic. In 1907 and 1908 some 4,757 East Indians immigrated to Canada. When the Stipulation became effective in 1909 only 6 East Asians were admitted to Canada in that year, and only 29 between 1909 and 1913.

This discriminatory policy was directly challenged on May 23, 1914 when a ship called *Komagatu Maru* arrived in Vancouver carrying 376 British subjects (12 Hindus, 24 Muslims and 340 Sikhs). They were never allowed to disembark. Canadian authorities detained the ship in harbour, claiming that because the ship had made numerous stops along the way, the terms of the *Continuous Journey Stipulation* had been violated. After a two-month standoff between government officials and the passengers, the ship was escorted to sea by a Canadian naval vessel and forced to sail back to India. From that point until 1947, a few wives of men already in the country were virtually the only South Asians allowed in to Canada. The community remained small.

The "Komagatu Maru Incident"

The story began when Bhai Gurdit Singh, an affluent Sikh businessman, chartered a ship in Hong Kong and filled it with passengers and 1500 pounds of coal (to sell or trade for lumber) and set off to Canada to challenge its immigration laws on the grounds that all British subjects had the legal right to travel and reside anywhere in what was then called the British Empire. In 1914, both India and Canada were still strongly linked to the Crown.

It was a challenge to England because of the possible political repercussions. At the time there was a growing movement for independence in India so any mishandling of the situation could inflame political passions. On the way over to Canada the ship picked up additional passengers in Shanghai, Yokahama, and other ports. Newspapers picked up on the story with lurid headlines such as "Boatloads of Hindoos on Way to Vancouver." Canadians were frightened about the possible "invasion" of Canada by these "foreigners." When the ship arrived off the coast of Vancouver, it was met by Canadian coast guard vessels and prevented from docking. Over the next two months passions ran high as supporters and opponents of the migrants clashed. Indians who had already settled in Van couver, before the passage of restrictive legislation, wanted to provide food, clothing and other supplies to the passengers as they waited offshore. Opponents of Indian immigration were determined to starve out the passengers and bar them from entry. At one point a force of 120 constables tried to board the ship and attach a grappling iron to it so they could drag it out to sea. They were forced back when passengers showered them with coal and bricks. Later a military ship equipped with 12 heavy guns was brought in, along with 200 bayonet-toting soldiers in an attempt to intimidate passengers. In the end an agreement was reached. Twenty-four passengers were allowed to disembark for legal and medical reasons. The remaining passengers were provided supplies and the ship was escorted out of Canadian waters by the HMCS Rainbow, to the cheers of a mob at dockside.

The ship headed back to Calcutta but was intercepted before reaching port and taken to a small harbour called Budge Budge, outside of the city. They were ordered by the authorities to board a train for the trip to the Punjab (the heartland of the Sikh faith in India) but refused. They attempted to march to Calcutta to protest this decision but were forced back by the police. When they again refused to board the train, police opened fire on the protesters leaving 20 people dead and many more injured.

Easing Of South Asian Immigration Restrictions

In 1919 the Canadian government issued an Order in Council that allowed the wives and children of Indians already in Canada to join them. After India and Pakistan won Independence in 1947, it became difficult for Canada to hold to a policy of exclusion with fellow Commonwealth countries. From that time on, a limited number of South Asian immigrants were allowed to enter the country. From a total of four individuals in 1949/50, the number increased to less than 200 per year by the end of the 1950s.

When restrictions based on country of origin were finally removed in the 1960s, South Asian immigration increased sharply. Among recent South Asian immigrants there is a high level of educational and professional achievement, including many teachers, doctors and engineers.

Apart from India, Pakistan, Bangladesh, and Sri Lanka, many South Asians who happen to live in other countries eventually find their way to Canada. For example, beginning in 1972, Canada took in over seven thousand South Asian refugees fleeing from persecution in Uganda under the notorious despot, Idi Amin.

The Jews

In the 1880s there was an influx of Russian and Eastern Europeans to Canada. Many of them were fleeing the murderous regime of the Russian Czar who had scapegoated Jews as being responsible for the economic hardships the country was experiencing. The Jews were largely concentrated in what were known as Shtetls (ghettos), which made them an easy target of hatred by the authorities who encouraged the non-Jewish population to engage in *pogroms* (massacres) against them.

The Jewish population of Canada doubled in the 1870s and 1880s with many of the newcomers taking jobs as unskilled labourers in trades and small businesses, often threatening the status and wage levels of Canadian-born workers because of their willingness to work long hours for less money. This is a pattern that is common to all new immigrants who are poor. Between the first and second World War (1918-39), about 40,000 Jews were admitted to Canada under special permits, but Jewish immigration was severely restricted. For example, Canada barred thousands of Jews who were fleeing the persecution of the Nazis in Germany in the 1930s. One of the worst incidents was Canada's refusal to admit 907 desperate German Jews on the ship *St. Louis* in 1939. The German government had tried to embarrass Jews by issuing visas to some German Jews to go to Cuba, which they knew beforehand the Cuban government wouldn't honour. When Cuba turned the boat away, they sought admission in the United States but no port on the eastern seaboard of the United States would accept them. When they arrived off the coast of Nova Scotia the Canadian government also turned down their pleas for admission. Their boat was forced to turn back to Europe. Some were allowed to land in Britain and France but many ended up in Hitler's gas chambers when he overran France at the start of the war. This incident has come to be known as the *"Voyage of the Damned."*

Widespread Anti-Semitism

Many politicians and other influential citizens in Canada were openly anti-Semitic until the end of World War II. They tolerated such blatantly discriminatory practices as *"restrictive covenants,"* whereby Jews were prohibited from owning property or renting in certain residential areas. During the 1920s and 1930s, Jews were excluded from public institutions or limited by a *quota system* (McGill University had a quota on the number of Jewish students it would admit right up until the late 1950s). The horror of the Nazi persecution and genocide of the Jews entered into public consciousness after the war resulting in a dramatic decline in anti-Semitism by the mid-1960s. By that time Jews (as an identifiable group) had attained an average level of income and education that far exceeded the Canadian average.

Ukrainians And Poles

About 180,000 Ukrainians and Poles immigrated to Canada from the villages of Eastern Europe in the 1890s. Ukrainians settled mainly on farms in Manitoba and Saskatchewan. Many of these settlers were induced to come to Canada through ads in European newspapers that promised blocks of free land. However, when they arrived in Canada, they were subjected to prejudice and discrimination on the part of the Canadian-born that viewed them as ignorant and less than human peasant people. Unscrupulous immigration officers often swindled newcomers denying them jobs, housing or other services. Some were later interned in prison camps during World War I as possible enemy sympathizers. In spite of these obstacles the Eastern Europeans eventually prospered as farmers and merchants. The descendants of Eastern European immigrants are now heavily concentrated in the city of Winnipeg.

The Irish

A "wave" of Irish immigration to Canada occurred in the 1840s when the potato crop in Ireland was ruined by a potato blight, leading to widespread hunger and starvation. Many were sick with cholera or typhoid fever when they boarded ships (later dubbed "coffin ships") to come to North America. Six thousand Irish migrants are buried on Grosse Isle, a small island in the St. Lawrence River about 30 miles east of Quebec City, which acted as a quarantine station for European migrants. The healthy arrived in Montreal and settled near the harbour in what was called Griffintown. They built the Victoria Bridge and later worked for the railroad. A typhoid epidemic once again raged through the community leaving many more dead in "fever sheds" around the port. To commemorate the victims, bridge workers dragged a huge Black Rock out of the St. Lawrence River, which still lies on top of a common grave. Many of the Irish settled in Quebec and intermarried frequently with French Quebecois. Irish orphans of the epidemics, often several brothers and sisters from the same family, were taken in by French Canadian families. The Catholic Church, under the direction of Father Charles-Felix Cazeau took great care to preserve the family name and history of each child. Today many visitors to Quebec are baffled when they encounter people with the surname Ryan or O'Neil that can't speak a word of English. Other Irish immigrants went to Ontario where they sought out wage labour. They were often viewed as dirty, unmannered drunks by the Canadian-born. But they were willing to do the hard manual labour that resulted in the construction of the Canadian canal system. Within a generation many of the Irish had prospered and with affluence came greater acceptance in Canadian society. The city of Montreal, in Quebec, now boasts the oldest St. Patrick's Day parade in North America.

Southern European Immigrants (Italians As An Example)

Italians first came to Canada in the late 19th century to work on the canals and later the railroad. Most only expected to remain in Canada a short time and then return to Italy with their savings. However, many stayed and migrated to urban centres like Toronto where they opened up small businesses. During World War II the loyalty of many Canadians of Italian descent was suspect because Italy, under the Fascist dictator, Benito Mussolini, declared war on Great Britain in 1940. Many were arrested by the RCMP as "dangerous aliens" and placed in "internment camps" in southern Ontario. It wasn't until the early 1950s that Italians were again recruited as immigrants after their status as enemy aliens was finally dropped. Between 1951 and 1960 about 250,000 Italians entered Canada, many taking up residence in Toronto where they quickly prospered in building trades and small businesses.

The Significance Of Refugees

There have always been many refugees among the immigrants to Canada. *United Empire Loyalists* (American colonists who wanted to remain loyal to the British Crown) sought refuge after the American Revolution. American blacks escaped slavery through the *"Underground Railroad,"* a network of "safe houses," organized by white and black sympathizers to facilitate their escape to Canada. Many settled in Nova Scotia, and around Chatham in southern Ontario.

The Underground Railroad

During and after the War of 1812 thousands of blacks fled the United States in search of freedom in Canada. These refugees were drawn here because of legislation that made Upper Canada (now Ontario) the first territory in the British Empire to abolish slavery. The *Abolition Act* of 1793 granted blacks the same protection under law as whites. American Abolitionists were willing to risk imprisonment to help blacks escape to Canada. Without much formal organization they established networks of paths through the woods and fields, river crossings, boats, wagons, and safe houses for people making the trip north. Railroad jargon was used to alert "passengers" when travel was safe. Runaways "commuted" either alone or in small groups, assisted by "conductors," white and black sympathizers to the cause, who risked their lives to escort the refugees to each "station" (located about fifteen miles apart) until they reached the final rail "terminal," which was freedom. One famous white conductor was James Fairfield, an abolitionist who helped many people escape by posing as a slave trader in the American south. One refugee who escaped by the Underground Railroad was Harriet Tubman. She became known as the "Black Moses" because she made 19 trips back to the American south to help 300 fellow captives escape to freedom.

The *British Imperial Act* of 1834 abolished slavery throughout the British Empire making Canada even more attractive as a destination for black refugees, particularly after the passage of the American *Fugitive Slave Act* in 1850. This legislation toughened penalties for people aiding and abetting the abolitionist movement within the United States.

Before the American Civil War (1860–65), about 75,000 blacks had migrated to southwestern Ontario, settling around London, Chatham and Dresden. Some acquired "Crown Land" to farm but very little government aid was made available. They lived in fear of bounty hunters who were hired by American slave owners to track down the "fugitives" and bring them back, dead or alive.

During and after the American Civil War, many of the fugitives returned to the United States either to fight for the Union side, or with the hope of a better life in their own home country after slavery ended. Blacks who remained in Canada often faced prejudice and discrimination by white employers who wouldn't hire them, and by hotels and restaurants that wouldn't serve them. However, they were considered "equal before the law" and were always able to vote and participate in civic life in Ontario in a manner that was not possible in the United States until well into the 1960s.

European Refugees

Jews fled, first from the Russian Pogroms and later from the Nazis. Various Russian and Baltic peoples sought refuge from Siberian labour camps in 1940. Some 1800 Estonians made their way to Canada by small boats immediately after World War II.

The "DPs"

After World War II, Canada took in thousands of Europeans who were homeless as a consequence of the conflict. More than 250,000 displaced persons (labeled DPs) and other refugees were admitted to Canada between 1947 and 1962, mainly Poles, Ukrainians, Germans and Austrians, but including smaller numbers of Latvians, Lithuanians, Czechs, Russians and Dutch.

"Cold War" And "Third World" Refugees

Much of the post World War II immigration to Canada is a consequence of political and economic factors associated with the "Cold War." For example, in 1957, there was a large influx (37,000) of Hungarians who fled their country after the Soviet Union crushed an attempt to establish a more democratic regime there. The same pattern was repeated in 1968 when the Soviets invaded Czechoslovakia. By late 1969 about 12,000 Czech refugees were admitted to Canada.

The "Cold War" turned hot in many "Third World" conflicts where civil wars broke out between rebel groups seeking independence from colonial powers and, or, socialist revolution, and other groups wanting to maintain the status quo. The major superpowers (Soviet Union, United States) usually backed one side or the other to help sway the outcome. In the case of Vietnam, the Americans intervened directly to try to prevent a Communist government from coming to power, and maintain its own influence in Southeast Asia. The resulting conflict, and subsequent ones in Laos and Cambodia, produced a food of refugees to Canada starting in the late 1970s. About 60,000 so-called *"boat people"* (an ethnic Chinese minority that was persecuted in Vietnam after the Communists came to power in 1975) settled in Canada in the aftermath of the war. The same war saw an influx of about 50,000 young Americans who came to Canada to avoid being drafted by the American army. Because they were not formally classified as refugees, the Canadian government at first refused entry to those who could not prove that they had been discharged from military service. This requirement was relaxed in 1968 after opposition to the war had grown. Canada received more immigrants from the United States than from any other country in 1971 and 72. About half of those fleeing the Draft (compulsory military service) remained in Canada even after an amnesty had been declared in 1976 in the United States.

An American Central Intelligence Agency (CIA) inspired coup against the democratically elected government of Salvador Allende in Chile, in 1973, led to civil unrest and the installation of a right-wing dictatorship under General

Augusto Pinochet. Seven thousand Chileans fled to Canada to seek refuge from possible reprisals when he came to power. Human rights groups criticized the Immigration Department for its slow response to the plight of Chilean refugees, charging that the delay was motivated by the fear that taking them in would antagonize the United States government, a major backer of the new regime. The same pattern occurred in the late 1940s and early 1970s in Greece when CIA supported right-wing regimes gained power and suppressed opposition parties.

In the 1970s and 1980s, Cold War inspired civil wars in the Middle East (Lebanon), Africa (Mozambique, Angola, Somalia, etc.) and Central America (Nicaragua, El Salvador, Guatemala) generated huge numbers of refugees, with many finding safe haven in Canada. The disintegration of the Soviet Union and the former Yugoslavia in the late 1980s resulted in an explosion of long suppressed ethnic and religious rivalries and an influx of immigrants and refugees from Poland, Croatia, Serbia, and many former Soviet republics such as Lithuania, Latvia, Estonia and the Ukraine. Between 1991 and 2001 the top ten source countries for immigrants and refugees have been China, India, the Philippines, Hong Kong, Sri Lanka, Pakistan, Taiwan, the United States, Iran, and Poland (Census of Canada, 2001).

Major Revisions To The Immigration Act Since 1910

While specific regulations and pieces of legislation were passed by the government that were blatantly discriminatory towards racial minorities, it was not until the *Immigration Act of 1910* that an implicit "colour bar" was formally introduced into federal legislation. *Section 38 (c)* of the *Immigration Act of 1910* denied entry to

> ...any nationality or race of immigrants of any specified class or occupation, by reason of any economic, industrial or other condition temporarily existing in Canada or because such immigrants are deemed unsuitable having regard to the climatic, industrial, social, educational, labour...or because such immigrants are deemed undesirable owing to their peculiar customs, habits, modes of life, methods of holding property and because of their probable inability to become readily assimilated or to assume the duties and responsibilities of Canadian citizenship within a reasonable time after their entry.

This piece of legislation was the main instrument of an implicit "White Canada" policy up until the passage of new, non-discriminatory Immigration Regulations in 1962. By that time the government position had shifted towards the promotion of a system favouring universal and equal treatment of all applicants based on certain entrance standards without regard to "race," religion, or country of origin. With this new policy, Canada became the first of the three major destinations for immigrants (Australia and the United States being the others) to remove discriminatory legislation. It wasn't until 1975 that the United States introduced similar amendments to its immigration policy. The "White Australia" policy was abandoned there in 1973, with a declaration that citizenship would be granted on conditions applying "equally to all."

The Point System

The removal of discriminatory criteria was further refined with the passage of the *Immigration Act of 1967* which created the "points system." The purpose of the points system was to establish an "objective" system to determine "who gets in" to Canada. Criteria for admission were: education and training, personal assessment; occupational demand; occupational skill; age; arranged employment; knowledge of French or English; relatives; and employment opportunities in area of destination. The nine factors have a combined potential value of one hundred. If an applicant received fifty points or more they would likely be settled (now the criteria is seventy points).

A new and independent appeal board was also established in 1967 with the passage of the *Immigration Appeal Board Act*. Anyone ordered deported from Canada could appeal to the Board, regardless of their status under the *Immigration Act*. For example, visitors to Canada could apply for landed immigrant status. If they were refused they could now appeal to the board. This quickly became a problem as large caseload backlogs developed. While they were waiting for a judgement, applicants could remain in Canada and enjoy the benefits of legally admitted immigrants, sometimes for several years. After residing in Canada for many years it became very difficult to deport such people. This was a harbinger of some of the controversies that continue to plague the immigration process to the current day.

New Barriers

Although the establishment of a formally "colour-blind" policy gave the impression that discrimination based on "race" had been eliminated, subtle discriminatory mechanisms were maintained such as the number and location of immigration offices located abroad. For example, overseas expenditures indicated that the commitment to recruitment of immigrants from "developed countries" was substantially greater than the commitment to recruitment from "less developed" or so-called "Third World" countries. This suggests that the preference of Immigration Canada was to recruit from the traditional "source countries," thus favouring "lighter skinned" populations. In response to criticisms of this nature a more formal commitment to the elimination of racial discrimination was enshrined in the *Immigration Act of 1976*. According to *Section 3(f)*

> It is hereby declared that Canadian Immigration Policy and the rules and regulations made under this Act shall be designed and administered in such a manner as to promote the domestic and international interests of Canada recognizing the need to...(f) *ensure that any person who seeks admission to Canada on either a permanent or temporary basis is subject to standards of admission that do not discriminate on grounds of race, national or ethnic origin, colour, religion or sex.*

Other Innovations

The revised *Immigration Act of 1976* recognized four basic categories of individuals eligible for landed immigrant status: Independent class, family class, humanitarian class (refugees), and assisted relatives class. The independent class is made up of individuals who apply (usually from abroad) on their own initiative and are selected if they can obtain the requisite number of points for job skills, education, etc. Family class is comprised of family members (immediate family and grandparents over 60, or, if widowed or incapable of earning a living, under sixty). Assisted relatives are more distant relatives (cousins, etc.) who are sponsored by a family member in Canada but who must also meet some of the selection criteria of independent class applicants. Humanitarian Class (refugees) included refugees defined as such under the 1951 United Nations Convention related to refugees (*Convention refugees are defined as a class of individuals who have left their country and cannot return because of a well-founded fear of persecution for reasons of race, religion, nationality, group membership, or political opinion*), and those who don't qualify under the UN definition but who are members of a specially designated class recognized by the Cabinet of the Canadian government for humanitarian reasons. With the creation of the Humanitarian class, the revisions to the immigration act for the first time included a formal recognition of a separate selection and admission process for refugees.

The New Era

The passage of the 1976 legislation and its implementation by 1978 marked the beginning of a new era in Canada's immigration history. Immigration policy was now seen as an important mechanism by which Canada could achieve certain demographic, economic, social, and cultural goals. Discrimination based on race or ethnic origins would no longer be tolerated. Canada would abide by its obligations under international human rights conventions and protocols. There would be federal-provincial cooperation in setting target numbers for the different immigration categories. The new legislation received unanimous support from all political parties in the House of Commons and was hailed by many commentators as a prototype for other countries to follow. In the decades that followed new challenges would emerge to test the commitment of Canadians to a "liberal" immigration policy.

Immigration And Refugee Protection Act

On June 28, 2002 the new *Immigration and Refugee Protection Act* (IRPA) came into force replacing the *1976 Immigration Act*, 1978 immigration regulations and subsequent amendments and regulations. Changes were made to certain categories to encourage a broader range of applicants with the skills and education needed to promote economic growth and development. For example, under the "Skilled Workers Category," more "points" have been allocated for applicants with a trade certificate or a second degree, more work experience, greater proficiency in both English and French, and to older workers with the requisite skills.

Census Trends

The extent to which Canada has become a cultural mosaic is evident from the responses to the 2001 Canadian census, where two hundred different ethnic groups were cited in response to a question on ethnic ancestry. As of May 2001, the proportion of foreign-born Canadians was at the highest level since 1931 (18.4% of the total population, see Figure 3.1). By contrast, only 11% of the population of the United States was foreign-born in 2001. The only country with a higher percentage of foreign-born was Australia, where, according to its 2001 census, 22% of the population was foreign-born.

Figure 3.1:Proportion of Foreign–Born, Canada, 1901–2001

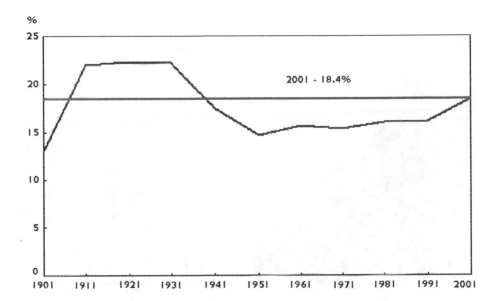

Of 1.8 million immigrants who arrived between 1991 and 2001, 58% arrived from Asia, including the Middle East, 20% from Europe, 11% from the Caribbean, Central and South America, 8% from Africa, and 3% from the United States. Up until the early 1960s, the major immigrant source countries were the United Kingdom (Britain, Scotland, Northern Ireland, and Wales), Germany, Southern Europe (Italy, Greece), the Netherlands, and the United States (see Figure 3.2). Before 1961, only 3% of immigrants to Canada were Asian-born.

Seventy-three percent of immigrants arriving in the 1990s were "visible minorities" (*"persons, other than Aboriginal peoples who are non-Caucasian in race or non-white in colour"*). In 2001, visible minorities represented 43% of the population of Toronto. Newcomers settle primarily in the three major urban centers of Montreal, Vancouver, and Toronto (73% of new arrivals between 1991-2001). In Toronto and Vancouver, immigrants who arrived between 1991 and 2001 made up 17% of those cities total population in 2001. Twelve percent of Montreal's total population is comprised of new immigrants who arrived between 1991-2001. The lower number attracted to Montreal relates to specific selection criteria (ability to speak French) that applies only to the province of Quebec.

Figure 3.2: Proportion of Immigrants Born in Europe and Asia by Period of Immigration, Canada, 2001

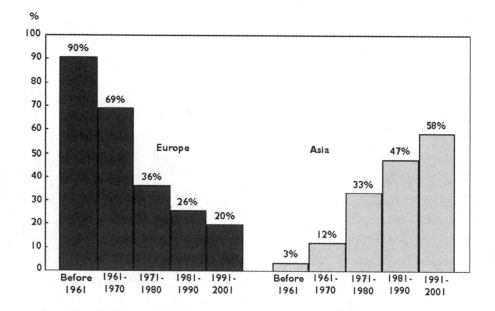

The Quebec Exception

With the election of the Parti Quebecois in 1976, under Premier Rene Levesque, one of the first issues to be raised with the federal government was the question of provincial powers with regards to immigration policy. The newly elected provincial government wanted a full range of powers in this area because of its eventual goal of total independence from the Canadian confederation. Within two years, an agreement was reached with the federal government (called the *Cullen-Couture Agreement*, 1978), which granted Quebec special powers with regards to the selection of independent class immigrants (skilled workers and businessmen with dependents), refugees, and the financial and other criteria required for family class and assisted relative sponsorship arrangements. These special powers of selection are unique to the province of Quebec and reflect a desire to control the cultural and social development of the province in keeping with its French character.

Chapter Four
IMMIGRATION DEBATES

Perhaps the most controversial aspect of Canada's immigration policy is the refugee determination process. This deserves special attention in light of the terrorist attacks on the World Trade Center in New York (September 11, 2001) and the subsequent response of the Canadian Immigration Minister and Department.

Refugee Claimants Outside Of Canada

Individuals seeking to enter Canada as conventional refugees (defined as refugees under United Nations guidelines) apply outside the country, at refugee camps or Canadian immigration offices around the world. Under the 1951 *Geneva Convention* definition a refugee is a person who is *outside his or her country of nationality or habitual residence and who cannot return because of a well-founded fear of being persecuted for reasons of race, religion, nationality, political opinion, or membership in a particular social group.*

Canada is also a party to the 1984 *Convention Against Torture* and the *International Covenant on Civil and Political Rights*. Under these obligations Canada also offers protection to people in certain designated countries who face persecution but are still in their country of origin and people who are affected by civil war, armed conflict and massive violations of human rights.

In the case of *Convention* refugees, Canadian immigration officers process their applications, guided by the provisions of the new *Immigration and Refugee Protection Act* (*IRPA*) of 2002, which replaced the previous *Immigration Act of 1976-77*, the 1978 Immigration Regulations, and subsequent amendments and regulations. Persons claiming refugee status outside of Canada are subjected to a rigourous selection process to determine their ability to adapt to Canadian society. Most of the people admitted this way are genuine refugees.

Between 1976 and 1986, Canada accepted more refugees per capita than any other country in the world and for this achievement was awarded the Nansen medal in 1986, the first country ever to receive this recognition. Roughly 25% of the new immigrants to Canada from 1978 to 1981 were in the refugee category and were mainly selected from overseas.

In-Country Refugee Claims

Refugee protection is also offered to people fleeing persecution who can somehow make their way directly to Canada to apply. According to Citizenship and Immigration Canada, they are persons whose "removal to their country of nationality or former habitual residence would subject them to the possibility of torture, risk to life, or risk of cruel and unusual treatment or punishment." Anyone arriving in Canada by land, sea or air is entitled to make such a claim and cannot be sent back to their place of origin until it is determined that the claim is not legitimate. To do so would be a violation of Canada's obligations under several international covenants.

Problems With In-Country Refugee Claims

Much of the current controversy surrounding the refugee determination process began in 1985. At that time the out of country system of selecting refugees for settlement in Canada was increasingly bypassed by growing numbers of asylum seekers (sometimes disparagingly referred to as "asylum shoppers") who came to Canada as visitors or students and then claimed that they could not return to their country of origin for fear of persecution. A few high profile incidents also involved refugee claimants showing up in boats off the coasts of British Columbia and Nova Scotia seeking asylum.

In the mid-1980s it became obvious that some claimants were not genuine refugees but rather individuals seeking to improve their economic prospects in Canada. These "bogus" claimants or "queue jumpers," as they were sometimes called, generated a strong anti-immigration "backlash" among some Canadians who felt they were taking advantage of a lax refugee determination system.

Critics saw the problems stemming from the complex procedural guarantees built into the 1976 *Immigration Act*, which resulted in processing delays and several avenues for appeal if an initial refugee claim was rejected. According to them, the resulting backlogs worked to the advantage of bogus refugee claimants, particularly when immigration officials were overwhelmed trying to adjudicate the increasing number of claims.

Ramifications Of The Singh Decision

The refugee determination process was further complicated by a 1985 Supreme Court of Canada decision (*The Singh Decision*) that guaranteed refugee applicants virtually the same social and legal protections accorded Canadian citizens under the *Charter of Rights and Freedoms*, except the right to vote. The result was that *all refugee applicants must be granted a full oral hearing before the Immigration and Refugee Appeal Board*, a procedural guarantee that is not available in any other refugee receiving country.

Before this change, refugee claims were decided by the Refugee Status Advisory Committee, which reviewed transcripts of interviews of refugee claimants conducted under oath by the immigration officers. Decisions and appeals were based on the written reports. Hearings could take place but they were not mandatory. Claimants who were denied refugee status were not entitled to an explanation for this decision.

Before the Singh Decision there were about 500 refugee claims made per month. Within five months of the Supreme Court decision in April 1985, the number of claims had risen to 700 a month and by January of 1987 there were 4000 refugee claims per month being made (*Globe and Mail*, February 25, 1987).

After the Supreme Court handed down the Singh Decision, the government decided it was impossible to provide a full hearing for each of the 20,000 refugee claimants who were entitled to one. They instead granted amnesty to all refugee claimants who had entered Canada before May 21, 1986, regardless of the validity of their claims. If they had a job or were likely to get one, posed no security or criminal threat, and passed a medical examination, they were allowed to remain in Canada as permanent residents.

Early Attempts To Change The System

In May of 1986 the Conservative government of Brian Mulroney introduced the *Refugee Reform Bill* (*Bill C-55*) to deal with the flood of new claimants. Refugee applicants would be denied refugee status if they had a criminal record or if they had refugee status in another country. They were also expected to have a "credible basis" for their claim.

The Safe Country Controversy

One of the most controversial aspects of the new legislation was the *"safe country"* provision, designed to discourage the practice of *"asylum shopping,"* whereby allegedly bogus refugee claimants move around, looking for the country that offers them the easiest entry and the best social benefits. Under this provision, refugee claimants would be prevented from entering Canada if they arrived from a "safe country," which, in theory, might grant them refugee status. A "safe country" is one that is democratic, committed to respect for human rights and the rule of law, and is a signatory to international conventions (*Geneva Convention*, 1951) on the fair treatment of refugee claimants.

Critics immediately attacked this provision because some countries deemed "safe" have friendly relations with countries whose governments have terrible human rights records. For example, in the early 1990s, a Salvadoran refugee in the U.S might be sent back to El Salvador to face death at the hands of a "Death Squad" because the United States government had a "friendly" relationship with the government of El Salvador and didn't recognize the legitimacy of refugee claimants from that country. Forty percent of the people who seek asylum in Canada each year arrive from the United States, supposedly a "safe country." Critics saw the "safe country" provision penalizing refugees from "right-wing" regimes who wouldn't get a fair hearing in the United States. Refugees fleeing from "left-wing" regimes such as Cuba are granted refugee status almost immediately. As a consequence of the widespread criticism, the "safe country" provision was later dropped.

Boat Arrivals

The growing concerns about asylum shopping intensified in the summer of 1986 when 155 Tamils from Sri Lanka were discovered adrift in lifeboats off the coast of Newfoundland. They claimed they had come all the way from Sri Lanka. Initial sympathy for their plight turned sour when people learned that they had paid an enterprising sea captain to ferry them from a refugee camp in Germany to Canadian coastal waters. A year later, a group of 174 Sikhs from India also made their way ashore from lifeboats off the coast of Nova Scotia.

In response to these unannounced arrivals the parliament of Canada was called into an emergency summer session in 1987 to amend the *Immigration Act*. The result was *Bill C-84*, the *Refugee Deterrents and Detention Bill*. This Draconian piece of legislation made it an offence to assist anyone to gain entry to Canada without the proper travel documents. Violators could be fined up to $500,000 and imprisoned for ten years. Transportation companies could be fined if it was discovered that their passengers did not have proper travel documents. Immigration officers were accorded greater powers to enforce the provisions of the *Immi-*

gration Act related to searches and seizures. The new bill contained a provision that permitted the government to turn away by force ships in Canadian waters that were suspected of bringing in bogus refugee claimants. Both *Bills C-55* and *C-84* were passed on July 21, 1988 and came into force on January 1, 1989.

The new legislation was greeted by a firestorm of protest from immigration and refugee advocacy groups, church groups, women's groups and trade unions. The critics drew attention to the fact that repressive governments often refuse to issue passports or travel documents to people who disagree with their policies. They could be jailed or even killed for requesting such documents. In such situations obtaining a false passport or travel document may be the only way to escape death or persecution.

Growing Backlog Of Refugee Claimants

By 1989, there were 125,000 people in the refugee backlog. The previous amnesty had the unintended effect, according to critics, of encouraging more people to show up at the border and claim refugee status. A new Immigration and Refugee Board (IRB) was established and a new two stage screening process was implemented in an attempt to speed up the adjudication of outstanding claims. Refugee applicants appeared before a two-member panel. Both panel members had to agree if a claim was to be refused. If one panel member believed a claimant deserved asylum, it was granted. In the case where both members of the panel refused a claim, they were required to provide a written explanation for the decision. Refused claimants were entitled to a second level review of the transcript of the proceedings by another IRB member and the right to seek an appeal to the Federal Court. If the purpose of the new screening process was to expedite the refugee determination process, it didn't work. The backlog persisted and the number of refugee claimants continued to increase.

By 1992, Canada was in the midst of a painful recession. Public attitudes towards the perceived laxity of the refugee determination process hardened as the labour market became more competitive. One flashpoint for controversy was the high acceptance rate for refugee claimants. In the early 1990s, Canada's newly created Immigration and Refugee Board granted refugee status to roughly 57% of the people who sought it compared to an average 14% for sixteen other countries that accepted refugees (*Globe and Mail*, December 28, 1993).

In June of 1992, the Conservative government of Brian Mulroney again responded by introducing new legislation (*Bill C-86*) to tighten up the process and "crack down" on "bogus claimants." There would be public hearings of refugee cases, harsher detention procedures, deportations without hearings, and finger-printing of refugee applicants to discourage possible welfare fraud. The new leg-islation also attempted to reintroduce the "safe country" provision.

The Conservatives argued that these changes were necessary because of the growing problem of transnational criminal activity and terrorism, and a dramatic increase in the worldwide refugee problem. However, underlying the motivation for a tougher policy were political considerations that were only rarely expressed explicitly. When the *Immigration Act* of 1976 came into force in 1978, Canada was receiving a few thousand refugee claimants a year, mainly people fleeing from Communist regimes during the Cold War era. The number of claimants had in-creased to 37,726 people by 1992, mainly from "Third World" countries.

Reforms Modified

After much criticism, several aspects of *Bill C-86* were modified. For example, the government reverted to the previous practice of holding refugee hearings in pri-vate because public hearings might risk the lives of refugee applicants. The gov-ernment also agreed to have refugee applicant's fingerprints destroyed once they became Canadian citizens. The "safe country" provision was once again shelved.

Recent Changes

The attempt to tighten up the refugee determination process and eliminate bo-gus claimants did not significantly stop the inflow of asylum shoppers. In 2001 the number of new refugee claims reached 43,990. If past experience is any guide, according to critics, a significant number of these claims were bogus. In response to continued criticism about the laxity of the refugee determination process, then Immigration Minister Elinor Caplan introduced new legislation in 1999. The *Immigration and Refugee Protection Act* (*Bill C-11*) was finally enacted on June 28, 2002, in the wake of the terrorist attacks on the World Trade Center in New York City. It increased penalties for existing immigration offences, cre-ated a new offence for human trafficking (people smuggling), raised the penalty to life in prison for migrant smuggling and trafficking, and changed the rules so that *a security check now starts when a person makes a refugee claim. Under the old legislation a security screening was carried out only after a person was granted refugee status*. The purpose of the change was to detect criminals and security risks at the start of the process and speed genuine refugees through the system. Under the new legislation claims are not eligible if the claimant has been recognized as a refugee in another country and can be safely returned to that country.

Canada and the United States have also negotiated a "safe third country" arrangement that makes it more difficult for people who pass through the United States to make a refugee claim in Canada. They are instead required to make their claim first in the United States. This continues to be a source of controversy. According to the Canadian Council For Refugees, "the 'safe country' concept is only one of a range of tools used by states, including Canada, to prevent refugees from successfully making a refugee claim. Visas are required, documents are checked before boarding aircraft, immigration control officers are posted overseas and airlines are fined for bringing refugee applicants to Canada. The government maintains that the measures are necessary to prevent the arrival of 'improperly documented travelers'. However, these measures also block refugees fleeing persecution, many of whom are forced to turn to smugglers to help them get to safety. The more sophisticated the interdiction measures, the higher the prices charged by smugglers, and the more dangerous the means of travel used by those desperate to save their lives. One of the likely effects of the 'safe third country' agreement is that some refugee claimants, unable to enter Canada at a port of entry, will attempt to enter Canada irregularly, perhaps at a risk to their lives" (Canadian Council for Refugees, Feb. 18, 2003). It is important to note that under the new *Immigration and Refugee Protection Act* (IRPA) no country will be considered "safe" if it has not signed the United Nations *Convention against Torture and Other Cruel, Inhuman, or Degrading Treatment or Punishment.*

Refugee Applications Fall In 2004

Roughly 43,990 people sought refugee status in Canada in 2001, but only 25,750 did so in 2004, a decline of 41%, according to Citizenship and Immigration Canada (*Canwest News Service*, April 15, 2005). The decline resulted from tighter security measures at the border, closer scrutiny of visitor visa applications and more intense airport security operations that screen out passengers holding forged or fake documents. In 2004 about a third of asylum seekers came from the United States but that number is expected to drop because of the "safe country" provision that was signed between the two countries on December 29, 2004. Refugee advocates believe that a consequence of the tighter regulations will be to drive legitimate asylum seekers underground and try to get to Canada via smugglers.

Other Changes To Immigration Policy

Other changes involve tighter screening of "investor" or "business class" immigrants in response to the "cash for visa" controversy, where both language requirements and extensive criminal background checks were sometimes waived for wealthy foreigners who wanted to invest or retire in Canada. It must now be determined that the "net worth" of an applicant in the investor category must be "legally obtained," and immigration officers will have discretion to examine the propriety of the accumulation of net worth.

Permanent Resident Card

The implementation of the new immigration act in 2002 also brought the introduction of a permanent resident card providing new and existing permanent residents with "clear, secure proof of their status." The purpose was to replace the old Record of Landing, a simple piece of paper that was easy to forge. After December 31, 2003, all permanent residents will need the card to re-enter Canada after traveling abroad. In January of 2004, the American government announced that biometrics—authentication of identity by scans of body parts (iris, fingerprints, etc.)—will be incorporated on the passports, visas or other identification documents being used by passengers entering or leaving the country under its U.S.-VISIT scheme (*Globe and Mail*, January 10, 2004).

Immigration And Social Change

During the 1990s, an annual average of about 220,400 immigrants came to Canada, up significantly from an annual average of 125,400 in the 1980s. The sources of immigration to Canada have changed dramatically over the past forty years. As of the most recent census (2001), European-born people account for less than half of the total immigrant population due to growing numbers from Asia, Africa and the Middle Eastern countries. This is a marked change from 1981 when 67% of immigrants living in Canada were born in Europe. These changes have introduced a "racial "dimension to debates over immigration policy. Historically, concerns about immigration have centered on economic insecurity and the structure of the labour market. Put bluntly, native-born workers were afraid that their standard of living would be undermined by a rapid influx of newcomers who would "steal their jobs," regardless of their skin colour. Although it is not always articulated explicitly, the new concern of many Canadians of European origin is cultural insecurity, which is the fear that increasing diversity undermines the dominant white Anglo/French culture. Immigration policy is, therefore, part of a larger debate over the nature of Canadian "identity," which unfortunately is not "colour-blind" but "colour-coded."

Immigration Debates

Up until 1962 Canadian immigration policy was explicitly exclusionary, denying certain people entry based on their skin colour or ethnic origins (see Chapter Three). Over the past forty years, official government policy has changed, opening up admission to people from Central and South America, Asia, Africa, and the Middle East. The new, more "liberal" immigration policy has both supporters and detractors. Although most Canadians have immigrant ancestors, opinion polls over the past fifty years have consistently indicated that a majority of Canadians oppose dramatic increases in the number of people admitted into this country as immigrants. Some people oppose liberal immigration policies on rational grounds, arguing that the labour market cannot absorb large numbers of newcomers in a short period of time, particularly if the economy is experiencing a recession. Others oppose immigration, particularly from "Third World" countries, for ethnocentric reasons, because they don't want people who cannot be easily assimilated to the dominant Anglo/French culture. A relatively small segment of Canadian society opposes liberal immigration policies for racialist reasons, because they don't like to see so many people with skin colour darker than their own. Although their motivations for opposing liberal immigration policy are different, all three groups are part of what is known as the "restrictionist" or "exclusionist" position when immigration and refugee policy is debated in public.

Restrictionist Arguments

Restrictionists believe that Canadian immigration and refugee policies are so lax that we have become an international joke. Restrictionists are most upset about the fact that about 60% of the approximately 25,000 refugee claimants who arrive in Canada every year does so without proper documentation. Many arrive at Canadian airports or border crossings with the United States claiming political persecution in their own home country. The Supreme Court of Canada ruled in 1985 (*The Singh Decision*) that anyone claiming refugee status *in Canada* is entitled to an oral hearing. This means that anyone arriving on Canadian soil can claim refugee status. Depending on security considerations, claimants either get a questionnaire to mail in to Immigration Canada, or are interviewed right away. Immi-

gration officers can detain people without documents until they establish who
they are. But unless they are found to have a serious criminal record, to pose a security risk (possible terrorist) or are under a previous deportation order, their
claim is passed on to the independent Immigration and Refugee Board (IRB) for a
hearing (The IRB is a quasi-independent tribunal set up in 1989. Members of the
IRB are political appointees appointed by Order in Council for a period of seven
years. They receive training and assistance from the refugee documentation center
in making decisions). While waiting for a hearing, refugee claimants are eligible
for medical care, welfare, and are allowed to work. In the United States, by contrast, asylum seekers are prohibited from working for the first six months after
their application and do not have any government supported legal representation
available to them.

Oral Hearings And Appeals

When the IRB hearing occurs, refugee claimants explain why they have fled their
country. They are entitled to paid legal counsel to help them with their claim.
Under United Nations guidelines (*Geneva Convention*, 1951), refugee claimants
must demonstrate that they have grounds to fear persecution because of their
race, religion, nationality, social group, or political opinion. Under the new *Immigration and Refugee Protection Act* a single person decides if the claim to refugee
status is legitimate. If the claim is accepted, the refugee can apply for permanent
residency within 180 days of receiving a written decision from the Board. If the
refugee claim is rejected, the person making the claim is expected to leave the
country within 30 days or face arrest and deportation. However, within fifteen
days they can appeal this decision and apply for a judicial review in the Federal
court, which can order a new IRB hearing. If this appeal fails, claimants are entitled to what is known as a Pre-Removal Risk Assessment (PRRA) before they are
ordered to leave the country. An official from Citizenship and Immigration Canada instead of an Immigration and Refugee Board official adjudicates this appeal.
The time required for oral hearings and possible appeals can drag on for months
and even years. During that time refugee claimants may marry a Canadian citizen or resident and apply to remain in the country on humanitarian and compassionate grounds. Even if all appeals fail, and refugee claimants are ordered to
leave, there is no mechanism in place to determine whether or not they have actually left the country. Many remain in the country, illegally, for years working
in the underground economy or supported by friends and families.

Persons Ineligible For Refugee Protection

According to Citizenship and Immigration Canada the following categories of persons are not eligible to have a refugee claim referred to the Immigration and Refugee Board:

- Persons recognized as *Convention* refugees by another country to which they can be returned;

- Persons already determined to be protected persons under the *Immigration and Refugee Protection Act* or its regulations;

- Persons who arrived in Canada, directly or indirectly, from a country other than their country of nationality or former habitual residence and designated by the *Immigration and Refugee Protection Act* regulations;

- Persons who were determined to be inadmissible on grounds of security, human rights violations, serious criminality or organized criminality;

- Persons who had a previous refugee protection claim rejected by the IRB, or persons who had a previous refugee claim determined to be ineligible for referral to the IRB, or persons who had a previous refugee protection claim withdrawn or abandoned (Citizenship and Immigration Canada, Sept., 2002).

Backlogs And "Bogus Claims"

The time consuming oral hearings and appeal process has resulted in such large refugee backlogs that the government, from time to time, has offered blanket amnesties to people waiting for their claims to be adjudicated. Critics claim that people have been permitted to remain in Canada even though their claims to political persecution are impossible to verify. It costs the Canadian government millions of dollars each year to process bogus refugee claims. According to James Bissett, a former Canadian Ambassador, and executive director of Canada's Immigration service from 1985 to 1990, "the yearly cost for processing and caring for 40,000 asylum seekers is estimated to exceed $1 billion per year. Compare this with the $20-25 million Canada donates annually to the United Nations High Commission for Refugees (UNHCR) whose caseload exceeds 22 million refuges per year" ("*Canada's Asylum System*," Center for Immigration Studies, May, 2002).

Critics believe that many bogus claimants are criminals, possible public security threats, or simply economic migrants using the right of political asylum to achieve their objectives without meeting the criteria set out in Canadian immigration law. For example, 599 Chinese migrants arrived in Canada in 1999, claiming refugee status. Most arrived in rusty freighter boats that appeared off the coast of British Columbia. The migrants had paid about $30,000 each to criminals (known as "snakeheads") to smuggle them into Canada. The Canadian government spent about $36 million incarcerating the Chinese migrants and in processing their claims. By July of 2000 only 16 of 576 applicants had been granted refugee status (*Globe and Mail*, July 22, 2000, p. A.7).

People Smuggling

People smuggling is a multi-billion dollar business. The "snakeheads" are part of organized crime groups, or triads, located in the Fujian province of Southeast China. They rent or buy ships in Singapore or Taiwan, obtain forged travel documents in Thailand, and obtain supplies for the journey in Hong Kong. Dozens of migrants are crammed together below deck in converted cargo ships, with little in the way of personal amenities. When the ships near American or Canadian territorial waters passengers may be discharged to smaller ships to take them close to the shoreline or designated drop-off points. Other members of the smuggling rings then arrange to take them across the country to their final destination, usually Toronto or New York City. In many cases, the smuggled migrants have paid a deposit ($15,000) to get on one of the boats, the remainder to be paid off once they start working in North America. While paying off their loans the migrants and their families back home are often at the mercy of the crime syndicates. Since they are not "legal" many end up working in sweatshops for less than the minimum wage. Women may be sexually exploited or abused.

The Terror Threat

Since the destruction of the World Trade Center on September 11, 2001, the concern over public security has focused renewed attention on the perceived laxity of Canada's asylum system. For example, critics cite the case of Ahmed Ressam, an asylum seeker from Algeria who did not show up for a scheduled refugee hearing and was later apprehended trying to enter the United States with a car trunk full of explosives. Ressam was a member of a Montreal cell of the Algerian Armed Islamic Group (tied to the al Qaeda network of Osama Bin Laden) who planned to blow up the Los Angeles International airport during the millennium celebrations in the year 2000. The case did not receive much public attention until after the events in New York, even though a Canadian Security Intelligence Service (CSIS) Annual Report in June 2000 warned of the possible threat of possible terror attacks that would result in high casualties.

Economic And Demographic Arguments

Restrictionists also take issue with other aspects of immigration and refugee policy. They argue that immigration levels (the number of new people accepted into the country in any given year) are now (2003) three times higher than in the mid-1980s, in spite of two wrenching economic recessions (1983-84 and 1989-92). Canadian immigration levels are twice as high per capita as Australia and the United States, the two other major immigrant destinations. Acceptance rates for refugee claimants are three to four times higher than the average refugee acceptance rates for other industrialized countries. Critics argue that it is not necessary to maintain the currently high levels of immigration to deal with such problems as declining fertility rates (one rationale for the high admission rates) among the existing Canadian population. They cite studies of population trends that found that, even with no net immigration, Canada is assured of a population that continues to grow until 2015 (Swan, Neil, et al [1991]) *Economic and Social Impacts of Immigration: A research report prepared for the Economic Council of Canada*, Ottawa).

Problems With Family Class Admissions

Restrictionists oppose changes in immigration policy favouring the admission of more family members of immigrants who are already here. They claim that only 23% of new immigrants (2001) are actually evaluated on the basis of their potential economic contribution to the country (Stoffman, Daniel (2002) *Who Gets In*, Macfarlane Walter & Ross, Toronto, p.87).

In 1971, in contrast, 32% of new immigrants were admitted under the *Independent Category* on the basis of a *point system*, which required that immigrants obtain 70 out of a possible 100 points, based upon their educational level, occupational skills, and ability to speak one of the two official languages. *Family Class* immigrants do not require any such qualifications. If they have relatives who are already Canadian citizens or landed immigrants, they may be admitted, providing their relatives agree to take care of them financially, without help from the government, for a period of ten years (three years for spouses or same-sex partners under the revised *Immigration Act* of 2002).

Restrictionists argue that changes in immigration policy since 1978 have resulted in much higher levels of family class immigrants who don't have the skills, education, or language abilities to readily adapt to Canadian society. Many end up on welfare when their relatives fail to live up to their sponsorship agreement to take care of them for ten years. This "sponsorship breakdown" costs the Canadian state millions ($700 million in 1994) every year in additional costs (Campbell, Charles (2000) *Betrayal and Deceit: The Politics of Canadian Immigration*, Jasmine Books, p.163).

Sponsorship Undertakings

According to Citizenship and Immigration Canada guidelines "Canadian citizens or permanent residents living in Canada, 18 years or older, may sponsor close relatives or family members who want to become permanent residents of Canada. Sponsors must promise to support the relative or family member and accompanying family members for a period of three to ten years to help them settle in Canada. To sponsor a relative or family member you must sign a legal contract with the Minister of Citizenship and Immigration. This is called an undertaking. You must also sign a Sponsorship Agreement with your relative or family member that outlines your mutual commitments to each other" (Citizenship and Immigration Canada, 2003).

Certain income requirements must be met. The low-income cut-off is the mandatory minimum amount of gross annual income that sponsors are required to have. For example, an individual sponsor required a minimum of $18,841 gross annual income in 2001 whereas a four-person family required a minimum of $35,455 in 2001 to be eligible to sponsor someone. In the province of Quebec the minimums were higher with an individual requiring $24,203 (2001) and a family of four requiring a minimum of $38,247 to be eligible to sponsor someone. People who have previously sponsored relatives that have received social assistance (welfare) may not be allowed to sponsor another person. Sponsored relatives must also promise to "make every effort to become self-supporting"(unless they are elderly). Sponsored relatives and family members can include spouses, common-law or conjugal partners 16 years of age or older, parents and grandparents, dependent children (including adopted children). Other categories include children less than18 years of age who the sponsor intends to adopt and brothers, sisters, nephews, nieces or grandchildren who are orphans (under the age of 18 and not married or in a common law relationship).

A dependent child (son or daughter) is defined as being a person under the age of 22 who does not have a spouse or common law partner or is a full time student and is substantially dependent on a parent for financial support since before the age of 22 (or since becoming a spouse or common-law partner if this happened before the age of 22). A son or daughter is also deemed dependent if they were financially dependent on a parent before the age of 22 because of a disability.

Family Class Critics

According to immigration critic Daniel Stoffman, current family class problems stem from the 1978 changes to immigration regulations that permitted parents under the age of sixty to be sponsored by their children already living in Canada. "The parent of a 20 year old immigrant from a wealthy country such as France or Japan has little reason to follow his offspring to Canada and will almost never do so. Such a person will probably be in his 40s or 50s and at the peak of his working years. A 40 year old living in a poor country, on the other hand, often upgrades his economic status by coming to Canada, which has social benefits far exceeding those available at home" (Stoffman, Daniel (2002), *Who Gets In*, MacFarlane Walter & Ross, Toronto, p.82).

Restrictionists argue that family class immigrants are more likely to be illiterate than the Canadian-born population, leading to higher costs for language training or remedial education (Costs for language instruction for newcomers was $93.6 million in 2001, down from $119 million in 1998-99. This represents about one-quarter of the total costs for integrating newcomers and resettling refugees).

However, a recent Statistics Canada study, based on information from the National Longitudinal Survey of Children and Youth, countered some of the concerns raised by restrictionists about language difficulties. Overall, children from immigrant families started school with less developed skills in reading, writing and mathematics. With the passage of years, however, children with immigrant parents caught up to, and sometimes surpassed, the academic performance of their classmates with Canadian-born parents (Statistics Canada, Census of Canada, 2001).

"Cash For Visa"

Restrictionists also object to people being admitted under what is called the Business Class Program. People are admitted into Canada solely on the basis of money. For example, in 1979, under the "entrepreneur program," provision was made for the fast-track entry of foreign businessmen who had a "net personal worth of $500,000 or more, were prepared to invest a minimum of $250,000 in a provincially approved project for three years, and had demonstrated success in the business they were in." Critics argue that this is a "cash for visa" program which allows rich people to jump the immigration queue and buy their way into Canada without even meeting the minimum requirement of being able to speak either of the two official languages or, more importantly, without an extensive background check of how they had made their money in the first place. Restrictionists argue that much of the money brought in by investor class immigrants ended up in real estate or financial vehicles that didn't create very many jobs.

Census Trends

Restrictionists see more problems arising from recent census trends. For example, the 2001 census revealed that while recent immigrants were better educated than immigrants who entered the job market a decade ago, they earned less (see Figure 4.1). The census counted 805,000 immigrants aged 25 to 54 who arrived in the past decade. About 40% of this group had a university education, compared with 23% of their Canadian-born counterparts. In spite of the higher educational credentials, newcomers lost ground by virtually every income measure. For example, male arrivals in 2000 could expect to earn 63.1 cents for every dollar that Canadian-born workers earned after one year in the country—down from 63.4 cents in 1990 and 71.6 cents in 1980. Female newcomers earned just 60.5 cents compared to 70.5 cents in 1990.

Even more discouraging was the fact that immigrants who had been in Canada for 10 years earned just 79.8 cents of the Canadian-born workers' dollar in 2000, compared with more than 90 cents in 1990 and dollar for dollar in 1980. This trend changes the traditional pattern whereby immigrants to Canada had caught up to or surpassed Canadian-born workers within ten years of their arrival. Female newcomers who had been here 10 years managed 87.3 cents in 2000, down from 93.3 cents in 1990 and $1.03 in 1980. According to Statistics Canada, "the earnings of recent immigrants compared with those of the Canadian-born have deteriorated sharply" (*Canadian Press*, March 12, 2003).

Restrictionists see the changes as a consequence of maintaining high immigration levels despite a significant economic downturn in the early 1990s. However, an alternative explanation is that the educational qualifications of immigrants from non-traditional source countries are not recognized as meeting the standards of Canadian institutions.

Figure 4.1: Average Earning of Recent Immigrants,* Aged 25 to 54, by Highest Level of Schooling and Number of Years in Canada, Compared with the Canadian-Born, Canada, 1990 and 2000

	1990		2000	
	High school and some post-secondary	University	High school and some post-secondary	University
Male immigrants who had been in Canada for:				
1 year	$21,581	$33,673	$21,363	$31,460
2 years	$24,587	$37,895	$23,987	$37,397
3 years	$26,520	$42,010	$24,069	$40,011
4 years	$28,077	$42,116	$26,036	$42,627
5 years	$26,439	$45,873	$27,472	$44,054
6 years	$28,126	$48,443	$26,313	$45,773
7 years	$28,144	$50,385	$27,480	$45,795
8 years	$32,978	$54,439	$26,717	$44,361
9 years	$34,190	$54,426	$29,020	$46,151
10 years	$32,428	$52,060	$28,572	$47,522
Average earnings of men aged 25 to 54 born in Canada				
	$38,941	$60,375	$38,999	$66,520
Average earnings of men aged 25 to 54 born in Canada, all levels of schooling				
		$41,954		$45,002
Female immigrants who had been in Canada for:				
1 year	$15,607	$21,059	$13,805	$19,829
2 years	$17,596	$24,356	$16,855	$23,066
3 years	$18,777	$27,808	$16,357	$24,731
4 years	$18,345	$27,681	$16,687	$26,348
5 years	$18,597	$28,724	$17,854	$28,739
6 years	$18,805	$28,741	$17,839	$29,616

7 years	$19,394	$28,905	$18,088	$28,387
8 years	$20,051	$32,193	$19,217	$30,193
9 years	$20,661	$32,015	$19,926	$30,948
10 years	$20,703	$32,522	$20,626	$32,473
Average earnings of women aged 25 to 54 born in Canada				
	$22,576	$37,235	$24,493	$41,062
Average earnings of women aged 25 to 54 born in Canada, all levels of schooling				
		$24,955		$28,745
*Immigrants who arrived in Canada from 1980 to 1989 and from 1990 to 1999.				

In a landmark 2001 study, the Conference Board of Canada estimated the country loses $4.1 billion to $5.9 billion in income annually because it does not recognize the professional qualifications of 540,000 people, including roughly 350,000 immigrants, mostly from China and India. The Conference Board of Canada drew attention to the fact that out of 10,279 arrivals, between 1991 and 1994, listing engineering as their intended job, only 56 are now practicing (*MacLean's Magazine*, July 21, 2003, p.41).

Immigrants arriving in the 1990s were the most highly educated cohorts ever yet it is not uncommon in Canada to find recent university-educated immigrants driving taxis, working as janitors, security guards, and truck drivers and building superintendents. Another factor might be the younger age of immigrants who arrived in the 1990s (see Figure 4.2). In 2001, roughly 46% of all immigrants were between 25 and 44 years of age in comparison to their Canadian-born counterparts who made up only 31% of the total population.

Labour Market Participation

Participation in the labour market is another important indicator of how the immigrant population is integrating into Canadian society. Employment rates for the most recently arrived immigrants have moved steadily down since 1981 (see Figure 4.3). Up until the early 1980s immigrants had higher labour force participation rates than the Canadian born (79.3% versus 75.5%). However, by 1991 the labour force participation rate for immigrants fell below the national average (77.2% versus 78.2%). This gap has persisted and grown wider for the most recently arrived immigrant despite the beginning of economic recovery in the late

1990s. Immigrants make up about 20% of the 3.2 million people in the Canadian workforce and those who arrived in the 1990s represented almost 70% of the total growth in the labour market during that decade.

Figure 4.2: Levels of Educational Attainment Among Immigrants of the 1970s, 1980s, and 1990s,* Canada, 2001

	Total	Men	Women
Immigrants of the 1970s			
All levels of education	100.00	100.00	100.00
Less then high school	32.53	26.50	38.26
High school	19.06	17.06	20.97
Trades	14.04	17.98	1.29
College	12.12	11.78	12.44
University	22.24	26.69	18.01
Immigrants of the 1980s			
All levels of education	100.00	100.00	100.00
Less then high school	27.19	24.43	29.82
High school	24.26	22.52	25.91
Trades	10.85	13.23	8.60
College	12.56	11.18	13.86
University	25.14	28.65	21.82
Immigrants of the 1990s			
All levels of education	100.00	100.00	100.00
Less then high school	20.17	17.95	22.12
High school	18.95	17.35	20.35
Trades	7.57	8.80	6.48
College	12.60	11.18	13.84
University	40.71	44.71	37.21

*Immigrants aged 25 to 64 who arrived in the ten years preceding the 1981, 1991 and 2001 Censuses, respectively.

Figure 4.3: Labour Force Participation Rates for Immigrants and Non-Immigrants
   (Percentage)

Employment rate	1981	1986	1991	1996	2001
Labour force	75.5	76.3	78.2	77.0	80.3
Non-immigrants	74.6	75.8	78.7	78.4	81.8
All immigrants	79.3	78.5	77.2	72.1	75.6
Recent immigrants	75.7	71.1	68.6	61.0	65.8
Unemployment rate			%		
Labour force	5.9	9.1	9.6	9.3	6.7
Non-immigrants	6.3	9.4	9.4	8.8	6.4
All immigrants	4.5	7.7	10.4	11.0	7.9
Recent immigrants	6.0	11.8	15.6	16.7	12.1

Open Door Arguments

Supporters of Canada's "liberal" immigration policies argue that immigrants, with the exception of a few "bad apples," make exemplary citizens. Up until at least the early 1990s, studies of immigrant populations in Canada have shown that, as a group, they are less likely to be on social assistance (welfare) and less likely to draw employment insurance, As a group, they earn more than the Canadian-born and pay more in taxes (Akbari, Ather H [1989]) "The Benefits of Immigrants to Canada: Evidence on Tax and Public Services," *Canadian Public Policy*, 15, No. 4, p.424–35, and by the same author, (1991) "Public Finance Impact of Immigrant Population on Host Nations" Some Canadian Evidence," *Social Science Quarterly*, 72, No.2, p.334–46). See also an article by Akbari (1995) "The Impact of Immigrants on Canada's Treasury, circa 1990" in Don Devoretz, ed., *Diminishing Returns: The Economics of Canada's Recent Immigration Policy*. Toronto and Vancouver: C.D Howe Institute and Laurier Institute, pp.113–27).

Family Values

Many immigrant groups place a high value on extended families with greater commitment to children, elderly parents and grandparents than many native-born Canadians demonstrate. This results in less reliance on publicly funded daycare and old-age homes. Immigrants, as a group, are more likely to be married and less likely to be divorced than the Canadian-born. They are seen as more likely to own their own home, to be self-employed, to save more, and have higher net worth than native-born Canadians (CICNet Publications: *A Profile of Immigrants in Canada*, 1997). They are also about half as likely to land in jail as the Canadian-born (*Toronto Star*, June 17, 1998).

The "Boat People"

Supporters of open door policies cite the example of the Vietnamese "boat people," who came to Canada as refugees in 1979-81, a few years after the Communist takeover in their home country. By 1991, 78% were in the workforce and employed. Only 8% were unemployed compared to about 10% of the Canadian-born. Most could not speak any English when they arrived (Beiser, Morton [1999]) *Strangers at the Gate: The Boat People's First Ten Years in Canada*, University of Toronto Press).

The same story applies to the155 Sri Lankans and 174 Sikhs who showed up off the East coast of Canada in the mid-1980s claiming refugee status. Most of them are today gainfully employed, and some have set up businesses that employ other Canadians (*MacLean's Magazine*, August 23, 1999). Some supporters of open door policies admit that many refugees are economic migrants and do lie to get into Canada but they don't necessarily see this as a problem. They argue that, in many cases, it took audacity and courage for people to leave their home countries in search of opportunities in Canada. It is exactly this type of young, creative, risk-taking person that Canada needs, particularly as the native-born Canadian population ages.

Immigration And The "Welfare State"

Some people argue that it is not a "liberal" immigration policy that is to blame for current problems but "liberal" social welfare policies. Eliminate generous employment insurance programs, welfare payments, and "free medicare" and the only people who will want to come to Canada are those who are willing to work hard and "pull themselves up by their own bootstraps." Canada should welcome such people with open arms regardless of where they come from, a view held by right-wing "libertarians" such as Terrence Corcoran, an editorial page writer for the *National Post*.

Immigration Fears Overblown

Irving Abella, an author and York University professor, urges Canadians to "get a grip. We are not the 'suckers' that some critics have claimed," even in the case of the refugee determination system. "In an average year, Canada accepts some 25,000 refugees. And in a nation whose population is approaching 30 million, that is hardly excessive, especially compared with some European countries that have absorbed many hundreds of thousands. In a world overflowing with millions of refugees, Canada's contribution is certainly not exorbitant" (*MacLean's Magazine*, August 23, 1999).

The American Experience

Canada is not the only country where immigration policy is the subject of heated debate. According to Virginia Abernethy of Vanderbilt University, high levels of immigration threaten the standard of living of American-born workers and contribute to environmental pressures. Other critics such as Roy Beck, Washington editor of the magazine *Social Contract*, believe liberal immigration policies contribute to "demographic Balkanization." However, the late Julian Simon of the University of Maryland saw high immigration levels as increasing the number of creative minds in the population, thereby facilitating innovation and social change. Historian Arthur M. Schlesinger believes that "any curtailment of immigration offends something in the American soul" (*Scientific American*, Sept.20, 1999).

The United States had an "open door" immigration policy up until the 1920s but then passed legislation that severely curtailed entry except for people from northwestern European countries. The restrictive policy ended in 1965 with a series of more liberal laws, including the *Immigration Reform and Control Act* of 1986, under which 2.7 million illegal aliens, mainly from Mexico were granted legal immigrant status. The changes resulted in the most prolonged and largest wave of immigration in American history with over thirty million new arrivals since 1965. Up until then the two largest "waves" had been from 1899 through 1914, with 13.6 million new arrivals, and 1880 to 1898, with 8.6 million. In any given year, the United States takes in roughly one million legal immigrants and about another 300,000 who arrive illegally. Since 1970, more than 30 million legal and illegal immigrants have settled in the United States. The foreign-born population of the United States is currently 33.1 million or 11.5% of the total population of the country. The two favourite immigrant destinations are California and New York. As in Canada, immigrants to the United

States tend to be younger than the average American-born. Roughly 65% of new legal arrivals in the United States enter under "family reunification" programs, 13% under "employment-based" preference programs, 14% are refugees or asylum seekers, and 8% under other categories.

According to the U.S Census projections, the American population will grow to about 394 million in 2050. Of the 122 million person increase between now and then, 80 million people will be added because of immigration. The projections also indicate that the United States will become an increasingly diverse society. In 1980 the U.S was 80% Anglo (non-Hispanic white) but the census projections indicate that by 2050 only 53% of the population will fit that description.

The Total Fertility Rate (the total fertility rate is defined as the average number of babies born to women in their reproductive years—roughly age 15-40) in the United States is currently 2.1335 births per woman, the highest it has been since 1971. By comparison, Canada's average fertility rate is 1.4 births per woman, the United Kingdom is 1.7 per woman and Germany's is 1.3 per woman. A Total Fertility Rate (TFR) of 2.1 is considered the replacement rate; once a TFR reaches 2.1 the population will remain stable assuming no immigration or emigration takes place.

Chapter Five
THE CHALLENGE OF DIVERSITY

Are certain groups in Canada more likely to experience the ill effects of prejudice and discrimination? In October of 2003 the results of the first large scale survey on this question were published by Statistics Canada. The survey asked respondents (interviewed by telephone in ten provinces) whether they felt they had experienced discrimination or had been treated unfairly by others in Canada in the five years prior to the survey because of their ethnicity, culture, race, skin colour, language, accent or religion. If respondents said they had experienced discrimination or unfair treatment, they were then asked how often they felt they had experienced this: often, sometimes, or rarely. The survey of 42,476 non-aboriginal Canadians aged 15 and over found that the vast majority of respondents, 86%, had not suffered discrimination or unfair treatment. Another 6% said they experienced it rarely, while 7% said they experienced it sometimes or often.

Prejudice And Discrimination In Canada

However, the survey showed that among respondents who identified themselves as belonging to "visible minorities," only 64% said they had not experienced discrimination in the five years preceding the survey (the survey was carried out from April to August in 2002). Fifteen percent of visible minority survey respondents said they rarely experienced discrimination but 20% had experienced it "sometimes" or "often." Thirty-two percent of black respondents to the survey said they had sometimes or often been victims of discrimination, the highest of any group. By comparison, 21% of South Asians and 18 % of Chinese respondents said they had experienced discrimination. Seventeen percent of blacks, 13% of South Asians, and 15% of Chinese respondents said they had rarely experienced discrimination.

According to the results of the survey, incidents of discrimination were most likely to occur at the workplace. Fifty-six percent of respondents said it had occurred at work or when they applied for a job. Thirty-five percent of respondents said they had experienced discrimination in a store, bank or restaurant. Twenty-six percent of respondents said they had perceived discrimination or unfair treatment on the street.

For people identified as visible minorities, there was little variation in the levels of discrimination or unfair treatment by length of time, or generation, in Canada. Roughly 20% of people in visible minorities who immigrated to Canada from 1991 to 2001 reported perceived discrimination or unfair treatment sometimes or often, compared with 21% of people identified as visible minorities who came prior to 1991 and 18% who were two or more generations in Canada.

The province of Quebec fared best in terms of the fewest perceived cases of discrimination or unfair treatment experienced by visible minorities. Sixty-nine percent of visible minority respondents in Montreal and across the province said they had not experienced discrimination while 19% reported experiencing it "sometimes" or "often" and another 12% "rarely" (Statistics Canada, *Ethnic Diversity Survey*, 2003).

"Hot Button Issues" In Canadian Society

There is little doubt that prejudice and discrimination exists in Canada as in every other society. However, the level of actual inter-ethnic conflict is insignificant when compared to many other countries around the world. The level of violence arising from the conflicts which do exist (English/French in Quebec) barely registers on the radar screen when compared to Bosnia, Rwanda, Northern Ireland, Israel/Palestine or any of the hundreds of other regional conflicts. However, the increasing "ethnocultural diversity" of Canadian society, particularly the increasing number of so-called "visible minorities," has brought to the foreground attitudes, issues, and policies, which have generated a potential for conflict. Among these "hot button" issues, which have emerged, are immigration policy, multicultural policy, employment equity, and "racial profiling." For example, changes in immigration policy, permitting more immigration from so-called "Third World" countries has generated a backlash among people who are alarmed or feel threatened by the rapidly changing "racial" composition of the country. This backlash has been exacerbated by certain high profile crimes committed by recently arrived refugees or immigrants of colour.

The "Just Desserts" Case

The shooting death of a Toronto police officer, Todd Bayliss, in 1994, created a huge uproar when it was discovered that Clinton Gayle, the person charged with the killing, had been ordered deported to Jamaica in 1991 for past criminal convictions, but was never removed. Gayle had been released from an Ontario jail on a two thousand dollar security bond while immigration officials tried to obtain the travel documents needed to send him back to Jamaica. However, his file had somehow been misplaced. Another high profile crime in the same year (1994) involved the shooting death of a 23-year-old woman named Georgina (Vivi) Leimonis, at a trendy Toronto restaurant called Just Desserts. Three robbers entered the restaurant and lined the customers up against the wall. One of the robbers panicked and fired his sawed-off shotgun, killing Leimonis. There was widespread anger again when people learned that one of the suspects in the case, O'Neil Grant, had been ordered deported to Jamaica in 1992, but was granted a five year stay of the deportation order. Ostensibly, the public uproar was over the shoddy record of enforcing a section of the *Immigration Act* that empowers authorities to deport immigrants convicted of a crime. However, the intensity of the public response suggested that the unspoken issue was the rapidly changing racial composition of Canadian society, particularly in the major cities.

Racialization Of Crime Incidents

"Racialization" of crime incidents is one of the ugly aspects of communities undergoing rapid demographic change. Entire minority communities can be held responsible for the behaviour of a few individuals. This occurred in the wake of the "Just Desserts" killing. In some cases, the media reaction to the case was inflammatory, with thinly concealed racial undertones, directed primarily against those of Jamaican origins. One columnist wrote that "the barbarians are inside the gate," which both reflected, and fed into, the fears of a certain segment of the population. The restaurant where Leimonis died was deluged with flowers. A note left at the scene of the crime urged people not to blame the black community but this was quickly scrawled out by another message, "kill your own, and leave us alone." The incident provided fuel for advocates of more restrictive immigration and refugee policies. Within a few months of the killing a bill (C-44) was passed by the Canadian parliament that made it easier to deport landed immigrants with serious criminal records. Three hundred and fifty-five criminals from Ontario were deported to other countries within two years of the bill's passage, 138 (38%) of Jamaican origin (*Colour Profiling: The Ultimate Just Desserts,* by Julian Falconer and Carmen Ellis, a paper presented to the 1998 American Bar Association Conference, Toronto, Ontario). One of the great ironies of the case was that O'Neil Grant, the source of much of the media uproar just after the killing, was acquitted of the crime five years later. No one paid much attention.

Racial Profiling

Another source of controversy has been the recurring charge that police forces in Canada engage in a practice known as "racial profiling," which is the practice of stopping and questioning people for little reason other than their skin colour.

Formally, the Ontario Human Rights Commission defines

...racial profiling (as) any action undertaken for reasons of safety, security or public protection, that relies on stereotypes about race, colour, ethnicity, ancestry, religion, or place of origin, or a combination of these, rather than on reasonable suspicion, to single out an individual for greater scrutiny or different treatment. Age and/or gender can also be factors in racial profiling.

This type of profiling assumes that the personal characteristics of an individual are indicative of his or her actions or of a tendency to be engaged in illegal activity. This differs from criminal profiling which relies on actual behaviour or on information about suspected activity by someone who meets the description of an individual (Ontario Human Rights Commission, Racial Profiling Inquiry, March 21, 2003).

For those who drive cars it is known, colloquially, as the offense of "driving while black" or "DWB." For many years, Professor Scott Wortley, a criminologist at the University of Toronto, argued that Toronto police routinely engaged in this practice. In his 1997 study, called "The Usual Suspects: Race, Police Stops and Criminal Justice," he surveyed a group of 1,300 randomly selected whites, blacks and Asian people in Toronto, and asked them about their contacts with police. In this survey, 28% of blacks reported being stopped at least once in a two-year period, compared to 14.6% of whites and 18.2% of Asians.

Wortley and a colleague, Julian Tanner, also surveyed 3000 Toronto high school students about their experiences with the police. They discovered that over a two year period black students were twice as likely as white students to be stopped by the police. Wortley and Tanner found "racial profiling directly contributes to the over-representation of black people in the criminal justice system."

Because Wortley's research was based on survey data, there was a tendency to dismiss or downplay the findings as being less than reliable. But in October 2002, a *Toronto Star* investigative team produced an analysis of police crime data that provided tangible evidence that Wortley's research was correct (see Figures 5.1 and 5.2). The Star reporters had obtained a police database recording more than 480,000 incidents in which an individual was arrested, or ticketed, for an offense dating back to 1996. It included about 800,000 criminal and other charges. This information was obtained through a freedom of information request that, for the first time, permitted access to these statistics to non-police personnel.

Figure 5.1: "Singled Out," Toronto Star, October 20, 2002

Blacks were more likely than whites to be charged with an "out-of-sight" offence.

■ **Proportion of race of those charged** □ **Proportion of race in population**

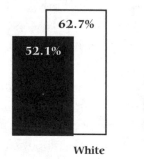

| | White | Black |

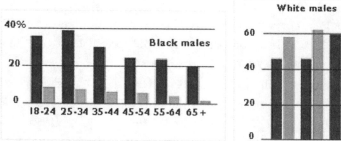

Young black males were even more over-represented in the arrest statistics.

Young white drivers were under-represented.

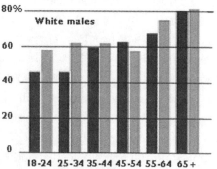

Driving While Black

The Toronto crime data showed that blacks were 4 times more likely to be charged for "out of sight" violations (driving without a license, driving without insurance, driving while under suspension, failing to update a driver's license with a change of address) than their proportion of the general population would warrant under a system of "random stops" by police. "Out of sight" violations are discovered only after the police stop a motor vehicle. Simply put, more blacks were being charged with "out of sight violations" because blacks, more than any other group, were more likely to be pulled over and stopped by police. The data also showed that blacks, charged with simple drug possession, are taken to police stations more often than whites facing the same charge. Once at the station, accused blacks are held overnight, for a bail hearing, at twice the rate of whites.

Figure 5.2: "Who Gets Arrested," Toronto Star, March 18, 2003

Who gets arrested for criminal or drug offences

■ **Percentage of those arrested** □ **Percentage in population**

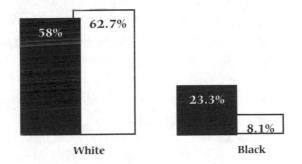

Different treatment: % of each social group

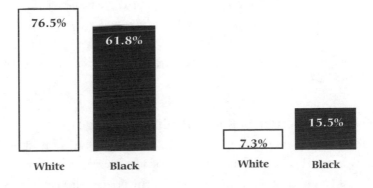

Released at the scene for simple drug possession.

Percent held for bail hearings for simple possession.

Explanations Other Than Profiling

Toronto police chief Julian Fantino disputed the findings. "We don't treat people differently," he said, in an interview. "Nor do we consider the race or ethnicity, or any of that, as factors of how we dispose of cases, or individuals" (*Toronto Star*, October 19, 2002).

Fantino suggested that social class and environmental circumstances, rather than skin colour, might explain the findings. To critics of the police force, Fantino's explanation appeared to be self-serving but there have been other cases where a rush to judgement proved premature. For example, a study of alleged racial profiling in the city of Minneapolis, in the United States, initially appeared to support the contention that police were stopping minorities for traffic violations far out of proportion to their numbers in the general population. But when statistical safeguards were applied, other reasons as to why minority drivers were stopped more often emerged. Black drivers in Minneapolis were more likely to drive older cars than whites—since their incomes were less than half that of white residents—and were therefore more likely to be pulled over for equipment violations. While blacks represented only 18% of the city's population, they were 31% of residents under 18, young drivers being more likely to speed and take greater risks, according to the automobile insurance companies. Finally, statistics showed that minority neighbourhoods were more likely to host serious crimes, which meant that police concentrate their resources in those areas, where minorities were overrepresented among the population of drivers ("Race to Conclusions," *Weekly Standard*, August 20, 2001).

Difficulties arise when trying to establish an adequate "benchmark" against which to measure if police are pulling over, searching, or arresting "too many" visible or ethnic minorities. If particular groups drive more recklessly, have older cars, are younger, are more likely to drive when police happen to be on the road, are less likely to wear their seatbelts, they are more likely to be stopped. Police usually pull someone over for an actual traffic violation. Data can be skewed by all these factors.

Police Force Reaction To Racial Profiling Charges

The Toronto Police Association launched a lawsuit seeking almost $2.2 billion in damages from The *Toronto Star*, alleging officers were defamed by the newspaper's series on police and race. A lawyer for the police, Tim Danson, said the Toronto police board of directors retained a team of experts from Ontario, British Columbia and the United States to study the *Star's* methodology. According to

Danson, "this team of experts confirmed the instincts of the police, namely that the *Toronto Star's* analysis is seriously flawed and unfair" (*The Canadian Press*, January 18, 2003).

The *Toronto Star* said it had its own experts help with the series and stood by its report, claiming the articles were "fair and balanced and accurate," vowing to "vigourously fight this lawsuit in the courts."

On June 24, 2003, the Police Association's lawsuit against the *Toronto Star* was thrown out of court. A judge ruled it wasn't reasonable to conclude that the data reported in the newspaper applied to every officer or any particular officer on the force.

The "Dee Brown" Case

A few months after the controversy involving the *Toronto Star* series, the Ontario Court of Appeal found that racial profiling exists in the province of Ontario, in a ruling that upheld a lower court decision to throw out a drunk driving conviction against former Toronto Raptor basketball star Dee Brown.

Brown was driving slightly over the speed limit on Toronto's Don Valley Parkway while returning home from a Halloween party in 1999, according to the evidence at his trial. He testified that a police officer drove up beside his sports utility vehicle, peered into the window, before signaling him to pull over to the curb. Brown failed a roadside sobriety test, after the police officer smelled liquor on his breath. Later, at the police station, Brown took a breath test that showed he had 140 milligrams of alcohol per 100 millilitres of blood. The legal limit is 80 milligrams. At his trial, Brown's lawyer argued that he had been stopped because he was a black man, wearing jogging clothes, a baseball cap, and driving an expensive vehicle. This was alleged to be a breech of the *Charter of Rights* because he had been stopped on the basis of his skin colour. Ontario Court Justice David Fairgrieve rejected any suggestion that Brown was a victim of racial profiling. He was convicted, ordered to pay a $2000 fine, and banned from driving for a year.

The conviction was overturned after an appeal hearing found that Justice Fairgreave appeared to show bias in dismissing the *Charter* application. At the conclusion of the initial trial, Fairgrieve had criticized Brown and his defense lawyer, Steven Skurka, for their "serious, nasty, and potentially malicious" allegations of racial profiling. The judge went on to suggest that Brown should consider apologizing to the police. The appeal court found the remarks "arguably showed a failure to appreciate that racial profiling can be a subconscious factor impacting on the exercise of discretionary power in a multicultural society" (*Globe and Mail*, January 18, 2000).

The original conviction was reversed based on a concession by the Crown that racial profiling does exist. According to Justice John Morden, of the Ontario Court of Appeal, "this was a responsible position to take. This conclusion is supported by significant social research. The attitude underlying racial profiling is one that may be consciously or unconsciously held. That is, the police officer need not be an overt racist. His or her conduct may be based on conscious or subconscious racial stereotyping" (*Kingston Whig Standard*, April 17, 2003).

At a news conference after this decision, Julian Falconer, who acted for the Urban Alliance on Race Relations, a group promoting racial harmony, and an intervenor in the case, said this was the first time an appeal court in Canada had taken "judicial notice" of racial profiling by police. He went on to add that the court was not accusing every police officer of racial profiling. But he said the judgement would allow those potentially mistreated by the police to raise issues of racial profiling. "Gone are the days of denial," he said, describing the judgement as a "watershed" (*National Post*, April 17, 2003).

The head of the Police Union in Toronto, Craig Bromell, was enraged by the court decision. In an interview with the *Globe and Mail*, he labeled the decision "politically correct crap," and said that black drivers could now commit infractions without fear of consequences. "Go do what you want," Bromell vented. "If that's what the system wants, go do what you want. You won. We give up. Quote me on all of that. If they're going to be using bullshit excuses like this then so be it. There's never been any proof of racial profiling" (*Globe and Mail*, April 17, 2003). Bromell suggested that police stop pulling over black motorists entirely.

In an opinion piece in the *National Post*, columnist Christie Blatchford saw the court decision as being less significant and "historic than either its supporters or detractors are claiming. It doesn't mean, as Mr. Bromell claimed, that blacks are outside the law or that police should stop pulling them over for valid reasons. It doesn't mean the officer who stopped Mr. Brown was engaging in racial profiling, only that because the judge never appeared to seriously consider the possibility, the case gives rise to a taint of potential bias.

It means that racial profiling may be a valid defense in some cases, and that judges ought to be open to seeing it. And that seems fair enough" (*National Post*, April 19, 2003).

The "Self-Fulfilling Prophecy"

Most people join the police force to do good work, to provide service to the community, and sometimes to put their lives on the line. Most police officers don't wake up every morning with the idea that "beating up on minorities" is an essential part of their job description. So why do charges of racial discrimination find such resonance in minority communities?

Scott Wortley uses an example that illustrates a common sociological phenomenon. He suggests picturing two groups, one black and one white, of equal size –say 1000 people. In each group, the rate of drug dealing is the same: 1 in 10 people deal crack cocaine, for a total of 100 in each group. If these two groups were being policed identically, meaning in a "colour blind" way, the number of dealers arrested should be the same in either group. However, when racial profiling occurs, the police assume that blacks are more likely to be dealing drugs, and therefore they are more likely to target them for special attention, resulting in more black stops. If the ratio of stops were 5-1, black to white, the police would charge 50 black dealers for every 10 white dealers. "What the statistics don't show," according to Wortley, "is that 90 per cent of the white drug dealers got away, and that half the black dealers got away." So, at the end of the year, the police statistics would "prove" drug dealing is rampant in the black community, which would, therefore, justify continued profiling. "It can be a *self-fulfilling prophecy*," Wortley claims (*Toronto Star*, Oct.19, 2002).

Wortley also believes that the higher proportion of blacks charged also affects attitudes. People who have experienced profiling, real or imagined, are less likely to be polite when confronted by authority figures. This leads to harsher treatment by the police than is justified in particular situations.

Public Attitudes Towards Racial Profiling

A Compas Inc. poll of 500 Ontario residents was conducted for *CanWest News* and Global Television in the spring of 2003 on the "hot button" issue of racial profiling. Compas researchers asked the survey participants whether profiling should be forbidden, optional or mandatory in campaigns against crime, violent crime, international terrorism and medical emergencies such as SARS (severe, acute respiratory syndrome). In the case of SARS, travelers from China had faced increased airport security because of concern they could be carrying SARS, and, in Ontario, parents who adopted children from China were forced into an automatic quarantine upon their return from that country regardless of symptoms.

Half of those polled said profiling by race should be an option or mandatory when a medical crisis, such as SARS, is involved. Thirty-seven percent of respondents said profiling should be absolutely forbidden in such circumstances.

Attitudes were virtually identical toward the use of profiling by religion and national origin in the fight against international terrorism. Forty-nine percent of those polled believed profiling should be allowed in such circumstances, while 39% were strongly opposed to such a practice.

But there is significant opposition to the practice as it relates to crime. Using race to identify people who have a statistically higher chance of committing a crime remains more controversial. On the question of whether profiling should be used to combat crime, a narrow plurality (46%) of those polled said profiling should at least be an option while an almost equal number (44%) said racial profiling should be prohibited. According to poll director Conrad Winn, "it shows that Canadians are torn between liberal democratic principles—which say everyone should be treated as an individual and not as a member of a group—and practical realities" (*Kingston Whig Standard*, May 24, 2003).

In the United States, profiling has become a routine part of the post September 11, 2001 world. The American Department of State has tightened the visa issuing process and now requires background checks of male applicants from most Muslim countries.

Employment Equity Policy As Social Control

One strategy that police forces have used in an attempt to control race relations and deflect criticism on issues such as racial profiling centres on hiring more people from visible minorities. However, in 2001, only 51 of 332 or15% of the new recruits to the Toronto police force represented visible minorities, in one of the world's most multicultural cities. In 2002, only 11% of the new recruits were from visible minorities (*Toronto Star*, October 19, 2002). Despite more intense recruitment efforts, particularly among women of South Asian origins, the percentage of visible minorities among total police officer personnel remained at 12.1% in 2004 (*The Globe and Mail*, April 10, 2004).

In Montreal, the Montreal Urban Community Police Department has been vigourously trying to diversify its staff as part of a decade long employment equity program. Job applicants require the usual basic qualifications, which include Canadian citizenship, a clean police record, fluency in French and a "functional ability" in English, a Class 5 driver's license, and good vision. They also need a bachelor's degree or a technical college degree. The police department gives priority to applicants who have an academic background in law, social sciences, criminology, psychology, sociology, business administration, and human resources or in industrial relations.

Unlike the United States, where *affirmative action* programs sometimes set *quotas* for the number of visible minorities to be hired, regardless of qualifications, employment equity programs seek a more equitable representation in the workforce of aboriginals, visible minorities, women, and persons with disabilities, providing they meet the qualifications for the job. It affects all employees of the federal government and federally regulated industries.

The attempt to make the Montreal police force more representative of the general population has been an uphill battle. Of 278 new recruits hired between May 1999 and April 2000, only four were aboriginals, 18 were from visible minorities, and 20 from ethnic minorities. Eighty seven women were hired during the same period. Policing is often viewed negatively in minority communities, and people who join the police are sometimes viewed as "sell-outs" or traitors who are "joining the enemy'." New recruits must also be prepared to face possible hostility and "backlash" from a police subculture that is still dominated by white "Anglo-Saxon" or "French Canadian" males, some of whom may feel threatened by what they might perceive as an attempt to diversify the workforce at their expense.

The Politics Of Canadian Identity

Underlying many of the "hot button" issues raised is an unspoken concern about the changing racial composition of Canadian society. This is evident in the often highly emotional responses of many people to government policies on *multiculturalism* or *employment equity*. It is based on a perception by some that *"visible minorities"* have become too bold in asserting their rights and that this is having an adverse effect on employment opportunities, particularly for young, white males. Political groups such as the racist "Heritage Front" and other skinhead groups have been only to willing to capitalize on these concerns to win adherents to their cause, which is the return of a "White Canada."

It might seem ironic that the very programs and policies designed to promote greater tolerance and integration have had the unintended effect of generating support for racist groups.

Multiculturalism And Marginalization

However, it is not just racists who have problems with policies that promote multiculturalism. In a stinging attack on such policies, Trinidadian born Canadian writer Neil Bissoondath believes the concept of multiculturalism "has been reduced to the simplest theatre. Canadians, neatly divided into 'ethnic' and otherwise, encounter each other's mosaic tiles mainly at festivals. There's traditional music, traditional dancing, traditional food at distinctly untraditional prices, all of which is diverting as far as it goes, but such encounters remain at the level of a folkloric Disneyland. We take a great deal of self-satisfaction from such festivals; they are seen as proof of our open-mindedness, of our welcoming difference. Yet how easily we forget that none of our ethnic cultures seem to have produced literature or philosophy worth our consideration. How seductive it is, how reassuring, that Greeks are always Zorbas, Ukrainians always Cossaks; we come away with stereotypes reinforced. Not only are differences highlighted, but individuals are defined by those differences. There are those who find pleasure in playing to the theme, those whose ethnicity ripens with the years. Yet to play the ethnic, deracinated and costumed, is to play the stereotype. It is to abdicate one's full humanity in favour of one of its exotic features. To accept the role of ethnic is also to accept a gentle marginalization. It is to accept that one will never be just a part of the landscape but always a little apart from it, not quite belonging"(New Internationalist, No.305, Sept. 1998, p.20).

Some recent immigrants to Canada are themselves concerned that they are the victims of a growing cult of racial and ethnic identity that places them in a ghetto that makes individual integration and acceptance more, rather than less, difficult.

Gurmant Grewal, a former Reform (now Conservative) MP from British Columbia, who moved to Canada from India in 1991, introduced a private member's bill in 1997 designed to scrap Canada's multiculturalism department. Grewal argued that, "when the focus is on defining us with different brand names the government tries to keep us separate. It's not the integration of communities it is segregation. That's what they are trying to do" (The Montreal Gazette, October 14, 1997).

According to these critics, the obsession with "identity politics" leads to "hyphenated Canadianism," whereby your identity as a Canadian is always fractured by your ethnic origins. So instead of simply being a "Canadian" you are always an "Italian-Canadian" or an "Irish-Canadian" or an "African-Canadian."

These divisions are reinforced by questions such as the one on the Canadian census (#19) that asks respondents to identify themselves as "White, Chinese, South Asian, Black, Arab/West African, Filipino, South East Asian, Latin American, Japanese, Korean or Other." In response to this directive, McGill University anthropologist Bernard Trigger argued that "we should be unlabeling ourselves, not labeling ourselves" and that our government is "taking scientifically illegitimate categories and giving them credence by putting them in a census" (*Montreal Gazette*, January 29, 2000).

The question was introduced in the 1996 Census and was designed to resolve some of the ambiguities associated with another question on "ethnic origins" (Question#17) which was producing confusing combinations of ethnic origin which did not provide reliable data on the number of "visible minorities" in Canada. This was considered important because of the federal *Multicultural Act*, and *Employment Equity* legislation that requires this information to carry out its mandate. The ethnic origin question has been included on the census since 1871 although until 1951, it was referred to as racial origin.

Census Question Debate

Jack Jedwab, of the McGill Institute for the Study of Canada, disagrees with Trigger. He believes that lifting the census question would "send out the wrong message about Canada's commitment to diversity and about what constitutes Canadian identity. It would also deprive Canadians of access to useful data" (*Montreal Gazette*, January 29, 2000).

Jedwab argues that the data can be useful in discovering patterns of job discrimination. In his view discrimination is not only a problem for members of visible minorities or language minorities, but also touches members of some ethnic groups. Canada's strength has been in allowing for the coexistence of various expressions of identity rather than implying that they are un-Canadian.

Some opponents of the ethnicity question argue that just asking it detracts from the centrality of being Canadian because it draws attention to our differences. They argue that such distinctions serve to segregate or ghettoize certain groups in Canadian society. They would prefer that permanent residents of Canada be referred to simply as "Canadians."

In 1991, when census respondents were asked to give their ethnic origin, they were provided for the first time with a checklist of 15 options (English, French, Russian, etc.), followed by a blank space. The option of "Canadian" wasn't available. This caused a considerable uproar, particularly among people whose families have been in Canada for several generations and resented being asked to rediscover some long-forgotten ethnic heritage. As a result, 3% of census respondents wrote "Canadian" in the blank space. As a result of the controversy, the question about ethnic origins was changed on the 1996 census. A list of 24 example groups including "Canadian" was provided and respondents were asked to specify as many groups as were applicable to them. Consequently. Census respondents claiming "Canadian" as their "ethnic origin" increased sharply to 19%.

The controversy didn't end. After the 1996 census, statistics Canada conducted a year-long consultation on the "ethnic origins" question. Several sociologists and demographers were critical of the inclusion of "Canadian" as an "ethnic origin," arguing that it is no such thing but rather a "self-identity," and defeats the whole purpose of a question designed to measure the different backgrounds of the Canadian population. Social Science researchers believed that the non-ethnic "Canadian" category would make it difficult to compare new data with historical data, as the ethnic origins question had been asked, in one form or another, as far back as 1871.

In the summer of 1999, Statistics Canada proposed that the "ethnicity question" be dropped because it was "demographically tainted." The argument was that the census questionnaire gives respondents the opportunity to describe themselves in their own terms rather than respond to clear-cut, unambiguous choices, which sometimes leads to multiple and confusing combinations of ethnic identifications.

In response to the Statistics Canada proposal, Alex Himmelfarb, then the Deputy Heritage Minister in the federal Liberal government, sent a letter to Statistics Canada's chief statistician, Ivan Fellegi, warning that dropping or radically altering the ethnicity question would deny the government valuable information needed to fulfill its legislative and policy obligations," particularly those related to federal multicultural legislation. He noted that the Canadian constitution states that the *Charter of Rights* must be interpreted in a manner consistent with the multicultural reality of Canada and "without reliable data, which only the census can provide, the courts cannot discharge the obligation." In addition, the ethnicity information is used not only by federal institutions, but also by medical researchers, ethnocultural and aboriginal groups, the media, and social scientists (*The Ottawa Citizen*, January 13, 2000).

The questions remained in the 2001 census but the criticism did not cease. On March 16, 2001, the then Reform Party's Deepak Obhrai introduced a private members bill (C-301—an Act to Amend the Statistics Act—ethnicity question). The purpose of the bill was to ensure that no questions be asked in the Statistics Canada population census to determine a person's ethnicity. Obhrai does not accept the use of ethnic statistics to formulate public policy. According to him, "any application based on racial lines is asking for trouble. You are not going to create policies for one segment that are different from those of another segment" (*House of Commons*, March 16, 2001).

Debate over whether questions should be asked about racial or ethnic origins on census questionnaires is not confined to Canada. Similar controversies have percolated to the surface in both the United States and the United Kingdom and have yet to be resolved to anyone's complete satisfaction.

Multiculturalism As A Policy

Multiculturalism, as a policy, was introduced in the early seventies by Prime Minister Pierre Elliot Trudeau. He argued that, "a policy of multiculturalism should help break down discriminatory attitudes and cultural jealousies. National unity, if it is to mean anything in the deeply personal sense, must be founded on confidence in one's own individual identity; out of this can grow respect for that of others" (House of Commons, October 8, 1971).

Defenders of the policy, like McGill University professor Jack Jedwab, argue that, "in democratic societies, citizens possess multiple identities and attachments. Multiculturalism policy acknowledges our regional and/or cultural differences and stresses the need to accommodate them when necessary. Such an approach is more likely to succeed in reinforcing a sense of belonging to Canada and unity than is the dismissal or rejection of differences (*Montreal Gazette*, Oct.10, 2001).

Multiculturalism has not resulted in any less loyalty to the idea of Canada, according to Jedwab. In fact, when asked about symbols such as the Canadian flag and the national anthem, "members of Canada's ethnocultural communities have higher levels of attachment to such markers of identity than do Canadians as a whole."

A survey of over two thousand people conducted in March, 2002, by the Montreal based Association for Canadian Studies (ACS) found that 85% of those who said they were from countries outside Europe saw the flag as a very important symbol of Canada, and 73% said the same about the national anthem. The study is considered accurate within 3.5 percentage points, 19 times out of 20.

Seventy-nine per cent of survey respondents who said they were immigrants from Europe, though not from the United Kingdom, said they consider the flag to be a very important symbol and 70% said the same of the national anthem.

Both immigrant groups expressed a stronger allegiance to the two national symbols than long-time English or French speaking Canadians. Only 37% of French-Canadians described the Canadian flag as a very important national symbol and 36% felt that way about the national anthem. Among Canadians whose mother tongue is English, 77% said the Maple Leaf flag was a very important symbol of Canada, and 67% felt the same way about the national anthem.

The survey also found that 44% of respondents "strongly agreed" that "multicultural policies" had made a contribution to Canadian identity. Younger Canadians tended to feel stronger about its benefits than older ones. Politically, those who described themselves as followers of the Liberal Party and the New Democratic Party showed the strongest support for these policies with less support from the Conservatives, and, not surprisingly, the least support from the Bloc Quebecois.

Jack Jedwab, the executive director of the ACS, hoped the survey would debunk the notion that Canada's multicultural policies risked diluting national pride. He believes that "immigrants, whether European or non-European, are very attached to some of the fundamental Canadian symbols like the flag and the anthem, which suggests there's a significant degree of patriotism amongst a lot of immigrants" (*Kingston Whig-Standard*, June 28, 2003).

Multicultural Politics

Not all "ethnocultural communities" are as sanguine about official multiculturalism as Jack Jedwab's upbeat assessment would suggest. When Prime Minister Pierre Trudeau first outlined his vision of multiculturalism in the early 1970s, it was greeted with extreme suspicion by many in the province of Quebec (and among aboriginal leaders) as an attempt to undermine the claim to "special status" in Canadian society as a *"Charter Group"* under the *British North America Act*. Trudeau had pushed hard for official bilingualism and biculturalism across Canada as part of his strategy to keep Quebec in confederation and undercut the arguments of Quebec nationalists. This emphasis on accommodating the demands of Quebecois, who wanted to remain part of Canada, offended members of other ethnic minority groups (Germans, Ukrainians) who argued that their cultural contribution was as important as Quebec's to the creation of the Canadian "mosaic." Trudeau attempted to allay these concerns by promoting a policy of "multi-culturalism within a bicultural framework," which would recognize and celebrate the contributions of all ethnic minority groups that helped build Canada.

Demographic Change

Supporters of multiculturalism argue that Canada has been transformed by profound demographic changes over the past 30 years. The number of ethnic and religious groups has increased dramatically. As Canadians, they should not be obliged to identify themselves by their ancestry but they also should not be stigmatized if they choose to acknowledge their origins and heritage. The Canadian *Multiculturalism Act* was proclaimed in 1988, making Canada the first na-tion to establish multiculturalism as a national policy. *Section 27* of the Canadian *Charter of Rights and Freedoms* explicitly recognizes the need to recognize and pro-tect the multicultural character of Canadian society.

Shifting Identities

According to the first ever Ethnic Diversity Survey carried out by Statistics Can-ada in the spring of 2002, one-half of the population aged fifteen and over had a strong sense of belonging to their ethnic or cultural group(s). The sense of be-longing to one's ethnic group was strongest among the first generation of arriv-als in Canada, particularly the most recent. Roughly 62% of immigrants who arrived from 1991 to 2001 declared a strong sense of belonging to their ethnic group, compared with 55% of those who came to Canada before 1991. By con-trast 47% of the second generation and 48% of the third generation in Canada re-ported a strong sense of belonging to their ethnic or cultural group.

The survey also found that first generation newcomers, regardless of time of arrival in Canada, were more likely than other generations to have partici-pated in ethnic or immigrant associations in the year prior to the survey. Roughly 6% of immigrants were members of or participated in these organiza-tions compared to just 2% of the second generation and 1% of the third genera-tion. However, those who had immigrated to Canada in the past ten years were less likely to participate in groups or organizations in Canada than immigrants who had been in Canada for more than ten years. The survey researchers specu-lated that more recent immigrants to Canada need time to adjust to their new country, establish networks and settle into new jobs in their communities.

Controversies

Multiculturalism as a policy, as well as other policies (employment equity) ostensibly designed to promote a more equitable representation of particular groups in the workforce and other institutions have generated opposition for a variety of reasons, some rational and within the boundaries of responsible debate, and some that are explicitly racialist and exclusionist in tone and content. On the political Left, such policies are often seen as a mechanism for social control or a form of minority cooptation which ultimately only reinforces existing institutional forms. On the political Right, policies such a multiculturalism or employment equity are seen as an attack on "classical liberal" ideals. One of the most vociferous opponents within this camp is George Jonas, a columnist and frequent contributor to the *National Post*. In Jonas' view, the 1960s produced "a new, sick parody of liberalism, instead of seeking equality and justice for individuals, (we) began seeking parity for entire groups. We no longer tried to minimize our differences, but started emphasizing them. We no longer wanted equal opportunity for human beings regardless of race, sex, ethnicity, lifestyle or religion, but demanded privilege and special status for belonging to some aggregate that we could then designate as 'disadvantaged' or a 'minority'. We no longer asked for a fair chance as persons, but for a free (or at least subsidized) ride as members of a particular group" (*National Post*, October 29, 1999).

Jonas accuses bureaucrats, consultants, activists and academics of specializing in the "politics of fragmentation" that emphasize divisions based on ancestry, language, race, ethnicity, sexual orientation, and gender rather than pride based on our shared citizenship as Canadians. In his view, attempts to redress historic injustices, through programs like employment equity, only cause more alienation and embitterment by creating new "victimized" groups.

Hate Groups And Hate Crime

Part of the reaction to the changing racial composition of Canadian society has been the rise of "white identity" or "white power" movements ranging from the Heritage Front to neo-nazi skinheads and "street punks." The more sophisticated groups bill themselves as a "white civil rights movement," with the rallying cry of "equal rights for all and special privileges for none." Ostensibly, this viewpoint resembles the classical "liberal" position articulated by George Jonas. However, the literature associated with these groups reveal extensive links with "white supremacists," Holocaust deniers, and other racists. The common thread uniting these groups is the belief that policies like employment equity, affirmative action and official multiculturalism are really weapons in a "race war" designed to disenfranchise and marginalize the white population. They use a variety of media to spread their message ranging from books, magazines and newsletters to telephone hotlines, Internet sites, and fax machines. Depending upon the group, and the level of sophistication, the material produced can be merely provocative or a thinly disguised "hate message," which tests the limits of "free speech." This presents a problem for police and the judiciary.

Hate Speech And The Criminal Code Of Canada

According to the *Criminal Code of Canada*, hate propaganda, which includes any writing, sign, or visible presentation, that advocates or promotes genocide *(defined by the criminal code as "killing members of a particular group or deliberately inflicting on the group conditions of life calculated to bring about its destruction")*, is an indictable offence under *s.318* of the *Code*, with an offender liable to imprisonment for a term not exceeding five years. This part of the law is straightforward. However, the issue becomes more complicated for a "hate message" (directed toward a racial or religious group) not explicitly promoting or advocating genocide. This falls under *s.319* of the *Criminal Code*, which is "public incitement of hatred." According to the *Criminal Code*, non-genocidal hate messages are also indictable offenses (punishable by two years) or a summary conviction offence (punishable by a fine of $500 or six months in jail or both) but there are so many loopholes in the legislation that it is difficult to get a conviction. For example, no person can be convicted of making hateful statements (other than advocating or promoting genocide) against an identifiable racial or religious group if they believe that what they are saying is true! This makes the legislation virtually unenforceable. In a democratic society, which places a high value on "free speech" and "freedom of expression," it is extraordinarily difficult to put restrictions on what people can and cannot say, regardless of how emotionally and psychologically hurtful these utterances can be.

Human Rights And Freedom Of Expression

Freedom of expression is one of the most important rights in a democratic society because most other human rights and freedoms depend on the ability of people to speak out about the contentious issues of the day. However, according to Justice Beverly McLachlin, absolute freedom of expression is impossible in a democratic society. Therefore, McLachlin sees the role of the courts interpreting the provisions of the *Charter of Rights and Freedoms* as a highwire act that "puts the balancing of the collective interests versus individual rights at the center of every issue" (*Toronto Star*, April 16, 2002). Obviously, freedom of expression does not include the right to yell "fire" in a crowded theatre when there is no threat of fire. Laws also protect individuals from libel and slander. The issue becomes more complicated when there is no immediate threat to life or public order, or when a particular individual is not targeted. Nowhere was this more evident than in several cases brought before the Supreme Court of Canada in the early 1990s.

The Keegstra Case

In the mid-1980s, an Alberta high school teacher, James Keegstra, was charged with unlawfully promoting hatred against an identifiable group under *s.319 (2)* of the *Criminal Code of Canada*. According to testimony by former students, Keegstra had taught his classes that Jewish people were out to destroy Christianity and were responsible for economic depressions, anarchy, war and revolution. On occasion he had characterized Jews as "deceptive,""secretive" and "inherently evil," and alleged that the holocaust was merely a historical fabrication to "gain sympathy." The statements were made in a classroom setting and former students testified that they would receive lower grades if they didn't parrot Keegstra's views on the subject.

The case eventually ended up in the Supreme Court. Keegstra's lawyer, Douglas Christie, argued that the section of the *Criminal Code*, *s.319 (2)*, under which Keegstra had been charged, was a violation of his right to free expression under the *Charter of Rights and Freedoms*.

Keegstra lost the case but only by one vote. The Supreme Court justices ruled by a 4-3 margin that, although *s.319 (2)* was an infringement of the freedom of expression outlined in s.2(b) of the *Charter*, it was justified as a "reasonable limit" on the right to of free expression under *s.1* of the *Charter* because (a)" there is obviously a rational connection between restricting hate propaganda and fostering harmonious social relations between Canadians (b) it doesn't unduly impair freedom of expression and (c) its harmful effects don't outweigh the advantage gained from limiting freedom of expression." Put simply, the victims of hate propaganda deserved added protection from this type of public slander. However, the three dissenting judges argued, "that any reasonable benefit of the legislation is outweighed by the significant infringement on the constitutional guarantee of free expression effected by *s.319 (2)* of the *Criminal Code*" (Keegstra, [1990] 3 S.C.R 697).

The Zundel Case

Two years after the Keegstra decision the delicate "balancing act" of the Supreme Court would be tested again in the case of Ernst Zundel. Zundel is a German immigrant to Canada who specializes in the publication of literature that denies that the Nazi extermination of European Jewry under Hitler actually occurred. He was charged in 1983 in Toronto with the offense of "publishing a statement that he knows is false and that causes injury to a public interest," which was contrary to *section 181* of the *Criminal Code of Canada*. The people who had brought the charge against Zundel would have preferred to use *s.319* (willful promotion of hatred), as in the Keegstra case, but that would have required the consent of the Attorney General. The then Attorney General of Ontario, Roy McMurtry, refused to give his consent, claiming that he thought that the use of *s.319* might violate the *Charter of Rights and Freedoms* (*Globe and Mail*, August 29, 1992). Given the narrow majority in the Keegstra case, this perception was not incorrect. In 1985 the case went to court under *section 181* of the *Criminal Code*, which did not require the consent of the Attorney General.

Section 181 of the *Criminal Code of Canada* stated that

> ...every one who willfully publishes a statement, tale or news that he
> knows to be false and that cause or is likely to cause injury or mischief to
> a public interest is guilty of an indictable offence and liable to imprison-
> ment for a term not exceeding two years.

In a degrading public spectacle that included Zundel's defense attorney trying to discredit the eyewitness testimony of holocaust survivors, the jury decided to convict Zundel of the charge. He was sentenced to three years imprisonment and three years probation. The Ontario Court of Appeals overturned the decision on the grounds that he could be convicted only if he "knew" that his publications were false and not merely if he was "reckless." A second trial ensued which focused on certain specific claims contained in Zundel's publications rather than the larger issue of whether or not the holocaust actually occurred. The jury in this trial also convicted Zundel. He was sentenced to nine months in jail. This time the Ontario Court of Appeal upheld his conviction and sentence.

Zundel appealed to the Supreme Court of Canada claiming that his conviction under *s. 181* of the *Criminal Code* was a violation of his freedom of expression under *s.2 (b)* of the *Charter*. The court heard the case and ruled that *s.181* of the *Criminal Code* infringes *section 2(b)* of the *Charter* which guarantees the right of freedom of expression providing that the expression is "not violent." The Court did not consider Zundel's publications to be violent, regardless of the odious nature of the content. A majority of the justices found that censoring every statement that might be "likely to cause injury or mischief to a public interest" cast too broad a net and represented an infringement on the *Charter*.

As a result, Zundel's conviction was overturned. However, in a minority dissent, three justices argued to "deliberately lie about the indescribable suffering and death inflicted upon Jews by Hitler is the foulest of falsehoods and the essence of cruelty. *Section 181* provides protection, by criminal sanction, not only to Jewish Canadians but also to all vulnerable minority groups and individuals. It achieves this goal by expressing the repugnance of Canadian society for the willful publication of statements known to be false that are likely to cause serious injury or mischief to the public interest" (*Zundel, 1992 2 S.C.R. 731*).

"Libertarians" Versus "Egalitarians"

The cases described above serve to illustrate a persistent and unresolved tension between two "conflicting visions" on the question of "free speech" and its limitations in a democratic society. The absolute "libertarian" vision fervently upholds the right to free speech, no matter how vile and offensive, as the cornerstone of all our rights and freedoms. Any interference with this right, even if well intentioned, will eventually result in tyranny. The opposing "egalitarian" vision believes there are sometimes justifiable limitations on the right to free speech to protect vulnerable individuals or groups in a population from vilification, and in the interests of greater social harmony. It is unlikely that the tension between these opposing visions will ever be completely resolved, therefore presenting a continuing challenge when cases of this kind are brought before the courts.

Canadian Human Rights Legislation

While the limits of "free speech" and "free expression" remain contentious issues, Canadian human rights legislation prohibits discrimination based on race, national or ethnic origin, colour, age, sex, marital status, disability, sexual orientation, or conviction for an offence for which a pardon has been granted (*Canadian Human Rights Act, 1977*—amended in 1996 to include sexual orientation as a prohibited ground of discrimination). This legislation extended the protection of individual rights and freedoms outlined in the Canadian *Bill of Rights* introduced by Prime Minister John G. Diefenbaker on July 1, 1960. Provincial governments have also developed their own human rights codes. Both federal and provincial jurisdictions have commissions responsible for investigating and adjudicating complaints about violations of the codes. In 1982, the Canadian *Charter of Rights and Freedoms* established the protection of a wide range of basic rights and freedoms, which incorporated many of the previous human rights protections.

International Human Rights Agreements

Canada has also been a signatory to a variety of international human rights declarations and covenants including the *Universal Declaration of Human Rights* in 1948, which requires a commitment to have legislative protection to deal with racism directed towards identifiable groups. It is also a signatory to the 1970 *International Convention on the Elimination of All Forms of Racial Discrimination* and the *International Covenant on Civil and Political Rights* of 1976. Both documents contain provisions that attempt to prohibit hate speech and hate propaganda.

Appendix

Employment Equity Legislation and the *Charter of Rights and Freedoms*

Employment Equity Act 1995, c.44 (2) The purpose of this Act is to achieve equality in the workplace so that no person shall be denied employment opportunity or benefits for reasons unrelated to ability and, in the fulfillment of that goal, to correct the conditions of disadvantage in employment experienced by women, aboriginal peoples, persons with disabilities, and members of visible minorities by giving effect to the principle that employment equity means more than treating persons in the same way but also requires special measures and the accommodation of differences.

Section 15.2 of the Canadian *Charter of Rights and Freedoms* protects employment equity. *(Section 15 (1) Every individual is equal before and under the law and has the right to equal protection and equal benefit of the law without discrimination and, in particular, without discrimination based on race, national or ethnic origin, colour, religion, sex, age or mental and physical disability*

(2) Subsection (1) does not preclude any law, program or activity that has as its object the amelioration of conditions of disadvantaged individuals or groups including those that are disadvantaged because of race, national or ethnic origin, colour, religion, sex, age or mental or physical disability.)

Chapter Six
CULTURES IN CONFLICT:
THE HIJAB AND KIRPAN CONTROVERSIES

According to the 2001 Canadian census, the largest gains in religious affiliations in Canada over the last ten years occurred among Muslims, Hindus, Sikhs,
and Buddhists. This is consistent with changing immigration patterns as more
people from regions outside of Europe make Canada their preferred destination.
Among this group, respondents to the 2001 census who identified themselves as
Muslims recorded the biggest increase, more than doubling from 253,300 in
1991 to 579,600 in 2001. Muslims comprised 2% of the total population in Canada in 2001, up from under 1% a decade before. People who identified themselves
as Hindus increased 89% to 297,200, while the number of Sikhs rose 89% to
278,400, each representing about 1% of the total population of Canada.

Figure 6.1: Immigrants by Major Religious Denominations and Period of
Immigration, Canada, 2001

	Period of immigration (%)				
	Before 1961	**1961-1970**	**1971-1980**	**1981-1990**	**1991-2001****
Total immigrants	100.0	100.0	100.0	100.0	100.0
Roman Catholic	39.2	43.4	33.9	32.9	23.0
Protestant	39.2	26.9	21.0	14.5	10.7
Christian Orthodox	3.8	6.3	3.8	3.0	6.3
Christian, not included elsewhere*	1.3	2.2	3.8	4.9	5.3
Jewish	2.7	2.0	2.2	1.9	1.2
Muslim	0.2	1.3	5.4	7.5	15.0

Hindu	0.0	1.4	3.6	4.9	6.5
Buddhist	0.4	0.9	4.8	7.5	4.6
Sikh	0.1	1.1	3.9	4.3	4.7
No religion	11.0	13.5	16.5	17.3	21.3
Other religions	2.1	1.0	1.1	1.3	1.4

*Includes persons who report 'Christian,' as well as those who report 'Apostolic,' 'Born-again Christian,' and 'Evangelical.' **Includes data up to May 15, 2001.

The proportion of immigrants entering Canada from countries where these religions are practiced has increased steadily since the 1960s, when immigration restrictions based on country of origin were removed. According to the 2001 census, of the 1.8 million immigrants who came to Canada in the 1990s, Muslims accounted for 15%, Hindus roughly 7%, and Sikhs and Buddhists about 5% each (see Figure 6.1).

Roughly 73% of the Hindus in Canada live in Ontario, as do 61% of Muslims, and 38% of all Sikhs. About 50% of Sikhs reside in British Columbia. Adherents to these faiths are somewhat younger than the overall Canadian population (see Figure 6.2). The median age of Muslims was 28 years in 2001 compared to 37 for the overall Canadian population. The median age for the Sikh population was 30, and 32 for Hindus.

Figure 6.2: Major Religions by Median Age, Canada, 2001 Census

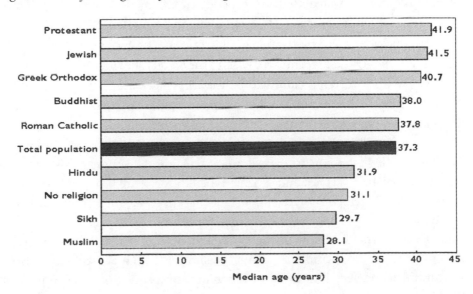

Islam

With the significant upsurge of newcomers to Canada who identify with these faiths, it has become increasingly important to understand the origins and key components of this religious diversity. This quest has taken on added urgency because of the events of September 11, 2001, and also because of the conflicts involving many of the countries from which hundreds of thousands of new Canadians have recently fled.

There are many misunderstandings about the nature and activities of these religions, and stereotypes abound. For example, some people in Western countries automatically assume that people of the Muslim faith are all "terrorists" or "misogynists" mainly because of sometimes lurid and sensationalist media coverage of events in the Middle East. The notion that violence and Islam are inextricably linked does a great disservice to the more than 1 billion people worldwide that identify with this faith and have never committed a violent or misogynist act in their lifetime.

Islam is no more a violent religion than is Christianity and Judaism, and all share common roots, originating at different times among the people of the Middle East. Abraham, a key figure in the Jewish religion lived about 2000 years before Christ. The prophet Mohammed established the Islamic faith about 622 years after the birth of Christ (Islam means "submission to the will of Allah." A Muslim is "one who submits").

Mohammed was a prosperous merchant living in the village of Mecca (in what is now Saudi Arabia) when he experienced visions that he believed to be a message from God. The archangel Gabriel is said to have described to Mohammed a set of principles governing the functioning of a society and how people should behave, which eventually formed the basis of the *Koran* (The Holy Book of Islam).

Mohammed merely claimed to be the messenger and not the author of these teachings. His followers believed him to be the last and greatest of the prophets, in the tradition of many Jewish prophets before him, including Jesus.

Islam, like Christianity and Judaism, is a monotheistic religion, meaning a belief in one God whom Muslims call Allah. Muslims, like many Christians, believe there will be a "Day of Judgement" when the dead are brought back to life to be judged. Therefore, it is very important that they take the ethical and moral teachings in the *Koran* seriously. There is an afterlife of eternal bliss for those who abide by the teachings of the *Koran* and eternal torment for those who don't. There are no sacraments in the Muslim faith such as baptism or Holy Communion and very little ornamentation in the Mosque (the Muslim place of worship). Muslims are expected to wash before praying. Friday is considered to be the Muslim holy day. All Muslims are expected to abide by the five pillars of the faith (acknowledgement of one God, Allah, and his messenger Mohammed, daily prayer—five times a day facing the holy city of Mecca, almsgiving to the poor, fasting during Ramadan, and pilgrimage to Mecca at least once in a lifetime, if it can be afforded).

Like traditional Jewish or Christian families, the Muslim social structure is deeply patriarchal, meaning that it is assumed that the father will play the leadership role in the family and wield most of the power in decision-making. The primary responsibility of women is to care for the family. The veiling of women is common in some Muslim countries but there is a dispute over whether it is actually a requirement of the faith. It is seen as an expression of modesty that the teachings of the *Koran* urge for both men and women. As in many other religions, there are dietary restrictions and prohibitions. Alcohol is prohibited, as is the consumption of "unclean" meat such as pork. Other meat can be eaten provided that it is *"halal"* (slaughtered according to Islamic tradition).

Muslims take great pride in the achievements of the Arab and Islamic civilization that dominated the Middle East for several hundred years after the death of the prophet Mohammed. A philosopher of that era, Avicenna of Baghdad, is considered by many to be the founder of modern medical science. It was a civilization that invented algebra, simplified arithmetical calculation, and helped preserve the culture and civilization of Europe during the Dark Ages.

In all religions of the world there are different ways of interpreting the holy texts, and the *Koran* is no exception. Although the message of the *Koran* is generally one of peace, there are militant passages, as in the Bible, which are seized upon by extremists to justify violence or self-sacrifice in the pursuit of certain ends. In the same way, the humane and compassionate teachings of Jesus were ignored by many of his followers during the "Holy Wars" of the 11th, 12th and 13th centuries. The Ten Commandments include one against the taking of human life yet this did not prevent the horrendous atrocities carried out by the armies of Israel in ancient times.

Divisions Among Muslims

The most important division within the Muslim world is between the Sunni and Shiite branches of the Islamic faith, although there are many other smaller sects. The prophet Mohammed never appointed a successor when he died in 632 A.D., which resulted in a power struggle among his followers. One faction, that came to be known as the Sunnis, believed that the Caliphate (Islamic priesthood) should be an elective office. Another faction, the Shia, believed it should be a hereditary office.

In 680 A.D, Hussein, a grandson of the prophet Mohammed claimed the Caliphate for his family against the wishes of the majority of Muslims who opposed him. Although outnumbered 10 to 1, Hussein decided it was more honourable to die for his beliefs than to live as a victim of what he perceived as an injustice. In the resulting conflict, Hussein and his army were massacred and he became the Supreme Martyr, the symbol of struggle against tyranny. From that point on, Hussein became an inspiration for militant Shiites.

In the contemporary era, the mainstream Sunni branch of Islam represents about 90% of the Muslim population worldwide. It encourages the faithful to worship Allah on an individual basis in conformity with the Five Pillars (duties) of the Faith, and the *Koran*. This branch of Islam is more tolerant of ethnic and religious diversity and has been adopted by people well beyond its birthplace in the Middle East. There are significant Muslim populations in over seventy countries around the world, including over fifty million people in the republics (now individual countries) that made up the former Soviet Union. The world's most populous Muslim country is Indonesia where close to 190 million people are believers.

The Sunnis believe that any Muslim can be a leader and that religious leaders do not necessarily have superior wisdom. The more fundamentalist Shia branch of the faith does not share this pragmatic approach. The Shiites claim that Mohammed passed on his hereditary rule to his son-in-law Ali and his descendants, and through him to a line of "Imams" or spiritual leaders. Orthodox Shiites believe that there were twelve divinely appointed "Imams." The last one disappeared in the 878 A.D. and they await his return as Mahdi (guided one) who will fill the earth with social justice. Contemporary Shiite leaders are expected to be able to communicate with the last Imam who continues to exist in the spiritual realm. This special ability allows them to interpret Islamic law and govern the believers.

Muslim Stereotypes

There are about 50 million Shiites, mainly located in Iran, Lebanon and Iraq. The religious and political differences between Sunni and Shiite branches of the faith provided the fuel for many conflicts in the Middle East over the past twenty-five years, such as the civil war in Lebanon and an eight year war between the Shia majority of Iran and the Sunni dominated government of Iraq between 1980 and 1988. Many of the common stereotypes about Muslims in the West are a consequence of these conflicts. For example, some members of the fundamentalist minority Shia sect of Islam believe that self-sacrifice in the defense of Islam is a form of martyrdom that guarantees a special place in heaven. Although most Islamic scholars disagree with this interpretation and insist that the Koran forbids suicide, it did not prevent thousands of young Iranians from running over minefields to detonate explosives and clear the way for regular soldiers during the Iran/Iraq war in the 1980s. It is exactly these images along with the horrific memory of such events as the destruction of the World Trade Center in New York by another group of fundamentalists (*Wahhabis*), mainly from Saudi Arabia, that have shaped North American perceptions of Islam. A disturbing by-product of these events has been an increasing amount of suspicion, paranoia, and outright hostility directed at people who practice the Muslim faith in North America but are in no way connected with the extremists, and, in fact, came here to escape some of these conflicts.

Islam And Social Change

Islam offers believers certainty and continuity in a world undergoing rapid economic, technological and cultural transformation. Religious devotion is not something separate from day to day living or from forms of political expression. This explains why Arab nationalism is very much bound up with the Muslim faith and often resonates in a militant fashion. The strong and unchanging moral code of Islam poses a challenge to the secular philosophies and goals of the West, particularly in the liberal democracies that uphold the idea of a separation between church and state.

The West is viewed by many Muslims, particularly in the Middle East, as materialistic, decadent, and corrupt. The United States, in particular, is singled out, not only for its perceived moral laxity but also for its continued support for the state of Israel. Until September 11, 2001, extreme anti-western sentiment was mainly associated with such groups as *Islamic Jihad* (Islamic Holy War) and *Hizbollah* (Party of God). *Hizbollah* took part in suicide bomb attacks that resulted in the death of 250 American servicemen in 1983, and its activities also caused Israel to withdraw from land it had occupied in Lebanon. Islamic Jihad was responsible for the assassination of Egyptian President Anwar Sadat, allegedly because of his pro-western views and willingness to negotiate with Israel.

Islamic Justice

Islamic justice is also based on the teachings of the *Koran*. It is codified in the *sharia*, a text that is believed to be an expression of divine will. Under the *sharia*, Muslims have most of the rights that people in western societies take for granted such as the right to be presumed innocent until proven guilty, the right to be free from arbitrary arrest and detention; the right to a fair and public trial; the right to present evidence and call witnesses in one's defense; the right to counsel of one's own choosing; the right to a decision based upon legally admissible evidence; the right to have the decision rendered in public; and the right of appeal. A guilty verdict cannot be rendered the same day as the evidence is presented, but an innocent verdict can.

Islamic law (*sharia*) is a comprehensive behavioural guide that is designed to cover virtually all aspects of a Muslim's life from birth to death. Under Islamic law there are six crimes with fixed punishments: death for apostasy (the abandonment of one's faith); death for highway robbery; death by stoning for adultery; one hundred lashes for fornication (meaning here having sex outside marriage or in inappropriate circumstances); eighty lashes for drinking alcohol. Islamic civil justice also calls for restitution or, in the case of assault, punishment equal to the crime.

The severity of some of these punishments is a source of consternation to many westerners. It is important to remember, however, that barbaric and unusual punishments are not unique to Muslim countries. Death by lethal injection and hanging is still practiced in many states in the United States. Corporal punishment was still practiced in prisons, and even schools, up to thirty years ago, and prison confinement for extended periods of time for minor crimes (drug possession) is actually increasing in North America (see Chapter Eight).

Marriage And Divorce

One of the more controversial aspects surrounding the Islamic faith involves the role of women and marriage. A Muslim may have as many as, but not more than, four legal wives at any one time. If a man has more than one wife he is enjoined to treat them with equal respect and consideration. According to traditional interpretations, a Muslim should not have more than one wife if he cannot financially support them or treat them with the consideration they deserve. Consequently, most modern Muslims believe that the prophet Mohammed was essentially advocating monogamy. The prophet Mohammed established many regulations for inheritance, dowries, divorce, and the protection of orphans. A traditional interpretation of the *Koran* suggests that divorce is relatively easy for men. On pronouncing a traditional formula, a divorce is attained but a man can take a woman back if he changes his mind. However, Muslim women can also seek a divorce, own and inherit property, and participate in political life, depending on the country they happen to live in. While many Muslim women in countries like Saudi Arabia live highly restricted lives and may not even be allowed to drive a car, others live in countries where they may aspire to the highest leadership positions such as Tansu Ciller who was elected Prime Minister of Turkey in 1993.

The *Sharia* Controversy

A report prepared by Marion Boyd, an attorney general in a former New Democratic Party government in the province of Ontario, was made public in December of 2004. The report recommended allowing *sharia* law to help settle family disputes among Muslims. This prompted an immediate response from groups like the Canadian Council of Muslim women who warned that allowing *sharia* law to be used to resolve domestic disputes would open the door to polygamy and infringe on women's rights in a marriage.

A provincial cabinet minister and several prominent Members of the National Assembly (MNAs) in the province of Quebec also denounced Boyd's report. At a conference held in Quebec City in March of 2005, International Relations Minister Monique Gagnon Tremblay urged all political parties in Quebec to say "loud and clear that not only do we not want it (*sharia* law) in Quebec, we don't want it in Ontario and we don't want it Canada" (*Montreal Gazette*, March 11, 2005).

Tremblay, a former immigration minister in the province went further arguing, "Muslims who want to come to Quebec and who do not respect women's rights or who do not respect whatever rights may be in our civil code should stay in their country and not come to Quebec, because that's unacceptable. On the other hand, if people want to come to Quebec and accept our way of doing things and our rights, in that instance they will be welcome and we will help them integrate."

At the same conference, Liberal MNA Fatima Houde-Pepin, suggested that Marion Boyd should live in an Islamic country for a few months to really understand the significance of *sharia* law. According to Houde-Pepin "we've seen *sharia* at work in Afghanistan, with the odious Taliban regime. We've seen it in

Sudan where the hands of hundreds of innocent people were cut off. We've seen it in Nigeria with attempts at stoning."

In Houde-Pepin's view, lobbyists for *sharia* law are trying to impose a political agenda rather than a religious one. "Their objective," according to Houde-Pepin," is not to integrate into Canada; it is to integrate Canada to their values. One of the strengths of Islamists is that they know you very well. They know our history, they know our culture, and they know our justice system, the *Charter of Rights*" (*Montreal Gazette*, March 11, 2005).

When informed about the comments made by Houde-Pepin, Salam Elmenyawi, Chairperson of the Muslim Council of Montreal, reacted angrily. In a phone interview with *Montreal Gazette* reporter Mike de Souza, Elmenyawi responded, "When you talk like that, you are attacking me and my faith. This is total ignorance. Bigotry and ignorance have no limits" (*Montreal Gazette*, March 11, 2005, p. A9).

Elmenyawi went on to say that debate over *sharia* law had nothing to do with Quebec's *Civil Code*. Quebec's Muslim community see family tribunals, independent of the courts, as a way to settle religious issues and to protect the rights of both men and women. In his view, Houde-Pepin's comments reflected a desire to assimilate Muslims rather than integrating them into Quebec society.

In the province of Ontario, people have been practicing religious based arbitration to settle civil disputes since 1991. The *Arbitration Act, SO 1991,c.17*, passed in that year (Marion Boyd was provincial attorney general at the time) permits two parties to mutually agree on an arbitrator to settle family or business disputes, *as long as they are in accordance with Canadian law* (my italics). The *Act* allows anyone, including former judges, lawyers or religious leaders to act as arbitrators. However, Homa Arjomand, coordinator of the International Campaign Against *Sharia* Court in Canada (ICASCC), has criticized allowing consenting parties to avoid courts by choosing arbitration based on a shared set of religious values. She objects to anyone but government carrying out the law. "Religion should not interfere with justice and the justice system. As an activist, I want family law removed from the *Arbitration Act*" (*Mississauga News*, Nov.5, 2004).

In Arjoman's view, Muslim arbitration in Ontario has meant women have no options. Even if they know their rights, they won't speak up for fear of consequences, which could mean isolation from their family and community.

Although Jewish and Christian-based arbitration already exist in Canada, similar concerns about the treatment of women have been raised. For example, Rabbi Lawrence Englander, of Sobel Synagogue in Mississauga, Ontario, doesn't believe rabbinic courts should handle family disputes, as could be the case in Judaism. "It's my belief that women don't get fair treatment in rabbinic court, as they would in Ontario Court. I believe that one of the tenets of western society is that we're all equal under the law and, therefore, there should be only one law for all citizens" (*The Mississauga News*, Nov.5, 2004).

The Ontario government is now studying Boyd's report on allowing *sharia* law to help settle family disputes. In her report, Boyd said she found no evidence of "an erosion of rights" in cases where *sharia* law has been used but suggested a continuing review of decisions to monitor any cases of possible abuse.

Quebec Justice Minister Yvon Marcoux said any decision made by Ontario to allow sharia would have no impact on what the Quebec government already has decided to do. "Certainly not in Quebec. The door is closed, and it will remain closed" (*Montreal Gazette*, March 11, 2005).

Muslim Women And The *Hijab* Controversy

In Western society where fashion is a way of life, the traditional garb associated with the Muslim faith often elicits a variety of responses, ranging from benign curiosity to outright hostility. Even within the Islamic faith there is controversy, particularly over the appropriate clothing requirements for women. Nowhere is the tension more evident than in the debate over the *hijab*, the traditional head covering worn by Muslim women (*hijab* comes from the Arabic *hajaba* and means "to hide from view" or "to conceal"). Some traditionalist Muslims believe that a woman should cover up everything but her face and hands while more liberal interpretations do not see even the *hijab* as a mandatory requirement for women.

Shariat (Islamic law) recommends loose clothing for both men and women as a symbol of modesty and integrity. But for many people in the West, particularly women socialized in the post–feminist era, the *hijab* signifies subjection and second class status for Muslim women. However, Tahira Anwar, a young Muslim Canadian woman, does not see the traditional garb as subjection but rather as a type of liberation. According to Anwar, "for years I was enslaved by beauty and sexuality. My life centered around lipsticks and high heels, till one day I gave it all up and chose to wear a scarf (*hijab*) over my head and *abhaya* to cover my body. My life changed forever. Personally, the *hijab* gave me an identity of my own and people began to see the real me. They saw beyond my physical attributes and that is the greatest freedom any woman could ask for" (*Rediffcom*, May 11, 2000).

Jawad Jafry, a Canadian filmmaker, who made a documentary on the *hijab*, agrees with Anwar, and sees the wearing of a head scarf as "simply a woman's assertion that her physical persona plays no role, whatsoever, in her social interaction." In researching his documentary, Jawad "found many career women wearing the *hijab* with considerable ease. To them the *hijab* was a way of life and a decorum for modesty." In his film, Jawad also interviewed women who don't wear the *hijab* and don't see their faith compromised by this omission.

Seis Elsheikh of the *Islamic Information and Dawah Center International* in Toronto sees the traditional garb as protecting women from exploitation and sexual abuse. He believes that "women are used and misused as objects in today's consumerist world. You have a woman selling soaps, detergents, even things men use. She is often seen as an object of sexual desire. The *hijab* protects her sexual rights and is the best safeguard she can have against all demeanors" (*Rediffcom*, May 11, 2000).

Women who choose to wear the *hijab* must still be prepared to face the fact that their decision is perceived by some Canadians as a highly symbolic gesture, either as an indicator of militancy or an unwillingness to accept the more secular nature of Canadian society. For example, Rukhsana Khan, an award-winning author of children's books, initially confronted negative reactions when she began to wear the *hijab*. According to Khan, "many children in high school made fun of me. Until a few years ago, students were suspended for defying the dress code. Today it's a lot easier to wear the *hijab* and yet get accepted in a western society" (*Rediffcom*, May 11, 2000).

The *Hijab* In Schools Controversy

In September of 2003, a young girl, Irene Waseem, returned from summer holidays to attend College Charlemagne, a French private school in Pierrefonds, Quebec. Although she had attended the same school for the previous four years it was the first time she had chosen to wear the *hijab*. She did not make it to her first class as the school's pedagogic director and another member of the administration told her to remove her *hijab* or leave the school. Waseem refused and the school officials called her father and told him to come and pick her up.

When interviewed by the local press Wassem said that "they (the school officials) told me that I should abide by the contract I had signed which said that it is part of the uniform that you cannot have anything on your head. I signed this paper, but I also know that it is within my rights as a Canadian citizen to wear a *hijab* to school. It is my religious right and freedom" (*Montreal Gazette*, September 24, 2003).

It was not the first time that the wearing of the *hijab* stirred controversy in Quebec schools. In 1995, the *Quebec Human Rights Commission* dealt with a similar case of a young woman sent home for wearing a *hijab*. At the time, the Commission ruled that banning *hijabs* in a *public school* violated Quebec's *Charter of Rights and Freedoms*. The Wassem case is different in that the ban on the *hijab* is in a private school. The law on private schools doesn't allow the Quebec Ministry of Education to intervene in such cases. The Human Rights Commission is investigating the case and will issue a report.

The school's decision to ban the *hijab* was condemned by the Muslim Council of Montreal, the Quebec Human Rights Commission, the Canadian Jewish Congress, and the League for Human Rights of B'nai Brith. According to Salam Elmenyawi, the President of the Muslim Council of Montreal, "it is sad to see that there are some people who continue to make Muslims feel they are not welcomed. Muslims always look to build bridges of understanding and respect, but apparently some people in the community insist on making a stand against us. The government finances public and private schools and should be able to use that as leverage to prevent schools from abusing children's rights like that" (*Montreal Gazette*, September 24, 2003).

Both the *sharia* law and *hijab* controversies illustrate some persistent underlying tensions concerning the changing ethnocultural composition of Quebec society. For example, in 1990, the chairperson of the Montreal Catholic School Commission, Michel Pallascio, created a firestorm of controversy by suggesting that Quebec would be better off trying to attract immigrants with Judeo-Christian values because they could be more easily integrated into Quebec society. According to Pallascio, "people leaving their countries expect to adopt a new language, but are much more reticent to abandon their spiritual values or their religious convictions" (*Montreal Gazette*, Sept.24, 2003).

Although the opinions expressed by Pallascio were roundly criticized by Quebec's Ministers of Education, Language, and Immigration, immigrant rights groups, and members of the city's cultural communities, the concerns about cultural integration remained a "hot button" issue. In 1995, for example, delegates at a meeting of the Centrale de L'Enseignement du Quebec (CEQ), the province's largest teacher's union, passed a resolution urging that skullcaps, *hijabs* and turbans be banned in Quebec public schools.

Other groups see the *hijab* controversy as essentially settled and inconsequential. According to Diane Guibault, a spokesperson for the Quebec Council for the Status of Women, "it's a Montreal thing, and it's generally accepted. The more we're used to seeing a *hijab*, the less it surprises us. Some women might be offended. For women who don't share the Muslim religion, the *hijab* sends a message that women should be kept in their place. But we should be able to accept that lots of women live in accordance with their religion, and wear it. They have their own reasons" (*Montreal Gazette*, Sept.24, 2003).

Cultural Conflict Or Teenage Rebellion

While some commentators might view the *hijab* controversy as an example of cultural conflict other less complex motivations may be at work. Diane Guilbault wonders if it's merely a coincidence that teenagers who wear the *hijab* cause the most controversy. In Guilbault's view, it may just be an act of teenage rebellion and what could be more ingenious than choosing a traditional symbol to make a personal statement. According to Guilbault, "the *hijab* impulse will pass. We've noticed that by the end of the school year some girls aren't wearing them anymore. Sixteen, 17 years old is the age when you want to take a stand on things. If a girl wants to keep wearing the *hijab* for the rest of her life, that's her choice. But if she decides to take it off and keep it off, our society is not going to say no"(*Montreal Gazette*, Sept. 24, 2003).

There is little doubt, however, that the decision to wear the *hijab* was freighted with cultural significance for Suhail Wassem, the father of Irene, the young girl at the center of the most recent controversy. According to him, "my daughter made a decision and I support what she chose for herself. In Islam, it is an obligation to wear the *hijab*" (*Montreal Gazette*, Sept.24, 2003).

Irene's French Canadian mother also supported her decision but worried that she would stick out among friends.

"She went to Tim Horton's and I was like, 'oh my god, what will happen?' But she came back and everything was all right.

"I know she is focused on education, not parties, because the *Koran* says so. I also know she will not spend her time partying or taking drugs like other teenagers.

"I wish the school tried to have some time to listen to Irene the same way I did. I wish they knew her reasons and why she decided to wear it" (*Montreal Gazette*, Sept.24, 2003).

The International *Hijab* Controversy

The wearing of the *hijab* is very controversial in France, which has a strong assimilationist tradition and is resolutely opposed to the idea of multicultural-ism. In the fall of 2003, two Muslim schoolgirls plunged the country into a bit-ter and divisive debate when they decided to wear the *hijab* to school. In response to the controversy French President Jacques Chirac set up a commission on sec-ularism to determine whether or not to ban the *hijab* completely, not only in schools but also in all public offices.

In Germany, A German teacher of Afghan origin went to court in an at-tempt to overturn a decision by school authorities not to hire her because she in-sisted on wearing a *hijab*. The courts ruled that wearing the headscarf was enough to bar a female teacher but only if the state concerned had established a legal basis for the ban.

In the Netherlands *hijabs* are generally accepted but can be banned if schools are able to cite a security risk. In Belgium, the decision whether or not to allow the *hijab* has been left to the discretion of individual schools. In Denmark and Greece both teachers and students are permitted to wear it. In Great Britain, workplace laws banning discrimination on religious grounds have been inter-preted to permit the wearing of *hijabs*. Italy and Spain have no ban in public schools but private schools may enforce a dress code. Although Turkey is the largest Muslim country in Europe, its government maintains a strict secular policy and bans the *hijab* not only in schools but also in all public places (*The Economist*, October 23, 2003).

Female Circumcision And The Limits Of Cultural Relativism

The controversy over the wearing of the *hijab* is a minor culture clash compared to the issue of female circumcision, which provides a major challenge to the con-cept of *cultural relativism*, where all beliefs are considered to be equally valid (de-pending on their context) and that none can be considered wrong or inferior. Female circumcision is the practice of removing the clitoris, labia minor, and la-bia major of the female genitalia, and, in some cases, stitching together the sides of the vulva to insure fidelity to the husband. The procedure is carried out on rel-atively young girls and is seen as a coming of age ceremony in several African countries. There is a religious dimension to this practice because many of the practitioners believe it to be part of Islam, even though there is no mention of it in the Koran.

An estimated 2 million girls, mainly between the ages of 4 and 12 (but some as infants and some as adults before marriage) undergo this procedure every year (*Toronto Star*, March 8,1997). The World Health Organization (WHO) estimates that 85 to 115 million women have been subjected to this ritual worldwide. It is a female that performs the surgery and it is seen as a way by which females can differentiate themselves from males by removing their "male parts."

Needless to say the practice is reviled in the west and is usually referred to as Female Genital Mutilation (FGM) rather than the more benign sounding circumcision to avoid any confusion with a routine, and much less controversial, procedure carried out on many infant males. Apart from the health risks associated with the procedure, and the psychological effects, opponents of female circumcision see it as a practice clearly designed to put women in a subordinate position to males and in a subservient role in the larger society. For this reason, female circumcision is viewed by many in the West not only as a vile practice but also as a fundamental violation of the rights of women. *Article 5* of the *United Nations Convention on the Elimination of All Forms of Discrimination* says unambiguously that governments must strive for "the elimination of prejudice and customary and all other practices which are based on the inferiority or the superiority of either of the sexes."

Defenders of this practice believe it to be an integral part of their culture which has both a social and religious meaning to the literally tens of millions of women who have undergone the procedure. Women, in fact, are often the biggest defenders of this practice because they all have shared the same experience and consider it to be a "normative" part of their culture.

Strong village traditions in several countries make it difficult for parents to say no to the practice. However, in 1993, a Somali woman, Khadra Hassan Farah, fled her country because she feared that her daughter, Hodan, age 10, would be forced to undergo the procedure. She applied for refugee status in Canada and was granted it based on a ruling by immigration officials that the young girl's "right to personal security would be grossly infringed" if she was returned to Somalia.

In March of 1993, the Chairperson of Canada's Immigration and Refugee Board issued *Guidelines on Women Refugee Claimants fearing Gender-related Persecution* making Canada the first country in the world to establish such guidelines.

In a letter to the British Refugee Legal Center on July 8, 1994, *the United Nations High Commission For Refugees (UNHCR)* outlined its position on female circumcision. The letter stated that: "Female Genital Mutilation, which causes severe pain as well as permanent physical harm, amounts to a violation of human rights, including the rights of the child, and can be regarded as persecution. The toleration of these acts by the authorities, or the willingness of the authorities to provide protection against them, amounts to official acquiescence. Therefore a woman can be considered a refugee if she or her daughter/daughters fear being compelled to undergo FGM against their will; or she fears persecution for refusing to undergo or allow her daughters to undergo the practice" (Crawley, Heaven (1997) *Women as Asylum Seekers: A Legal Handbook*, p.71, Immigration Law Practitioners Association and Refugee Action).

Ethics, Culture And The Law

Female circumcision, of the kind practiced as a coming of age ritual in some countries, is not permitted in medical institutions in Canada and is not condoned. In February of 2002, a couple in Ontario was charged with forcing their daughter to undergo the procedure at the hands of a non-medically recognized practitioner. The girl went to the police to tell them about the operation, which had been performed two years earlier in the family home. In Canada, female genital surgery is prohibited by the *Criminal Code of Canada* except where "the procedure is medically necessary and performed by a doctor or where the subject is 18 years of age and consents to the procedure and no bodily harm results"(*Toronto Sun*, Feb.15, 2002).

The prohibitions on this cultural ritual and the unwillingness of western medical practitioners to perform the procedure, raises some interesting ethical, cultural and legal questions. On the rare occasions when a request for a female circumcision is made in Canada it is usually an adult woman speaking on behalf of her child for religious/cultural reasons.

Dr. Eike-Henner Kluge, in an article in the *Canadian Medical Association Journal*, presents the issue as an ethical dilemma that poses a challenge to aspects of Canada's commitment to multiculturalism. She writes that "suppose that the request (for female circumcision) is so deeply rooted in the cultural background of the woman making the request that the mere suggestion that the procedure is inappropriate would be regarded as deep insult to her cultural identity. Furthermore, suppose that the woman claims that failure to perform the procedure would harm the girl's self-esteem and cultural identity, and affect her societal integration, and suppose she points out that the World Health Organization's (WHO) definition of health includes the notion of social well-being."

Kluge argues that "with due alteration of detail the same ethical reasoning holds for male circumcision. There rarely are medical reasons for performing the procedure; personal preference or religious values of the parents usually underlie the request."

In Kluge's view, "Canada is not a melting pot of cultures: it is a mosaic. The people who live here are not forced to abandon their cultural heritage and adopt a homogeneous cultural identity. In fact, at its best Canada encourages its people to preserve their cultural heritage. By *"Charter"* (*Section 27–Canadian Charter of Rights and Freedoms*: *This charter shall be interpreted in a manner consistent with the preservation and enhancement of the multicultural heritage of Canadians*), "and law, it is illegal to discriminate on the basis of that heritage or background. This cultural attitude is the reflection of a fundamental ethical principle. Every person is someone of incommensurable value, and the beliefs of that person are worthy of respect."

Kluge argues for "respect but not unreflective acceptance. Some of the countries where female circumcision is common have accepted that it is a violation of the dignity and integrity of a woman. They have outlawed the practice, tradition notwithstanding. The United Kingdom and France have done the same" (*Canadian Medical Association Journal*, Volume 148, Number 2, pages 288-289, January 15, 1993).

This legal/ethical dilemma, while admittedly an extreme example, illustrates the fact that even a country like Canada, which encourages its people to preserve their cultural heritage through public pronouncements and legislation, cannot reflexively accept all the cultural practices associated with other countries and traditions.

Alternatives To Female Circumcision As A Cultural Practice

In an attempt to deal with the issue of female circumcision, Save the Children Canada, in partnership with Ntanira Na Mugambo CNNM—a community based women's organization—undertook a program, in Tharaka, Kenya, to try to discourage the practice by educating girls and their families about an alternative rite of passage. Instead of undergoing the mutilation, the girls achieve their status of womanhood by 'Circumcision through Words', which involves a one week program of counseling and community celebration. The aim of the project is to not only reduce the number of mutilations but also to discourage early marriages so that young girls will have the opportunity to continue with their education. The rate of female circumcision has fallen from 95% to 70% in communities where the program has been implemented.

Immigrant Women And Domestic Abuse

Psychological and physical abuse has no ethnic, cultural or social class boundaries. All women who are abused face similar issues relating to economic and social powerlessness, fear of abandonment and the need to protect children and
family relationships. However, a number of factors make some immigrant
women particularly vulnerable to abusive situations and outcomes. A woman's
duty in many cultures and religious traditions is still to subordinate herself
completely to her husband and to childrearing. Working outside the home, unless related to the extended kinship circle, is often viewed as undermining the traditional patriarchal family structure. Tensions often arise when financial
commitments and pressures require both partners in a relationship to participate in the workforce. In cases where domestic abuse occurs many women are
reluctant to speak out fearing that public knowledge of such an event will bring
shame and disgrace on them. Separation or divorce is virtually unthinkable
given the insularity of some immigrant communities. Women who complain or
speak out face the possibility of being shunned by their own community. The
stress of maintaining a discreet silence exacts a heavy emotional and psychological toll that can result in anxiety and mental health problems. Problems are com-
pounded for women who are not fluent in either the English or French language
and lack sufficient education to find a job if they leave their partner. Immigrant
women may also lack information on their legal rights both under the *Criminal
Code of Canada* and immigration law.

According to Marsha Sfeir of Education Wife Assault, "in many cultures, including my own which is Lebanese, if there is a separation or divorce, the children
are automatically given to the man. There is nothing more important to a Lebanese
woman than her children, so if she doesn't know that in Canada the law doesn't
automatically give the man the children, she would rather stay with him than
jeopardize her relationship with the children" (*Varsity News*, October 14, 1997).

Immigrant Women And Canadian Immigration Policy

Adding to the vulnerability of many immigrant women in Canada are some features of Canadian immigration and refugee policies. Of particular concern are requirements under what is known as the sponsorship program, which enables
Canadian citizens or landed immigrants to sponsor close relatives or family
members who want to become permanent residents of Canada. Sponsors must
promise to financially support the relative or family member or family members

for a period of three years, in the case of a spouse, common-law partner or same sex partner, and ten years for most other family members. To sponsor a relative or family member, the sponsor (person already living in Canada) must sign a legal contract with the Minister of Citizenship and Immigration. This is called an undertaking. Sponsors are expected to provide enough support that the relative will not have to rely on social assistance (welfare). Sponsored relatives (except the elderly) must promise to make every effort to become self-supporting.

This presents a serious challenge for many immigrant women, particularly those lacking adequate language abilities, education or specific job skills. In the time needed to acquire these skills the sponsored spouse remains financially dependent on her husband. Under such circumstances it is unlikely that she would be eager to lay charges if domestic abuse occurs. This is particularly true if she also needs her husband's financial help to sponsor other relatives with whom she wishes to be re-united. In such a situation even an employed woman may be willing to endure abuse if the financial commitment needed to bring over a close relative requires two incomes.

The case of refugee women reporting domestic abuse is even more hazardous because of the risk that her husband could be sent back to their home country under the exclusion clauses of the refugee convention. He may be refused landed immigrant status or rendered ineligible until he has served a five-year rehabilitation period or legally pardoned. The concern that family reunification will be jeopardized by a battering charge against a partner is so great that proposed reforms to the new *Immigration Act* (*Bill C-11*) had to be amended before the legislation came into effect. In the original proposed legislation *"people convicted of a crime related to domestic abuse (would) not be able to sponsor (a relative) unless a pardon (had) been granted or rehabilitation (had) been demonstrated"* (Citizenship and Immigration Canada, Feb. 21, 2001). When the legislation was finally passed on June 28, 2002, the wording had been amended to read *"people convicted of a crime related to domestic abuse will not be able to sponsor, with flexibility to exempt particular cases on compassionate grounds"* (*Immigration and Refugee Protection Act*, 2002).

The Sikhs Of Canada

Almost a half million Canadians identify with the Sikh faith. Sikhs have a long history in Canada going back to Queen Victoria's Diamond Jubilee celebrations in 1897 when they were welcomed in Canada as members of the British Indian Army. This positive experience encouraged a few of the soldiers to consider immigrating to Canada, which they did about three years later settling mainly in

British Columbia, finding work in the sawmills or with the Canadian Pacific Railway. Like the Japanese and Chinese before them, the Sikhs, and other South Asian immigrants, experienced prejudice and hostility from a segment of the Canadian-born for their willingness to work long and hard for low wages as well as their unique clothing and religious practices. By 1908, limitations were placed on the number of South Asians who could immigrate to Canada through the *Continuous Journey Stipulation* and they lost their right to vote.

Changes in immigration policy beginning in 1947, when restrictions on immigration from Commonwealth countries were eased, resulted in a trickle of South Asian immigration followed by a larger influx after restrictions based on country of origin were finally removed in 1962. Although Sikhs make up only 2 % of the population of India, they are a significant component of the South Asian immigration to Canada, which includes people from India, Pakistan, Bangladesh, and Sri Lanka.

Origins of the Sikh Faith

Sikhism originates in a northwestern province of India known as the Punjab. The founder of the faith was a man called Nanak who was born in 1469. Although born to Hindu parents, Nanak became disillusioned with the injustices associated with the Hindu caste system and was inspired by the idea of universal brotherhood preached by Muslims. Rather than abandon Hinduism, he preached the unity of the two religions because he believed the basic teachings of both faiths were essentially the same. As a consequence, modern Sikhism incorporates aspects of Hinduism such as beliefs about Karma and rebirth with ideas of communal harmony and egalitarianism drawn from Islam. Nanak's charismatic personality and the notion of universal brotherhood attracted many followers and he became known as Guru (teacher) Nanak. His disciples (Sikh means disciple) came together to form the new religion of Sikhism. The teachings of Nanak are contained in the Sikh Holy Book, the *Guru Granth Sahib (the "Granth")*, which is highly revered, and symbolic of a living God to believers. The Sikh places of worship are known as *Gurdwaras*.

In the Sikh faith, there are ten recognized Gurus (teachers) who followed Nanak, each one contributing something that served to spread and consolidate the faith. Of particular importance was the fifth Guru, Guru Arjun, who was responsible for the building of the Golden Temple in Amritsar, which became the holiest of Sikh shrines. The last of the ten Sikh Gurus was Gobind Singh, who died in1708 after years of warfare against Muslims. He advocated the importance of military training to help believers to defend themselves. Much of the distinctive dress associated with modern orthodox Sikhs originates with Gobind and his creation of a new brotherhood of believers known as the *Khalsa* ("the pure"). The *Khalsa* are expected to abide by what is referred to as the "Five k's" (*pang Kakars– (1) Kes– unshorn hair which is regarded as akin to saintliness because the founder of the faith Guru Nanak started this practice (2)– Kanha– a comb to keep the hair tidy (3) Kara– steel bracelet worn on the right wrist symbolizing restraint from the commission of evil deeds (4) Kachh– undergarment to be worn to symbolize modesty and restraint over passions and desires (5) Kirpan– ceremonial dagger emblematic of courage and willingness to defend the weak and oppressed*) and the four taboos (*Kerehats (1)– trimming saving or removing hair from the body is forbidden (2)– use of alcohol is forbidden (3)– eating livestock that has been slaughtered in a particular way is forbidden (4)– adultery is forbidden*).

Sikhs who have been formally baptized are referred to as *Amridharis*. This means they have undergone a ceremony known as taking *Amrit* (a mixture of water and sugar that is blessed). Many members of the Sikh community in Canada can be described as non-traditionalists and are not identifiable by the traditional dress requirements of "orthodox" Sikhs.

Politics

Sikhs represent only 2% of India's population but they form a majority in the Northwestern state known as the Punjab. In 1983, some Sikh militants began agitating for a separate Sikh homeland, which they wanted to call Khalistan. The Indian government in New Delhi was determined to prevent this from happening because the Punjab borders on the neighboring country of Pakistan, an arch-enemy of India. Allowing an independent Khalistan would encourage other separatist movements in the area and create even more problems for India.

In 1984, the Indian Army launched an attack on the Golden Temple in Amritsar in an attempt to oust some militant Sikhs who were present. The Indian government claimed the temple was being used as a base to hoard weapons and plan terrorist attacks. This action generated outrage because the Golden Temple is the holiest shrine in the Sikh faith. In retaliation, the Prime Minister of India, Indira Gandhi, was assassinated later the same year by two of her bodyguards who happened to be Sikhs (about 15% of the Indian military is comprised of Sikhs). Thousands died as anti-Sikh violence by Hindus, the religion of the majority in India, followed in the wake of Gandhi's death.

In 1987, the new Prime Minister of India Rajiv Gandhi, Indira's son, dismissed the state government in the Punjab and imposed direct rule from New Delhi. He ordered Indian troops to lay siege to the Golden Temple in another attempt to remove the militants. This did not work. When the siege was ended the level of violence only intensified as thousands of well-armed militants had become entrenched in bases all over the Punjab. Terror tactics increased resulting in a significant loss of life as anyone who was seen as an enemy of an independent Khalistan was targeted.

Effects Of Overseas Violence On Canadian Sikhs

Unfortunately, the political conflicts over independence for Khalistan have affected the Sikh community in Canada where squabbles between rival factions have sometimes led to violence. Although most Canadian Sikhs are not involved in the disputes and have a well-deserved reputation for their extraordinary entrepreneurial abilities and industriousness, they are an easily identifiable minority and have sometimes been vilified because of the actions of a few members of the community. Negative perceptions have been reinforced by several high profile violent events such as the Air India crash of 1985 that took the lives of 329 passengers. The RCMP alleges that Sikh militants based in Canada were responsible for planting the bomb that brought the plane down as an act of revenge for the Indian army's attack on the Golden Temple in 1984. The case involving two of the accused Canadian Sikhs ended in a not guilty verdict on March 16, 2005, after one of the longest, most expensive criminal investigations and trials in Canadian history.

In another incident, in May of 1986, police arrested 5 Montreal area Sikhs and charged them with conspiracy to blow up an Air India jet out of New York City. Two of the five men were tried, convicted and given life sentences for participating in the conspiracy.

In May of 1987, an attempt was made on the life of India's Minister responsible for the Punjab who was visiting Vancouver Island at the time. Four suspects were arrested at a police roadblock and later charged with attempted murder. They were convicted and sentenced to twenty years.

Violence has also erupted over election disputes at *Gurdwaras* (Sikh places of worship). In 1982, a Canada-wide warrant was issued for the arrest of a Sikh man who was charged with two counts of attempted murder in connection with a shooting inside a courtroom (Osgoode Hall in Toronto) after a judge ruled against the man in an election dispute at a Sikh *Gurdwara*. The man opened fire and then fled. No one was killed.

In the 1990s, the RCMP focused on the use of charitable organizations as a cover for the financing of extremist activities in India. In 1993, a group called the *Babbar Khalsa* Society registered as a religious and charitable organization. The group held power at many Canadian Sikh *Gurdwaras*, thereby controlling much of the revenue brought in. However, the group's charitable status was revoked in 1996 when it failed to comply with requirements of the Income Tax Act and Revenue Canada auditors raised questions about several expenditures. The RCMP alleged that the group raised money in Canada to buy weapons for extremists in India. In 1995, police officers from six Toronto police divisions had broken up a violent episode between rival groups of *Babbar Khalsa* and International Sikh Youth Federation supporters.

Culture Clashes Within The Sikh Community

Within the Canadian Sikh community there are also disputes between "liberal" and orthodox or "conservative" Sikhs. One explosive issue in recent years has been the presence of tables and chairs in the Sikh temples. For 500 years Sikhs had always sat on the floor while eating *langar* (a communal meal) after religious services in the *Gurdwaras*. This tradition derives from the teachings of the founder of the faith, Nanak, who stressed the importance of humility among the faithful.

In the 1970s some Sikh temples broke with tradition and brought tables and chairs into the *Gurdwaras*. Some orthodox Sikhs were offended because the practice of eating at a table was considered elitist and went against Nanak's egalitarian teachings. In the mid-1990s, they demanded the removal of chairs and tables from the temples and a return to sitting on the floor during meals. "Liberal" Sikhs objected citing difficulties for the disabled and the colder temperatures in North America that made sitting on the floors uncomfortable, particularly for older people. Disputes between the factions became so bitter that a riot broke out at one Vancouver temple in early 1997. The RCMP was brought in to subdue the brawl involving about seventy people.

The issue was brought before the Jathedar of the Akal Takhat Sahib, the acknowledged leader of the Worldwide Sikh Movement, who issued an edict against the use of furniture in the temples. "Liberal" Sikhs appealed the decision but the edict was maintained. The leaders of 21 Sikh societies in British Columbia and Alberta vowed to keep the furniture, even if it meant risking ex-communication for their actions. On June 8, 1998, three reform priests were suspended for defying the ban on tables and chairs. They complained to the *British Columbia Human Rights Commission*, arguing that they had been discriminated against on religious grounds. At the same time, many Sikh priests in the Vancouver area started a strike in an attempt to persuade temple executives to remove the furniture in the *Gurdwaras*.

Throughout 1998 disturbances broke out at several temples in Vancouver including one at the Ross Street Temple, the oldest Sikh temple in North America established in 1905. Police closed the temple down following a ruckus when conservative Sikhs tried to prevent a "liberal" excommunicated executive member from addressing the congregation.

Tensions increased further when the wheelchair bound publisher of a Sikh newspaper, Tara Hayer, a well known supporter of the "liberal" side of the issue, was gunned down in his garage by an unknown assassin on Nov.18, 1998. On October 27, 2000, the RCMP arrested two men in connection with the 1985 Air India bombing. One of the two was also charged at the same time with the attempted murder of Hayer.

In November and December of 1998, "liberal" candidates were elected to fill a number of management positions within several Sikh temples in British Columbia. Since then, attempts have been made to bridge the differences between the factions through dialogue and community wide meetings.

Some observers in the Sikh community see the dispute over tables and chairs in the temples as a "symbolic issue" which essentially masks a deeper concern among traditionalists that accommodating to modern practices, in other words the "Canadian Way," will undermine or weaken the faith.

Sikh Youth

The most troubling development in the Sikh community in the past decade has been the rise of youth gangs and associated violence which has claimed the lives of over sixty young people in British Columbia. As a consequence, important questions have been raised about family structure, the role of women, and the attitudes and expectations of young people within the community.

South Asian families, in general, are male-centered with important decisions usually left to the father. Women tend to stay in the background and play traditional supportive or nurturing roles. Arranged marriages are still common in South Asian families. Although individual families might engage in arranging marriages themselves, there are also companies such as Sanjog Marriage Services which act as intermediaries making introductions to prospective spouses. However, young Sikhs in Canada increasingly reject unsatisfactory matches and don't face the social sanctions they once did for such a decision. Marital disputes often erupt as a consequence of a decision by South Asian women to enter the labour market.

Conflicts between parents and children, particularly girls, arise over such issues as dating, clothing fashions, make-up, and the influence of peer groups in school situations. Young people are increasingly taking their cultural cues from American and Canadian television programs as well as sometimes violent and sexually explicit unrated videos produced by the thriving Hindi movie industry in British Columbia.

The conservative moral code of many South Asian families stands in sharp contrast to a liberal, secular mainstream culture governed by situational ethics. Young women must do nothing that would bring shame or disgrace to the family. Boys, on the other hand, are raised more permissively, even indulgently, and are praised for their independence and risk-taking qualities. These family patterns, along with some of the militant aspects and traditions of the Sikh faith, have, in the view of some observers, produced a volatile mixture that has led to a youth culture that thrives on bravado and violence.

In a blistering critique of the complacency of the Sikh community in the face of youth related gang violence, Renu Bakshi, a CTV reporter and journalist of Punjabi background, wrote in *MacLean's Magazine* that, "from the moment a Punjabi boy opens his eyes, his parents hand him the keys to the Porsche of life. From now on, his mother will ride in the back seat, literally and figuratively, putting her son ahead of the world. Her boy will have the privilege of eating a warm meal, without the chore of clearing the dishes alongside his sister, In a fit of childhood rage, he will kick and punch his mother, as his father and grandfather look on, taking great pride in their boy's supposed courage" (*MacLean's Magazine*, Feb.21, 2000).

Vancouver police inspector Kash Heed sees a pattern whereby violence is used as a means by which the head of a household settles disputes with his wife and other members of the family. Growing up in these highly patriarchal family structures lead young men to believe that disagreements are best resolved through force rather than through dialogue. According to Heed, "you have fathers and mothers praising their sons when these boys are involved in illegal activities—drug trafficking and murders. But these parents are still going 'that's my boy' based on that old family principle"(*MacLean's Magazine*, Feb. 21, 2000).

In Renu Bakshi's view, the community has attempted to protect itself by denying that a problem exists. Parents would rather look the other way than admit that some young males in the community are out of control. "Even after their sons are murdered in drug related shootings, parents have often spoken on record to reinforce their son's 'innocence'. Police officer's have also described incidents where parents have slammed the door in their faces when they tried to deliver the news of a murder" (*MacLean's Magazine*, Feb. 21, 2000).

In June of 2000 a forum took place between police and members of the Sikh community in Vancouver. The idea was to build trust and help solve the gang problem. Tensions arose immediately as police officers complained of a "conspiracy of silence" in the Sikh community to protect their sons at the expense of solving murder investigations. Accusations of racism were hurled at the police as members of the Sikh community resented being singled out for special attention. However, the fact remained that no other South Asian sub-community in Canada, which includes large numbers of Hindus and Muslims, has lost as many young men to violence. A similar gang problem is emerging among Sikh youth in Britain and in the United States. In California, only 25% of the Indo-American population is Sikh, yet the violent, Indo-American street gangs are made up almost entirely of Sikh young people. The same cycle of denial is evident among parents in California, where they claim their sons are not part of gangs, they're just "boys being boys." One result of the forum in Vancouver was a call by all present to stop further bloodshed and begin an examination of the elements of Sikh culture, religion, and family values that might be contributing to the problem.

The Kirpan Controversy

The distinctive clothing and religious requirements of orthodox Sikhs have sometimes been a source of controversy for those practicing the faith in Canada. The most recent example occurred in Lasalle, Quebec, near the city of Montreal. In November of 2001, a young Sikh, Gurbaj Singh Multani, fell down in the playground of the school he was attending. As a result, the kirpan, the ceremonial dagger the wearing of which is an important component of the faith, dropped out of its wrapping under his clothes. Upon learning of this event from students and school monitors, the authorities at Ste. Catherine Laboure School in Lasalle decided it was dangerous and banned him from wearing it while attending school. The young man then refused to go to school. Discussions ensued between the School Board and the family about some way that the school rules against the possession of concealed weapons and the religious obligations of the young man could be reconciled. Both the young man and his father, a devout Sikh, ruled out any compromise such as wearing a plastic kirpan or a miniature one on a necklace. They offered instead to keep the kirpan beneath the boy's shirt, sewn into a cloth sheath, at all times, a proposal which was rejected by the school board, prompting the family to challenge the school's policies in court, on the basis of religious freedom. They hired a prominent civil rights lawyer, Julius Grey, who argued that the kirpan was no more dangerous than a geometry compass. The family obtained a temporary injunction in April of 2002 that allowed Multani to return to school wearing his original kirpan.

However, the controversy generated strong emotions on both sides of the debate. A police presence was required to escort the young man into the school with fellow students shouting abuse as he went by them. Dozens of parents kept their children at home on the day of Multani's return to protest the decision to allow him back. For many of the parents the issue was a concern over safety. They saw the kirpan as a weapon that posed a real threat to their children. According to Sylvie Blais, one of the members of the school's board of governors, "the kirpan represents violence because it's a knife. Since September 11 and the World Trade Centre we realize that we aren't beyond the reach of such acts" (*British Broadcasting Corporation News*, May 18, 2002).

The Sikh community in Quebec felt that the taunts leveled at Multani when he returned to school demonstrated ignorance and even racism by the majority French speaking community in Montreal and that Quebec's education policy had failed to keep up with the new reality of different cultures arriving in the province. According to Manjit Singh, the Director of the Canadian Sikh Council, "the good name of Quebec has been sullied" by the controversy and compared it to the civil rights conflicts in the United States in the 1960s (*BBC News*, May 18, 2002).

In May of 2000, the Superior Court of Quebec ruled that Multani should be allowed to wear his ceremonial dagger thereby overturning the decision by the school and the school board in Lasalle. In what amounted to a compromise decision, the court outlined certain conditions that had to be met to take into consideration both the security concerns of the school as well as respect for religious liberty. The kirpan must be no longer than ten centimeters in length, it must be kept in its wooden sheath and wrapped in fabric that is sewn shut, and it must be worn under the clothing of the student.

The decision was based on precedents that had been set elsewhere in Canada. The right to wear a kirpan at school was upheld in 1991 after an Ontario school board challenged the province's *Human Rights Commission* decision that reasonably sized kirpans could be worn at school. In 1988, a Sikh man had filed a complaint with the Ontario *Human Rights Commission* alleging that he had been discriminated against because of his religion. The man's employer, the Peel Board of Education had forbidden him from wearing a kirpan on school property, after it had introduced a no-weapons policy following several violent incidents involving knives. The Peel Board argued that the kirpan can be used as a weapon and is considered as such by non-Sikhs. A Commission board of inquiry ruled in 1991 that the ban on the kirpan discriminated against Sikhs finding that although the policy was enacted in good faith, it was not reasonable under the circumstances because there had never been a case of violence in any Canadian school involving a kirpan. It ordered the school board to allow Sikh pupils, teachers or staff members to wear kirpans to school subject to certain safety restrictions (similar to the ones delineated in the Quebec decision). The Peel School Board appealed the ruling to the Ontario divisional court but lost. The Ontario Court of Appeal then refused to hear the case (*Montreal Gazette*, Feb.21, 2002).

The decision by the Quebec court did not placate some of the members of the school community opposed to the wearing of the kirpan who saw the conflict as a symptom of the failure of the boy's family to integrate into Quebec's increasingly secular society. According to one parent, religious groups "can do what they want at home and in their churches—but not at school...When (immigrants) arrive here, there are certain laws they should respect" (*Montreal Gazette*, April 18, 2002, A-3).

Quebec's Minister of Justice announced on May 27, 2002, that the government had decided to appeal the decision asserting that it had adopted a policy of "zero tolerance" to the wearing of weapons in schools and that, even symbolically, a weapon is still a weapon. On March 4, 2004, the Quebec Court of Appeals overturned the lower court decision and banned the kirpan in public schools as a "reasonable limit on religious freedom." In a unanimous decision, the court concluded that Multani's religious rights had to give way to school safety. Stripped of its religious symbolism, the court concluded that the kirpan had all the physical characteristics of a weapon and was therefore dangerous not only to Multani but fellow students and staff members (*CBC news*, March 5, 2004). The case has now gone to the Supreme Court of Canada. For the time being, Multani attends a private school in Quebec that permits the wearing of the kirpan.

The Turban Controversy

Another controversy involving the clothing requirements of *Khalsa* Sikhs occurred in the late 1980s and centered on the uniform requirements of the Royal Canadian Mounted Police (RCMP). Earlier in the decade, the Canadian Armed Forces, Canadian National Railways, and Minister of Correctional Services had all been challenged under the *Canadian Human Rights Act* by Sikhs claiming that these organizations had dress regulations and codes that preventing them from gaining employment, thereby discriminating on the basis of religion. In all these cases, judgements had been made in favour of the Sikh complainants, with the decisions being upheld in the case of appeals. In 1988, Baltej Singh Dhillon challenged the RCMP when the Force told him he could join only if he didn't wear the turban his Sikh faith demands. As a consequence of this challenge, and aware of the court decisions in previous challenges, the RCMP amended their uniform regulations the following year to enable detachments to hire orthodox Sikh officers. The changes permitted the wearing of turbans instead of the customary RCMP Stetson or forage cap.

Although motivated by the desire to more accurately reflect and represent the ethnic and cultural diversity of the country, the decision immediately generated controversy. Opponents circulated a petition that was signed by more than 200,000 people protesting the changes. In 1994, several former RCMP officers launched a lawsuit claiming that the changes to the uniform regulations violated provisions of the *Charter of Rights and Freedoms (s.2 (a), s.7, s.15)*.

Kirsten Mansbridge, a spokesperson for the group, argued that the RCMP has always presented a neutral and impartial image. "If you allowed one religious symbol, then every other religious symbol should be allowed. It would no longer be a 'uniform', it would be more like a costume" (*Calgary Herald*, January 26, 1994, A1). A lawyer representing the plaintiffs said there were "constitutional limits to the government's obligations and rights to accommodate and incorporate religious symbolism"(*Calgary Herald*, January 26, 1994, A1).

In 1995, the Supreme Court of Canada rejected their application to prevent turbans from being worn by RCMP officers on the grounds that there *was no*

constitutional barrier to the RCMP Commissioner acting to amend the uniform regula-
tions on the basis of existing jurisprudence and the evidence that was brought before
the crown (Grant v. Canada, 1995). On the other hand, the crown also noted that
nothing in the Canadian *Charter of Rights and Freedoms* had required the Force to
alter the uniform regulations.

Church And State

The opponents of the revised RCMP uniform requirements tried to frame the issue in terms of separation of church and state. Dr. Antonio Gualtieri, a professor
of philosophy and religion at Carleton University, argued that religious tolerance and mutual respect are best guaranteed when the state maintains as much
neutrality as possible towards all traditional religions. Such neutrality is fostered
when the symbols of the state are not mixed with those of any religion and, in
his view, this is particularly important in those state institutions which exercise
the coercive power of law enforcement (*Grant v. Canada, 1995*).

However, the Canadian Constitution does not contain an explicit textual requirement that there be a separation of church and state as exists, for example,
in the Constitution of the United States. Defenders of the revised policy that permitted turbans cited several examples where the role of church and state in Canada had been inextricably linked such as denominational (religious) schools
which are constitutionally protected in some provinces, exemptions to military
service which have been made for conscientious objectors, and the partnership
between church and state which existed in the province of Quebec right up until
the Quiet Revolution of 1960.

By the time the Supreme Court had rendered a decision several municipal
police forces had also revised their uniform regulations in an effort to attract recruits from the Sikh community. In October of 1993, baptized Sikhs employed
as municipal policemen in British Columbia were permitted to wear turbans
with a municipal badge number centered on its front (as well as a *kangha*—
comb—under the turban), a replica of the *kirpan* (the Sikh ceremonial dagger),
and a *Kara* (steel bracelet) on the wrist. A spokesperson for the Sikh community,
Aziz Khaki, said that the changes had been sought for years. "We felt there was a
barrier facing the Sikh community but now in B.C. that obstacle has been removed. Now it's a challenge to the Sikh community—this will allow you to participate fully and I'm sure many will accept that challenge" (*Vancouver Sun,*
October 13, 1993, B1).

Other Jurisdictions

Other municipal police forces and the Canadian Armed Forces permit Sikhs to wear turbans subject to certain conditions. For example, the Toronto Police Force does not allow officers wearing turbans to perform traffic duties or go on industrial sites where hard hats are required. They are also restricted from duties where a gas mask or respirator is required. Sikhs in the Canadian Armed Forces must conform to requirements where special equipment necessitates the removal of the turban. Since the Armed Forces will not transfer an individual into a position so as to avoid the wearing of special equipment, this presents something of an obstacle to the recruitment of *Khalsa* Sikhs. This is rather ironic since changes that allowed turbans and uncut hair occurred after a complaint (under the *Canadian Human Rights Act*) by a Sikh applicant to the Canadian Armed Forces in 1979. The Armed Forces had agreed to comply with the religious demand after the Human Rights Commission cited the turban ban as a discriminatory infraction (*Grant v. Canada, 1995*).

Hindus And Buddhists

A significant number of new immigrants to Canada are from mainland India and Sri Lanka, an island off the southern coast of India. Many identify with either Hindu or Buddhist religious traditions. Of all the world's religions, Hinduism has perhaps the richest mythology and from the standpoint of many westerners is the most difficult to understand. Prayers, wedding ceremonies, funerals and many other rituals associated with the faith are incredibly ancient. Specific practices such as the worship of tools and the sacredness of certain plants, animals, and even rivers are often baffling to many in the West. Of particular significance is the veneration of the cow by many Hindus who are vegetarian and will not slaughter or eat beef.

Hinduism is notable for its lack of rigid orthodoxy, which hampers any discussion of basic beliefs. A variety of religious writings that include hymns of praise, sacred teachings, epic legends and myths, and sacrificial rituals are associated with the faith. One of the most significant and highly revered works is the *Bhagavadgita*, which is actually a poem consisting of only 700 verses. Mohandas "Mahatma" Gandhi considered the holy book "*Gita*" to be as important to Hindus as the bible is to Christians.

Unlike Christianity, Islam and Sikhism, the Hindu temple (*Mundir*) is not a place of congregational worship but the abode of God, or the Gods, as many

Hindus subscribe to the idea of a three-fold deity that is depicted on idols by one body with three heads. Hindu temples often contain elaborate ornamentation, pictures and carvings that in one way or another pay tribute to God. There are no set times for prayers. Women are expected to wear a head covering before entering a temple and shoes must be removed. Since all aspects of bodily functions are thought to be impure and polluting, Hindus consider it important to wash or shower before prayer. In Canada, many Hindu religious activities are also carried out in the home with a special room sometimes set aside for meditation. Large gatherings occur to celebrate festive occasions such as *Holi* or Hindu spring festival, which occurs in February/March and *Diwali*, the Festival of Lights, which occurs each year in late October or November.

One of the central components of Hinduism is the concept of reincarnation (rebirth after death) and its close association with the doctrine of Karma, according to which the nature of one's rebirth after death is determined by one's thoughts, words, or deeds during life. This belief has been the historical underpinning of the *caste system* in India, a hierarchical social structure in which status and occupation are fixed on a hereditary basis. The caste system is believed to have emerged after conquering tribes from the north, known as the Aryans, subdued the indigenous population of India. The Aryans were of lighter skin colour and the word for caste is *Varna*, meaning colour. They regarded themselves as superior to the native inhabitants and so established a system of social stratification. Originally, four distinct castes emerged: The Brahmans were the highest caste comprised of priests and thinkers; the *Kshatriyas* or warriors; the *Vaisyas*, comprised of merchants, artisans and peasants; the *Sudras* or serfs. In modern India the main castes have been divided into hundreds of sub castes. There are also literally tens of millions of "outcastes" that live a hardscrabble existence and are considered by other Indians to be "ceremonially unclean" or "untouchable." A person is born to a particular caste and must remain there until they die. Only upon rebirth will they move up or down to another caste based upon their actions in their previous life. People are born into the highest caste because of their good behaviour in a previous life. Similarly, those born into poverty are in that position because of misdeeds in a previous life. One important consequence of this fatalistic view of life is that the inequalities of the caste system and virtually all other differences in human life are both explained and justified. Poverty and riches, good health or bad health, fame or obscurity, are all ascribed by *Karma*. Attempts to redress the inequalities that exist and lay the groundwork for a broader conception of social justice are essentially futile and even wrong-headed. It becomes heretical to even question the fate that has befallen people.

In modern India, the development of industry, and increased foreign travel, has served to undermine the rigidity of the caste system but many in the West attribute the continued widespread poverty and lack of social mobility to the legacy of old habits and customs.

The emphasis in Hinduism is the development of the inner life, meaning that humility, simple living, and intellectual reflection take precedence over the pursuit of material goods, pleasure, and social striving. This is directly at odds with the social and cultural ethos of Western societies where the legacy of the Protestant Reformation stresses the need to earn one's eternal salvation through personal ambition, striving and worldly success.

Buddhism

Buddhism is today the religion of Burma, Cambodia, Tibet, Sri Lanka, half of Japan and much of China. There are significant numbers of Buddhists in many western countries and its influence is worldwide. Its founder was Siddhartha Gautama (Buddha), the son of a privileged member of India's warrior caste, who was born about 500 years before Christ. He was a man born into a privileged position. Shortly after his marriage and the birth of a son, he became restless and renounced his family and all his worldly possessions to become a penniless wanderer in search of enlightenment. Through his experiences and encounters with others, Gautama concluded that the cause of all suffering in the world was selfish craving or desire. As long as humankind was captivated by the desire for material goods or sensual pleasures they never would escape the endless cycle of death and rebirth and they would have no peace. True spirituality and inner tranquility could only be attained by the renunciation of everything that one was attached to.

Gautama's message eventually attracted disciples who were encouraged to spread the Word (*Dharma*). The disciples were known as the Order of the *Sangha* who were expected to lead by example. There were no priests, rites, or creeds associated with the practice of Buddhism. Members of the order possessed only a saffron robe, a razor, a begging bowl, a water strainer and a needle to mend their robe. Disciples were not to be bound by social ties but instead were to devote themselves to the service of all living things. A council of 500 Enlightened Ones, who had studied the Buddha's teaching, were responsible for spreading the practice after his death.

The practice is based on a kind of mental discipline that avoids extremes and seeks to find a "middle way" (moderation) by way of an "eightfold path" (a code of conduct) on the road to "*Nirvana*" (enlightenment). Individuals strive to find for themselves the "Right Knowledge, The "Right Thought," the "Right Speech," the "Right Conduct," the "Right Means of Livelihood" (work), the "Right Effort," the "Right Mind Control," and the "Right Meditation." Along this "eightfold path" the individual must overcome the three cardinal sins: sensuality and greed; anger and ill will; illusion and stupidity.

The teachings of the Buddha were mainly passed on by an oral tradition and were not written down until about four hundred years after his death. The Doctrine incorporates aspects of what we now call Hinduism such as the notions of *Karma* and rebirth along with the Buddha's unique philosophical and intro-spective musings about the nature of human existence.

In the modern world the practice of Buddhism takes many forms, sometimes completely inconsistent with the original doctrine. Monasteries contain statues of the Buddha and followers lay flowers or light candles as a sign of devotion. Cere-monial bowing and praying is common. On entering Buddhist shrines people take off their shoes and sit on mats often facing a statue of the Buddha. Monks may chant in a low monotone with the congregation bowing or joining in the chant at certain times. The atmosphere is solemn and contemplative.

Political Issues

Many Hindu and Buddhist immigrants to Canada have come to escape social and political turmoil in their homelands. One of the most troubled areas is the is-land of Sri Lanka, an island just 50 km off the southern coast of India. Sri Lanka used to be known as Ceylon until it was renamed in 1972. The population of Sri Lanka comprises 19 million people and is divided into two main ethnic/religious groups. About three-quarters of the population are Sinhalese, members of a largely Buddhist, Sinhala-speaking ethnic group that have dominated the coun-try since its independence in 1948. Another 18% belong to a minority known as the Tamils, mainly of the Hindu faith, and are linked to ethnic Tamils who live on the southern mainland of India. There are also small numbers of ethnic Mus-lims as well as Tamil and Sinhalese Christians.

Before independence the British ruled the country for 150 years with the Tamil minority playing an important role in the administration of the colony. Influence shifted to the majority Sinhalese after independence. In the late 1950s

the Sinhalese majority attempted to make Buddhism the country's official religion and impose quotas on the number of Tamils in educational institutions and
the civil service. This led to several violent incidents. Violent incidents arose again
as a consequence of certain economic reforms in the early 1970s when many
Tamil agricultural workers lost their jobs. As a minority, many unemployed
Tamils also faced discrimination in the labour market, particularly young people in the urban parts of the country. In response, a movement arose seeking independence for the northern and eastern parts of Sri Lanka where the Tamil
population is concentrated, particularly the province of Jaffna, and the development of closer ties with the ethnic Tamil population in southern India. In 1983
full-scale war erupted as the demands for an independent state intensified. The
group pushing for independence is known as the Liberation Tigers of Tamil
Eelam (LTTE) or the Tamil Tigers. They have used guerrilla and terror tactics, including several hundred suicide bombings, in a bloody, two-decade civil war
that has claimed the lives of over 60,000 people, and generated thousands of refugees and displaced persons, many of them coming to Canada. The group is renowned for the ferocity of their tactics that include the bombing of buses
carrying civilians, attacks on Buddhist shrines and the assassination of prominent politicians, including one Sri Lankan President, Ranasinghe Premadasa, India's Prime Minister Rajiv Gandhi, and Ministers in the Sri Lankan government.
In October, 1997, a suicide truck bomb killed 18 people at the 39-story World
Trade Center in the Sri Lankan capital of Colombo. The Tigers were also accused
of a massacre of women and children in a majority Sinhala village in late 1999.
Suicide bombers are highly motivated individuals who turn themselves into human bombs by strapping explosives to their bodies, tactics that they pioneered
and are now also used by groups in the Middle East and elsewhere. Tiger recruits, including women and even young children, are subjected to vigourous
military training and ideological indoctrination, and are handed a cyanide cap-
sule to be worn around their neck in case of capture. Since martyrdom can be
achieved by avoiding capture through suicide very few have been taken alive by
Sri Lankan security forces.

   After horrendous losses of life on both sides, a cease fire began in the fall of
2001. In February 2002, the Sri Lankan government and the Tigers signed a
truce, finally acknowledging that neither side could actually win. Since then
talks have been conducted to resolve the outstanding issues but disputes have
again arisen over who will control U.S.$4.5 billion in foreign aid pledged to re-
construct the country.

Fund Raising Activities Abroad And In Canada

Much of the finance for the activities of the LTTE is raised in expatriate Tamil communities in Western Europe, the United States and Canada. This has become a major political issue as the heightened security concerns in the wake of the World Trade Center attack has focused attention on fund raising and charitable organizations that may be a front for groups raising money for terror activities in other countries or within Canada itself. Accusations have been made that Tiger controlled organizations in Canada and elsewhere use terror and intimidation tactics to extort money from the expatriate Tamil immigrant population to fund the activities of the group in Sri Lanka. The Canadian Security and Intelligence Service (CSIS) asked the federal cabinet to ban the LTTE as a terrorist group claiming that Canada's strategic importance to them as a base to raise illegal funds, recruit terrorists and gain political legitimacy increased significantly after Britain and Australia recently joined the United States in banning the group's activities. However, Bill Graham, Canada's Foreign Affairs Minister, blocked the listing of the Tigers as a terrorist group under Canada's counter-terrorism laws on the grounds that they do not pose an immediate security threat to Canadians. Graham claimed that a ban would hurt fragile peace negotiations between the group and the Sri Lankan government that have been ongoing since the cease fire in 2001 (*The National Post*, September, 11, 2003).

Former Ontario Premier Bob Rae led a delegation to Sri Lanka in August, 2003 to offer advice to the opposing factions on federal systems, constitutional reform, and ways in which other countries have resolved seemingly intractable cultural, linguistic and religious divisions. Based on earlier efforts by Rae and his group before peace talks were held in Oslo in 2002, both parties in the conflict had "agreed to explore a solution founded on the principle of internal self-determination based on a federal structure within a united Sri Lanka" (*MacLean's Magazine*, August 11, 2003, p.29). If this experiment in Canadian style federalism worked it would permit the return of tens of thousands of Sri Lankan refugees who have fled the country over the past twenty years.

The Tsunami Disaster Adds A New Dimension To Fund Raising Controversies

On December 26, 2004, Sri Lanka was one of many countries in the region devastated by a giant ocean wave known as tsunami. In the immediate aftermath of the disaster controversy arose over how aid to the area would be organized and distributed. Groups in the northern Tamil controlled areas of the country accused the Sri

Lankan government in Colombo of withholding or interfering with assistance to their part of the country. The government responded by calling the accusation LTTE propaganda and charged that the Tigers were using the disaster to recruit young survivors to their cause from relief camps that had been set up in the afflicted areas.

Once again the controversy reverberated back in Canada where leaders of the 200,000 strong expatriate Tamil community aggressively lobbied Ottawa politicians to provide more help to the northern part of Sri Lanka. Officials from Immigration Canada offered to send Canadian visa officers to Tamil areas to find disaster victims with close relatives who wanted to immigrate to Canada if those people had difficulty getting to Colombo (the nation's capital) to file their applications. This infuriated Sri Lankan deputy foreign minister W.H Wiswa Warnapala who complained that such a gesture "(would) be interpreted as a special attempt to get to Tamil areas, It would lead to criticism, discontentment and disgruntlement by the Sinhalese majority" (*Globe and Mail*, January 13, 2005, p.1).

Canadian immigration officials argued that the government's aim was to ensure that the Sri Lankans who qualified to be expedited through Canada's immigration system were reunited with their families. Warnapala countered that Tamils had already disproportionately taken "full advantage" of Canada's immigration system and expressed his government's point of view that Tamils had been extended special preference because of "pressure groups associated with the LTTE operating in Canada, particularly in Toronto and Scarborough" (*Globe and Mail*, January 14, 2005).

Given the accusations that Ottawa had grown too "cozy" with supporters of Tamil militants, Prime Minister Paul Martin agreed not to visit northern parts of Sri Lanka when he went there to survey relief efforts. The *Sri Lanka Lanka Daily News* said that Martin's decision not to visit the north "has taught another lesson in international diplomacy to the LTTE" (*Globe and Mail*, January 14, 2005, p.2).

The Tamil Tigers were disappointed by Martin's decision but even more furious when the Sinhalese dominated government in Columbo refused to give UN Secretary General Kofi Annan permission to visit Tamil-held areas in the Northeast of the country citing security concerns.

Gary Anandasangaree, a representative of the Canadian Tamil Congress, said that Mr. Warnapala's suggestion that the Canadian government was becoming too friendly with Tamil militants in Canada was absurd. "I'm a Tamil and militant is not a word that's been used to describe me. If democracy scares the Sri Lankan government, it's really not my problem. I have an obligation to express my views to the Prime Minister and I think that's what the community is doing at this time" (*Globe and Mail*, January 14, 2005, p.2).

Chapter Seven
CANADA'S ABORIGINAL POPULATION

The ancestors of today's aboriginal population entered North America by way of the Bering Strait, apparently in search of game, some 30-40,000 years ago. They slowly migrated southward. Evidence of the existence of eastern tribes goes back about 12,000 years. Early settlers engaged in hunting, fishing and trapping. As groups moved further south some tribes took up agricultural pursuits, growing maize in what is now known as Ontario and Quebec.

When Europeans "discovered" North America there were probably about 1 to 3 million "Indians" living here, with roughly 250,000 in what we now call Canada. As a result of European settlement or "colonization," the indigenous population was often crowded out of their lands, exposed to diseases for which they had no natural immunity (small pox, measles, diphtheria) and often involved in violent confrontations with white pioneers. After a long period of decline, the aboriginal population again began to rise, and has tripled in the last century. In 2001, those who identified themselves as aboriginal persons made up 3.5% of the total population of Canada compared with 2.8% in 1996. The "registered Indian" population (about half of the total aboriginal population) now numbers about 558,180 (Census of Canada, 2001), with an expected increase to about 750,000 by 2005 (see Figure 7.1).

Figure 7.1: Persons Registered Under the Indian Act, provinces and territories

Definitions and notes	2001		
	Total	Total living on reserve	Total living off reserve
		number	
Canada	558,180	274,215	283,955

About half of the aboriginal population of Canada is under the age of 25, which is a consequence of a much higher birth rate compared to the non-ab-original population (see Figure 7.2). The median age of Canada's aboriginal pop-ulation was 24.7 years in 2001, compared to 37.7 years for the non-aboriginal population. One-third of the aboriginal population is comprised of children un-der the age of fourteen.

Figure 7.2: Population Reporting Aboriginal Identity, by Age Groups, Canada, 1996 and 2001

	2001			**1996**
	Number	*%*	*Number*	*%*
Total	976,305	100.0	799,010	100.0
0-14 years	323,960	33.2	280,420	35.1
15-24 years	169,065	17.3	143,795	18.0
25 to 64 years	443,600	45.4	346,485	43.4
65 years and over	39,680	4.1	28,310	3.5

Early Relations

At the outset, the contacts between the aboriginal population and the Europeans produced many commercial partnerships. For example, certain characteristics of beaver fur made it highly fashionable in Europe. The demand for beaver pelts could not be satisfied without the knowledge, skill, and active cooperation of the aboriginal population. Initially the partnerships between the Europeans and the indigenous population were mutually beneficial and sometimes even harmoni-ous. However, conflicts between the major European powers spilled over into the New World, with the aboriginal tribes forced to make military alliances. The major conflict was between the British and the French for control of the eastern half of North America, with the British finally prevailing in 1760. Several tribes continued to play an important role as military allies to one side or the other during the American War of Independence (1776-83) and the War of 1812. When the major wars for control of the North American continent ended, the re-lationship between the aboriginal population and the white colonists changed dramatically. They were no longer needed as military allies and their usefulness as intermediaries in the fur trade ended after the amalgamation of the major fur-trade companies in 1821. Increasingly, they were seen by the large influx of white settlers as an obstacle to land development and control of natural resources. This change marked the beginning of a significant period of economic and cultural decline for the aboriginal population in Canada, which has only recently been reversed. Government policies were developed which attempted to regulate and control all aspects of aboriginal life. The idea was to get them to give up their traditional way of life and assimilate to the dominant white culture.

Assimilation And The *Indian Act*

The Indian Act of 1876 is often seen by traditional aboriginal leaders as a policy explicitly designed by the Canadian government to assimilate the indigenous population. For example, the *Indian Act* only recognized elected *Band Councils* as political representatives of the aboriginal population rather than the hereditary chiefs or other traditional forms of self-government (such as the longhouse in the Mohawk tradition). The *Indian Act* was also used to encourage the removal of aboriginal children from the reserves to be placed in what were called *Residential schools*, which were run by Christian clergy. This attempt to forcibly assimilate them to the white culture left a bitter legacy, which still reverberates in current debates. The *Indian Act* banned traditional cultural ceremonies, undermined traditional methods of self-government, and essentially turned the aboriginal population into wards of the state through control of their finances, education and social services. All of this was rationalized by an ideology of white racial superiority.

Land Treaties

In 1760 the British took control of what is now eastern Canada. Pre-Confederation treaties include The *Royal Proclamation of 1763* issued by England's King George III, which was created in part to protect the territory of the indigenous population from incursions by Anglo-American land speculators. The nature of this treaty was different from subsequent ones in that the interests of the aboriginal population were considered. Consequently, this treaty it is often cited by aboriginal leaders when modern land claims disputes arise. The Canadian government began to make a number of small land treaties (The Robinson Treaty of 1850—Treaty No.13) with Indians in what is now northern Ontario in the 1850s. As settlers moved west, the areas covered by the treaties increased in size. Between 1870 and 1899, Treaties One to Eleven covered most of the territory from West of Lake Superior to the Rocky Mountains, and north to Great Slave Lake.

There was a deep misunderstanding about the nature of the treaties. From the government's standpoint, the treaties were agreements to surrender aboriginal rights. In return, Indians were given cash varying from $3 to $12 per member, with more sometimes for chiefs and heads of families. The government also set aside land (reserves) for the use of the bands and granted hunting and fishing rights on parts of the land surrendered. The aboriginal population viewed the treaties as agreements to share the land. Land was not a commodity, which could be bought and sold, but a responsibility of the community, to be passed on to future generations. Although the aboriginal population had a strong territorial sense, the idea that anyone could actually "own," divide, surrender, transfer, or destroy the land of the creator was a foreign concept. Land was to be shared by all the living creatures.

The "reserve" land left to the aboriginal populations was virtually useless. Hunting and fishing rights were often violated, and the amounts paid for the land ceded were insignificant in relation to their true value. The end result was impoverishment and the loss of cultural identity, which was to plague many of these communities right down to the present day.

Modern Treaties And Land Claims Settlements

Present day treaties are negotiations between the federal government and aboriginal tribes in accordance with Canada's Lands Claim Policy established in 1973. Two broad classes of claims are recognized: comprehensive claims and specific claims. Comprehensive land claims are "based on the concept of continuing aboriginal rights and title which have not been dealt with by treaty or legal means" (Department of Indian and Northern Affairs). Rights include full ownership of land in the area covered by the agreement, financial compensation, guaranteed wildlife harvesting rights, resource management and revenue sharing, and measures to stimulate economic development and cultural affairs. Since 1973, some thirteen comprehensive claims have come into effect.

Specific land claims refer to "alleged non-fulfillment of Indian Treaties and other lawful obligations or from the alleged improper administration of lands and other assets under the *Indian Act*" (Department of Indian and Northern Affairs). Two hundred and seven specific claims have been settled since 1973, and another 120 specific claims are in negotiation.

One landmark comprehensive claims settlement was the Nisga'a Treaty of 1999. The government of British Columbia arrived at an agreement with the Nisq'a, which granted the tribe limited rights to self-government, including the right to establish an aboriginal government, police and judicial system, and make laws, with the proviso that they don't override the laws of the Canadian Parliament. However, Nisq'a laws concerning language and culture will override the provincial law of British Columbia. As part of the settlement, the Nisq'a were also granted $200 million dollars in financial compensation, 1930 km of land, the right to deliver federal and provincial social services, a share of the catch of the Nass Valley where they live, and also fishing and forestry rights in the surrounding area.

The Legacy Of Failed Policies

"Indians" did not have the right to vote (enfranchisement) in Canada until 1960 (up to that time they were characterized by the government as "resident aliens"), and are still struggling to gain control of their own affairs. Confused government policies have pursued both *assimilation* and attempts at cultural autonomy. Billions of dollars are now spent on social assistance and other programs ($7.5 billion in 2003) in an attempt to deal with the fallout from these failed policies. However, the problems of poverty, inadequate housing and sanitation, high suicide rates, domestic violence, and substance abuse, persist for large segments of the aboriginal population. In some cases, the effect of large infusions of cash has mainly served to generate new problems of cronyism, patronage, and familial nepotism on reserves where small groups of people monopolize positions of power and control of finances.

Status Or "Registered" Indians

According to the 2001 census about 274,215 *registered Indians* in Canada live on one of the roughly 2567 reserves and belong to one of the approximately 633 bands that are recognized by treaties or by the federal government's *Indian Act*, a piece of legislation dating back to 1876. Another 283,955 registered Indians live off the reserve. The size of reserves range from a few acres with several dozen people to thousands of acres with the population equivalent to that of a small town. Many reserves are in rural or remote areas, some accessible only by air. Only 31% of aboriginal people lived on reserves and settlements in 2001, down from 33% in 1996.There are some 1600 small reserves in British Columbia alone. Other reserves are located in close proximity to urban centers, with access to the same range of services and facilities available to other Canadians. In 2001, 49% of the aboriginal population lived in urban areas, up from 47% in 1996. The city of Saskatoon, Saskatchewan, registered the highest concentration of aboriginal inhabitants in the major Census Metropolitan Areas (CMAs) with 20,025 aboriginal people (about 9% of the city's population). Land on reserves is held in common by the Band but people have their own houses and, in most cases, recognize dividing boundaries, although they pay no municipal taxes. Since Indian matters fall under the purview of the federal government's Department of Indian Affairs, reserve land is seen as a federal rather than a provincial jurisdiction. For this reason, many Indians feel that they should not have to pay provincial sales tax on any goods they purchase.

"Registered" or "Status" Indians hold certain rights not only under the federal *Indian Act*, but also under specific treaties. For example, registered Indians living on reserves are exempt from paying taxes. They are also entitled to certain educational and health benefits under the regulations of the *Indian Act*. It is not possible for banks or other lending agencies to seize reserve land for the non-payment of debts. However, the same property cannot be used as collateral for a mortgage, thereby making it difficult to obtain business loans.

"Non-status" Indians

"Non-status" Indians are a second category of aboriginals who are not "registered" as Indians under the federal *Indian Act*. As such, they are not entitled to any of the rights and benefits accorded "registered" Indians. Most non-status Indians dwell off- reserve, mainly in the larger towns and cities of western Canada. There may be 100,000 or more people in this category. Some are the children of Indian women who married non-Indian men and moved off the reserve, thus relinquishing their official "status." Under the terms of the *Indian Act* of 1876 an Indian was any *man* of "Indian blood," his children, and his wife, whether or not she was an Indian. A white woman could gain Indian "status" by marrying an Indian male and their children would also have status. An Indian female would lose her status by marrying a non-Indian male and so would her children. This discriminatory practice ended in 1985 with *Bill C-31*, which amended the *Indian Act* so that women and their children who had lost their status this way could apply to be reinstated. Because of this amendment some 76,000 women who had lost their status through marriage were reinstated, resulting in 100,000 people being added to the registered Indian population of Canada. Despite the changes to the *Indian Act*, the effects of gender discrimination are still being felt in aboriginal communities. Some Band Councils, the governing bodies on Indian reserves recognized by the federal government, opposed the reinstatement of the women on the grounds that a dramatic influx of newcomers would increase the demand for already scarce resources. As a result, reinstated aboriginal women have experienced difficulties getting houses, community social services, and educational services for their children when they return to the reserve.

The issue of "Indian blood" can also become very controversial. For example, at one time some leaders on the Mohawk reserve near Montreal insisted that people who didn't have the required degree of Indian ancestry leave the reserve. A bylaw passed by the Mohawk Council, in 1981, threatened non-Mohawks with fines and imprisonment if they didn't leave the reserve immediately. This resulted in accusations of racism on the part of the Band Council by other residents and commentators off the reserve.

Uncertain Status

Kahnawake is a Mohawk reserve on the south shore of Montreal. In the fall of 1993, a community newspaper called "*The Eastern Door*" published an advertisement sponsored by the Mohawk Council of Kahnawake. It listed the names of 13 non-Indians who were living with Mohawks on the reserve and demanded that they leave the community immediately. The letter said the non-Indians were violating a bylaw passed by the Band Council in 1981—which stated that only Mohawks should live on the reserve—and threatened them with fines or imprisonment if they did not leave immediately.

One woman who appeared on the list beside the name and band number of her Mohawk common-law husband was defiant. "We bought this property and we are not leaving. At first when I got the letter, I didn't worry too much. But when I saw the list of names in the newspaper, that was the most upsetting" (*Montreal Gazette*, November 16, 1993). She said that other people who were named, especially those with children, were upset with the tone of the letter, which she said makes those listed sound like criminals.

When asked about the case, Band Council members said they intended to tell more than 30 other non-Indians to leave the reserve, because they feared their presence would erode Mohawk culture. They also claimed there was a shortage of housing space on the reserve.

Other Mohawks were concerned about the image the Council's move gave the reserve. One critic said the Council seemed to be picking on a few non-Indian community members and trying to embarrass them, instead of dealing with the issue in a manner that respected traditional Mohawk values. "The last time something like this happened was in Nazi Germany" (*Montreal Gazette*, November 16, 1993).

Metis

The 2001 census estimates that there are 298,480 Metis in Canada, the descendants of intermarriages between the indigenous population and early white colonists, usually French. They do not ordinarily live on reserves, nor do they have any land rights recognized by treaties, or benefits associated with the *Indian Act*. They are, however, recognized in the *Constitution Act* of 1982 as a member of Canada's aboriginal people. Some provincial governments (Ontario, Alberta) have also moved to recognize the Metis as full-fledged aboriginal people with constitutionally protected rights to self-government and self-determination. The Ontario provincial court ruled in 1998 that the Metis have as much right as status Indians to hunt and fish for food without a license. The case revolved around a Metis father and son in Sault Ste.Marie, Ontario, whose guns and a moose they shot were confiscated in 1993 because they lacked hunting licences. Steve Powley and his son Roddy, went to court to seek the same rights as Indians, who are allowed to hunt for food without licences and out of season.

The decision in favour of the two men was upheld at the Superior Court level. In 2001, the Ontario Court of Appeal upheld the two lower-court rulings, declaring the Metis have the same hunting rights as Indians. The case was taken before the Supreme Court of Canada. In a landmark ruling on September 19, 2003, the Supreme Court of Canada reached a unanimous judgement that the Metis are a distinct aboriginal group with a constitutional right to hunt for food. The Court's judgement stressed that the existence in the Constitution of the Metis —of mixed native and European descent—"protects practices that were historically important features of these distinctive communities, and that persist in the present day as integral elements of their Metis culture" (*The Globe and Mail*, September 20, 2003, A-1). The effects of the decision are likely to be far-reaching. Governments may eventually be compelled to negotiate with the Metis on a range of rights ranging from natural resources to health services and taxation.

The Supreme Court And Metis Rights

On September 19, 2003, the Supreme Court of Canada issued a landmark ruling on Metis hunting rights that is expected to have legal repercussions well beyond the immediate issue at hand. Highlights of the Supreme Court ruling:

- A Metis community is a group of Metis with a distinctive collective identity, living together in the same geographical area and sharing a common way of life.

- The development of a more systematic method of identifying Metis rights-holders for the purpose of enforcing hunting regulations is an urgent priority. That said, the difficulty of identifying members of the Metis community must not be exaggerated as a basis for defeating their rights under the Constitution of Canada.

- In addition to demographic evidence, proof of shared customs, traditions and a collective identity is required to demonstrate the existence of a Metis community that can support a claim to site-specific aboriginal rights.

- We recognize that different groups of Metis have often lacked political structures and have experienced shifts in their members' self-identification. However, the existence of an identifiable Metis community must be demonstrated with some degree of continuity and stability...to support a site-specific aboriginal rights claim.

- As Metis communities continue to organize themselves more formally and to assert their constitutional rights, it is imperative that membership requirements become more standardized so that legitimate rights-holders can be identified.

- In the meantime, courts faced with Metis claims will have to ascertain Metis identity on a case-by-case basis. The inquiry must take into account both the value of community self-definition, and the need for the process of identification to be objectively verifiable.

- The initial stay expired February 23, 2002, and more than a year has passed since that time. The Ontario Court of Appeal's decision has been the law of Ontario in the interim, and chaos does not appear to have ensued. We see no compelling reasons to issue an additional stay. (*The Globe and Mail*, September 20, 2003)

Inuit

The Inuit are native people whose ancestral home is in the far north. They are sometimes called "Inuk" or "Innuvialuit." The popular term "Eskimo" is considered an insult because it translates crudely as "raw meat eater." They are world famous for their kayaks, soapstone carvings, and the distinct form of ice-insulated housing known as the Igloo. There are some fifty different words in the Inuit language used to describe snow. The Inuit, numbering about 46,165 (Canadian Census, 2001) pay the same taxes as other Canadians and are not subject to the federal

Indian Act. In 1975, the Inuit and Cree of northern Quebec signed the James Bay Agreement with Ottawa and Quebec. This treaty permitted hydroelectric developments on aboriginal lands in return for full ownership by the Inuit and Cree of over 10,400 square kilometers of land and $225 million in financial compensation. Although they had never signed any treaty arrangements with the federal government, the Inuit have successfully negotiated land claims settlements to gain a certain amount of control over their homeland in the Eastern Arctic. On April 1, 1999, the territory of Nunavut (meaning "Our Land"), comprising about two-thirds of the Northwest Territories, came into existence. The Nunavut government is elected by all residents and includes a Legislative Assembly, a Cabinet, and a Territorial Court.

Social Problems

A report by the federal government in 2002 indicated that between 1979 and 2000, the life expectancy of First Nations populations on and off the reserve increased from 59.2 to 68 years for men, and from 65.9 to 76.6 years for women. Infant mortality for First Nations populations has been declining steadily. Between 1979 and 1999, the rate dropped from 27.6 deaths to 8 deaths per 1000 live births (*Healthy Canadians*, A Federal Report on Comparable Health Indicators, 2002).

The number of registered Indians enrolled in post-secondary institutions almost doubled between 1988/89 and 1997/98, rising from 15,572 to 27,100. According the Department of Indian and Northern Affairs, the total number of housing units has increased from 60,509 in 1989/90 to 83,008 in 1997/98. Over the same period the number of adequate units (properly insulated, etc.) has gone up from 24,659 (40.8%) to 45,153 (54.4%). In 1988/89, 85% of on-reserve dwellings had adequate water supply and 77% had adequate sewage disposal. By 1997/98 this had increased to 97% and 93% respectively.

These developments represent a significant improvement in the lives of Canada's aboriginal population. However, there are still problems to be overcome. The median pre-tax income for all persons indicating aboriginal identity is $13,526, or 61% of median income ($22,120) for all Canadians (Census, 2001). In spite of the positive upward trend in post-secondary enrollment noted above, only 8% of aboriginals aged 25-34 had a completed university degree compared to 28% of all Canadians in 2001. According to the Department of Indian and Northern Affairs, the unemployment rate for aboriginal Canadians is twice the rate of non-aboriginal Canadians. On reserves, the unemployment rate is about

29%, more than three times the national rate. The number of on-reserve welfare recipients rose by 20% from 1990-91 to 2000-2001 (Indian and Northern Affairs Canada, Basic Departmental Data, 2001). However, In 2000-2001, 148,236 Registered Indians were recipients of monthly welfare payments (social assistance), a drop of 5% from 1997-98.

Inequality In Health Outcomes
Between The Aboriginal And Non-Aboriginal Population

In response to a health survey in 2002, only 38% of aboriginal respondents reported "very good" to "excellent" health compared with 61.4% of all Canadians. In a survey by the *National Aboriginal Health Organization*, in 2002, 77% of aboriginal respondents reported having a regular family physician for 2001, compared to 87.7% of the overall Canadian population (Statistics Canada, *Access to Health Care Services in Canada*, 2001—National Aboriginal Health Organization, preliminary results of the *NAHO Public Opinion on Health Care*, July 2002).

Tuberculosis rates for First Nations populations on reserves are still 7 times the Canadian population as a whole but have declined from 70 cases per 100,000 in 1990 to less than 40 cases per 100,000 in 2000. The overall Canadian rate was 5.5 cases per 100,000 in 2000.

The prevalence of adult onset diabetes (Type 2 diabetes) among the aboriginal population is roughly two to three times higher than in the overall Canadian population, which has also seen an increased prevalence over the past decade. Being overweight or obese is associated with a higher incidence of Type 2 diabetes. Roughly 41.1 % of Aboriginal respondents to a telephone survey commissioned by Health Canada reported being overweight in 2002 compared to 32.5 % of the overall Canadian population in a Canadian Community Health Survey in 2001-02. In the same survey, the aboriginal population also reported higher levels of obesity at 36.6% compared to 14.9% of the overall Canadian population. Health Canada cautions that the aboriginal data might include pregnant women, whereas the Canada data do not (Health Canada, First Nations and Inuit Health Branch, secondary analysis of Ipsos-Reid, *Awareness and Knowledge Levels of Type 2 Diabetes Among Aboriginal Peoples in Canada*, 2002).

High accident and suicide rates continue to plague the aboriginal population in Canada with five times as many potential years of life (per 100,000 population) lost to unintentional injury, and three times as many years to suicide, compared to the overall Canadian population.

Sexually Transmitted Diseases

According to Health Canada, the annual proportion of AIDS cases attributed to ab-original persons increased from less than 1% before 1990 to 10% in 1999. Roughly half of those who test positive for HIV are female compared to the non-aboriginal population where 80% of positive HIV test reports are for males, the difference at-tributable to higher injectable drug use among the aboriginal population.

The rate of newly diagnosed HIV cases in Canada is about half the rate in the United States per 100,000 people, according to the Centers for Disease Con-trol (CDC) and Prevention. Positive HIV test reports declined in Canada from 10.2 to 6.9 per 100,000 people between 1995 and 2000, but increased in 2001 to 7.1 per 100,000.

The incidence (number of new cases per 100,000 population in a given year) of chlamydial infections increased significantly among the overall Cana-dian population between 1995 and 2001, but particularly among females aged 15-19 years with a reported rate of six times the national average for females of all ages. The incidence rates of reported chlamydial infections in the aboriginal population were seven times higher than in the Canadian population overall in 1999 (*Healthy Canadians*, 2002).

The Effects Of The *Indian Act*

Many of the social problems experienced by the aboriginal population can only be understood in a historical context. The cultural autonomy of Indian societies was continually subverted by government policies, from their earliest exposure to the Europeans. In a House of Commons debate on the *Indian Act* in 1876, Sir Hector Langevin remarked, Indians were "like children to a very great extent. They, therefore, required a great deal more protection than white men" (Canada, House of Commons, *Debates*, 1876, 752). Many clauses in the *Indian Act* illus-trate this patronizing approach. It consolidated all previous legislation with a host of regulations designed to undermine all vestiges of traditional aboriginal culture. For example, all traditional laws and systems of justice were banned, the government controlled personal finances, and ownership of land on reserves was prohibited. They could not sell crops or livestock without permission from the government appointed Indian agent. Cutting wood on the reserve was pro-hibited unless the Indian agent consented. The approval of the Indian agent was needed to work off the reserve. People who were not members of the Band were prohibited from visiting the reserve after nightfall. Liquor sales were strictly outlawed. Aboriginal women, in particular, were not allowed in bars. Indian agents had the right to control and even rewrite the last will and testament of many people. Ostensibly, many of the provisions of the *Indian Act* were designed to protect the population from exploitation by unscrupulous white men who might cheat them or take sexual advantage of women on the reserves for money. However, the effect of the many rules and regulations was to disempower the aboriginal population and transform them into wards of the State. Most of these rules remained in effect until 1951.

Traditional Ceremonies Banned

In 1884, the federal government amended the *Indian Act* so as to outlaw all traditional aboriginal cultural ceremonies. The most significant was the "potlatch" ceremony practiced by tribes on the West Coast of Canada. A potlatch ("gift giving") was a ceremony that celebrated a new marriage, a trade deal, or someone's good fortune. It involved gathering members of the community, and even neighbouring communities, for three days of ritual dances and gift giving. Missionaries labeled the ceremonies as "pagan rituals." Businessmen wanted an end to the ceremonies because it kept workers off the job. Politicians feared the tribes would use the rituals to organize politically and resist assimilation. The government called it a corrupt and destructive ceremony. Other traditional practices such as Sun Dances, Sweetgrass ceremonies, and Sweatlodges were also banned. Paraphernalia associated with the ceremonies such as masks, pipes, and feathers were confiscated. People who participated in such ceremonies or encouraged others to do so could be imprisoned from two to six months. These restrictions, which struck at the heart and soul of aboriginal cultures, were not removed until the *Indian Act* was again amended in 1951.

Residential Schools

The first schools of this type were set up in the 1840s in Upper Canada (Ontario). Some church groups had already opened mission schools on reserves but the government wanted to get involved after recommendations submitted to the Bagot Commission of 1842 and the *Gradual Civilization Act* of 1857. The federal government assumed even more responsibility for aboriginal education after the passage of the *Indian Act* in 1876.

In 1892, an Order in Council was passed that allowed the Department of Indian Affairs to set up Indian schools, which aboriginal children were encouraged to attend. It arranged government funding to provide $110-145 per student per year to church-run schools and $72 per student in day schools. The first schools to open were in western Canada in 1883–84. By 1898, 54 schools had opened nationwide, with the government imposing mandatory attendance for children aged 7–15. The idea was to accelerate the assimilation of young aboriginal children by removing them from what the government viewed as "deleterious home influences." Against the wishes of their parents, the children were rounded up in the fall, sometimes with the help of the RCMP, and sent to these schools to learn basic reading, writing and arithmetic skills. Boys also received religious instruction and were taught to be farmers, in keeping with government policy that Indians were to be indoctrinated with the twin virtues of the "bible and the plough." Girls went to separate schools where they learned to cook and sew. All lessons were conducted in English and the children were discouraged, sometimes brutally, from speaking their native language. Although many of the teachers were motivated by the best of intentions, they were participants in an abusive system. All aspects of traditional aboriginal culture were routinely denigrated at the schools. The effect on children attending the residential schools was profound. In some cases, they were subjected to physical, emotional and sexual abuse. Many attempted to run away but were forcibly returned and often beaten. When children returned home from school in the summer, they were strangers to their parents.

By 1946, there were about 76 residential schools in operation. Although conditions varied from school to school, the original goal of cultural assimilation was not succeeding. The church based curriculum and influences put children at odds with their parents. Children were told that their own culture was backward and worthless. Nothing their parents did was right. Many parents had turned to alcohol when their children were taken away from them. When students returned home they too were introduced to alcohol. Deprived of effective role models to emulate, the children perpetuated the problems when they became parents themselves. Psychologists of the time called it the "Residential School Syndrome."

By the early 1960s the federal government recognized that the attempt to forcibly assimilate aboriginal children to the dominant white culture was a dismal failure. By divorcing young people from their own culture the residential schools produced generations of lost souls, plagued by violence, alcohol and drug abuse, and with no effective family role models. Graduates of the schools (at grade eight) faced systemic racism in the labour market. No one would hire them. They were not welcome in white establishments or neighbourhoods.

Integration Attempts

Changes to the *Indian Act* in 1951 altered the approach to the education of aboriginal children. Rather than removal to distant residential schools, they were bused to the nearest public schools, run by the provinces. It was hoped that when they were integrated into white communities, many of the problems associated with the forced segregation of the residential schools could be avoided. It was yet another attempt at social engineering that was doomed to failure from the start. School textbooks rarely contained any positive references to aboriginal culture or traditions. The portrayal of indigenous peoples in the film, television and magazines of the era was crude and stereotypical. They were either savages, or lazy and shiftless. White parents were sometimes suspicious or hostile to the presence of aboriginal children in the classrooms, fearing that they would lower the quality of education for their own children. Aboriginal children often sat at the back of classrooms, acting withdrawn and isolated.

The "Sixties Scoop"

Another botched attempt at integration was the notorious forced removal of aboriginal children from their families to be placed in non-native foster homes or adopted by non-aboriginal families. This has come to be known as the "Sixties Scoop." Children were removed from their families and communities by Child Welfare authorities "in the best interests of the child." Parents were deemed to be "inadequate" because their child-rearing practices were too permissive and lacked discipline by the standards of white, middle class social workers. The slightest hint of alcohol abuse could result in a child being removed from a home. What the Child Welfare authorities did not understand was the extended family and community structures of aboriginal cultures, as well as the different cultural values and the accepted norms of raising children. Aboriginal families placed far less emphasis on individual ambition and "success" than did the dominant white culture. A social ethic of sharing and non-interference placed a high value on the equality of all members in the community. The idea of individual advancement, pervasive in the dominant culture, undermined this value of equality.

Many parents did not understand why their children were being taken away from them. The grief and anguish birth parents suffered often led to the abuse of alcohol as a way of trying to cope with the situation, which, in turn often led to the removal of yet more children. There is no doubt that some children did, indeed, need to be rescued from severely dysfunctional families. But later, with the advantage of hindsight, many social workers agreed that many of the removals were little more than state-sanctioned abductions, which would never have been justified in the case of the children of white parents.

It was not an uncommon experience for many native children adopted by white parents to later experience alcohol and drug abuse problems. Many are addicted to drugs, after running away from their adoptive parents to live on the street. In addition to confusion about their identities, many of the children came from alcoholic parents and suffer impairment of judgement and mental functions from forms of fetal alcohol effects, a disorder caused when mothers drank during pregnancy.

Cultural Genocide

By the 1980s, most provinces in Canada revamped their adoption policies after accusations of "cultural genocide" by many aboriginal leaders. They argued that the policy was bad for children who had grown up confused about their native identity, and bad for aboriginal communities because they had lost a disproportionate number of their children. Today, aboriginal leaders want recognition of what was done to their communities as a result of the residential school system and the forced removal of children from their parents in the 1960s. They have demanded, and received, official apologies from the Roman Catholic, Anglican, and United Churches, which ran the residential schools. The Canadian government issued a formal apology in 1998. Former students of the schools, particularly those who suffered physical and sexual abuse, have filed more than 4000 separate lawsuits over the treatment they received at the schools. Of these suits more than 1000 were settled out of court, with average payouts of less than $100,000. In 1998, more than 8000 victims came forward seeking some form of compensation from either the churches that ran the schools or the government, which funded them. In October 2001, the Canadian government offered a compensation package to the victims of abuse at the residential schools, offering to pay valid claimants 70% of the amount they were seeking. In return for compensation they had to drop their lawsuits against the government. The cash-strapped churches involved were not happy with this settlement, fearing that it obligated them to pay the remaining 30% of the claims or risk fighting the cases, one by one, in the courts. They claimed it was a unilateral decision by the government that broke off months of their own negotiations. Previously, the government had refused to consider making such large payments. The churches were committed to pursuing alternatives to litigation where possible to promote, "healing and reconciliation." However, in March of 2003, the Anglican

Church of Canada agreed to contribute $25 million towards compensating claimants in lawsuits filed since the federal apology of 1998. About one lawsuit per day is now being resolved out of court. The last federally run residential school closed in Saskatchewan in 1996.

The Indian Residential Schools Resolution

In 1996, a federal department called the Indian Residential Schools Resolution Canada was created to strengthen partnerships within government and with aboriginal peoples, religious denominations, and other citizens to address and resolve issues arising from the legacy of Indian residential schools. They work with former students, families and communities to promote healing and reconciliation. An effort is made to solve disputes in the least painful way and avoid the courts, if possible. They also work with the church organizations concerning their shared liability to compensate victims of sexual and physical abuse.

In response to the Royal Commission on Aboriginal Peoples in 1996, the federal government agreed to provide $700 million in compensation to aboriginal peoples for past injustices, $350 million to be devoted to "healing funds" for victims of sexual, mental, and physical abuse at the residential schools.

The Revival Of Aboriginal Culture

The apologies and financial settlements for abuses at residential schools illustrated the growing political effectiveness of aboriginal groups. The revival of political influence had begun in 1951 with amendments to the *Indian Act* lifting a ban on the creation and funding of Indian political organizations, which had been in force since 1927. The ban on traditional religious ceremonies and the pursuit of land claims was also lifted at the same time. The right of women to vote in Band Council elections was restored for the first time in seventy-five years, although they would still lose Indian status rights if they married non-treaty Indians or whites. Indians were also permitted to leave the reserve without the permission of the Indian agent.

As a result of the changes, political organizations like the Native Indian Council was formed in 1954. In 1968, this group split into the Canadian Metis Society, and the soon to be influential National Indian Brotherhood (NIB). The changes in legislation and the formation of new political groups did not mean that the federal government had altered its commitment to a policy of assimilation. It was evident in 1969 when the federal government's *Statement of the Gov-*

ernment of Canada on Indian Policy (later dubbed the White Paper) was presented to Parliament. It declared that the total assimilation of the aboriginal population was a worthy goal and one that was to be pursued as quickly as possible. The Department of Indian Affairs was to be abolished. Special Indian legislation was to be repealed. Treaties and land claims were to be considered insignificant. Title to reserve land would be granted to the Band who would divide it and distribute it to the people living there. Programs would be created to help Indians adjust to the changes. The federal government wanted to relinquish all responsibilities for Indians and transfer them to the provinces. They would be Canadian citizens like everyone else.

The policy was the brainchild of Liberal Prime Minister Pierre Elliot Trudeau, and his Minister of Indian and Northern Affairs, Jean Chretien. Trudeau was a classical liberal, in that he believed that individual rights were the cornerstones of a free society. Granting special rights to particular groups eventually undermined everyone's freedom. Indians should enjoy the same rights, no more and no less, than other Canadian citizens. It was a philosophy he also applied to his opposition to special status for Quebec in the Canadian Constitution.

Opposition To The White Paper

The response to the proposals contained in the White Paper proved to be a watershed event in the rebirth of Indian activism. Across Canada, Jean Chretien was greeted with jeers and boos wherever he went to sell the government proposal. Aboriginal leaders accused the government of preparing the document without adequate consultation from the people to be affected. In response to the "White Paper," the Indian Chiefs of Alberta presented a "Red Paper" that condemned the government proposals. They described it as "a scheme whereby within a generation or shortly after the proposed *Indian Lands Act* expires, our people would be left with no land, and consequently the future generation would be condemned to the despair and ugly spectre of urban poverty in ghettoes" (*Citizens Plus*, the "Red Paper," 1970).

The Indian Chiefs recommended that the *Indian Act* should be reviewed by Indian people but should not be repealed. They also wanted any treaties to be entrenched as part of the *British North America Act*. From the standpoint of the Chiefs, "the only way to maintain our culture is for us to remain as Indians. To preserve our culture it is necessary to preserve our status rights, lands, and traditions. Our treaties are the basis of our rights" (*Citizens Plus*, the "Red Paper," 1970).

Government Reaction To The "Red Paper"

Aboriginal reaction to the White Paper proposals angered Prime Minister Trudeau who felt that Indians were accepting permanent ghettoization instead of integration with the larger Canadian society, Trudeau commented at the time that "as for aboriginal rights, this means saying 'we were here before you. You came and you took the land from us and perhaps you cheated us by giving us some worthless things in return for vast expanses of land and we want to reopen the question. We want you to preserve our aboriginal rights and to restore them to us. Our answer is no. We can't recognize aboriginal rights because no society can be built on historical might have beens" (Comeau, P. and Santin, A. [1990]) *The First Canadians: A Profile of Canada's Native People Today. P.13*). Trudeau's remarks failed to sway a determined opposition by the aboriginal community, which forced the Liberal government to shelve its proposals within a year.

The aboriginal leaders believed that maintaining the *Indian Act*, despite its patronizing and racist assumptions, was necessary until the questions of aboriginal rights, treaty claims, and land claims, were settled. They recognized that eliminating the *Indian Act* would essentially absolve the federal government of any responsibility for the problems that existed. There were no treaties with provincial governments. Negotiating power would be weakened if they had to contend with 12 separate jurisdictions (the provinces and the Territories).

The Rise Of Aboriginal Militancy

In the decade following the rejection of the White Paper, a new unity arose among the aboriginal leaders of Canada. They succeeded in putting aboriginal issues on the national agenda in a way that would have been unimaginable a decade earlier. Land and treaty claims were pursued more forcefully through the courts. There was a rebirth of pride in Indian heritage. The growth of this militancy was evident when intense lobbying by aboriginal groups succeeded in obtaining recognition of "existing aboriginal and treaty rights" in the *Constitution Act* of 1982 (*Section 35*), making Canada the first country in the world to entrench such rights (In Pierre Trudeau's words, "clearly our aboriginal people occupied a special place in history. To my way of thinking, this entitles them *to special recognition (my emphasis)* in the Constitution and to their own place in Canadian society, distinct from each other and distinct from other groups." This represented a dramatic turnabout from his position during the White Paper controversy thirteen years earlier). Even more important for the Metis population was their inclusion, along with the Inuit, in the definition of "aboriginal peoples."

A Summer Of Discontent

A wave of aboriginal protest swept over Canada in 1990. On March 11, a group of Mohawk "Warriors" (a group comprised of idealistic Mohawk nationalists, as well as less reputable elements such as cigarette smugglers and gambling proponents) erected a blockade to stop the town of Oka, in Quebec, from expanding a local golf course on 55 acres of land they claimed as an ancestral Mohawk burial ground. One of the main roads into the town was blocked for three months as authorities and spokesmen for the protestors attempted to resolve the dispute. On July 4, with the negotiations stalemated, the provincial government ordered a force of 100 Quebec Provincial Police officers to remove the barricades. In the ensuing gun battle, one police officer, Corporal Marcel Lemay, was killed in the crossfire. The Warriors manned the blockade for 11 more weeks, finally surrendering in September, after the Canadian army had been brought in.

The Mercier Bridge, one of the four main bridges into Montreal, was also blocked by Mohawk Warriors from Kahnawake (a reserve on the South Shore of Montreal) as a gesture of support for the Oka blockade. Violence erupted there when a car convoy of elderly residents and children from the reserve was attacked by an angry stone throwing mob as they tried to make their way off the reserve and into Montreal during the standoff.

Other land claims disputes erupted across Canada in response to the Oka crisis. Militant groups blocked railway lines to disrupt freight and passenger service in Ontario and British Columbia. Five hydro transmission towers were toppled in Ontario, and a Canadian National Railway bridge was destroyed by fire. The Peigan Indians of Saskatchewan diverted a portion of the Oldman River to protest the construction of a dam, which they said would destroy their land.

It was the beginning of a new era for the aboriginal people of Canada marked by a much more militant assertion of treaty rights, land claims, and demands to redress past injustices by financial compensation. Self-government was the new rallying cry. However, the concept of self-government has proved almost impossible to define clearly. Does it mean transferring all powers currently exercised by the Department of Indian Affairs to the local Bands? Is it the signing of modern, comprehensive treaties such as the Nisq'a Agreement or the James Bay Northern Quebec Agreement? Does it mean the creation of a new third order of government within the Canadian Confederation?

Aboriginal leaders are generally supportive of the idea of self-government, but only if it does not represent the loss of currently recognized rights and privileges. Aboriginal women are less certain about the benefits of self-government if they come at the expense of equality rights, which they now enjoy under the Canadian *Charter of Rights and Freedoms*.

The Future

Progress will be slow and will require the resolution of longstanding issues such as the nature of aboriginal citizenship in a Canadian confederation, the location and amount of land controlled (and on what terms), the control of natural resources, and the powers that aboriginal communities will exercise in relationship to other levels of government (federal, provincial, and municipal).

One of the most positive developments of the past decade has been the increasing number of aboriginal historians, authors, playwrights, and filmmakers who are revitalizing the culture and history of indigenous peoples and are finding a receptive audience among the Canadian population at large.

Aboriginal entrepreneurs are also making headway in the business world. According to the Department of Indian and Northern Affairs, there are now over 20,000 businesses in Canada owned by aboriginals.

Some critics of the *Indian Act* believe that there would be even more aboriginal businesses if it were not for the fact that people on reserves are not allowed to own their own houses. According to Tanis Fiss, the Director of the Centre for Aboriginal Policy Change, "the vast majority of young start-up businesses use collateral, whether it's their car or their home. If Ottawa owns that land you live on, you can't mortgage that in order to get the capital to start businesses or attract investment to a particular reserve" (*National Post*, October 29, 2003).

Fiss also sees the *Indian Act* as a major obstacle to improving political and financial accountability on reserves. At present, the federal government allocates $7.5 billion towards services for Canada's status Indian population. Roughly 80% of the money is directed to the band chiefs and other band Council members on the reserve. According to Fiss, "the chief holds a tremendous amount, as does the council, of unchecked power, and who wants to give it up? Their entire livelihood is keeping the *Indian Act* alive and keeping the reserve system alive because that's where the federal money is coming. There is a plethora of lawyers, consultants, chiefs, councilors, etcetera, that have been making a tremendous livelihood out of keeping that going" (*National Post*, October 29, 2003).

Fiss believes that the federal government spending has created an "Indian industry" that rewards corrupt chiefs and perpetuates social problems on the reserves. Rather than spend money on ensuring basic services such as running water on the reserves, some chiefs instead use federal money for personal perks or to maintain their political influence in the community by rewarding friends and relatives. Fiss's solution is to phase out the *Indian Act* because it serves to shield native politicians who are rarely held accountable for the billions of dollars they receive every year. She would also scrap tax exemptions for aboriginals, and transfer property ownership to individuals living on reserves.

Phil Fontaine, the National Chief of the Assembly of First Nations denies the existence of an "Indian Industry" under the control of corrupt chiefs. The social problems on the reserve are attributable to insufficient resources, longstanding education gaps, and lack of private-sector partnerships. According to Fontaine, "we are accountable, we are transparent. We're no different than any other government. We make mistakes and we ought to be held accountable for the mistakes that we make" (*National Post*, October 29, 2003).

In October of 2003, Fontaine submitted a $300-million proposal that would result in the federal government transferring all responsibility for aboriginal housing to a new First Nations entity. The Assembly of First Nations is also studying the possibility of granting ownership rights to individual residents of the reserves.

Controversies

Although Canada's aboriginal peoples represent about three percent of the total population of Canada, they comprise about 12 percent of the inmates of federal prisons. At the provincial level, the picture is even bleaker. Aboriginals represented 55% of prison admissions in Manitoba in 1995-96 and 72% in Saskatchewan (*Globe and Mail*, April 29, 1999). About three quarters of male aboriginals will have been incarcerated in a correctional center for some reason by the age of 25.

What accounts for such a disproportionate representation of aboriginals in the criminal justice system of Canada and what can be done about it? Alcohol and substance abuse are widely recognized as key factors in explaining many of the problems both on and off the reserves. Until 1970, Canadian law prohibited the buying or possession of alcohol. In that year, however, the Supreme Court of Canada ruled (*R. versus Drybones*—1970) that enforcement of this restriction implied inequality on the basis of race. From then on, off-reserve purchase or possession of alcohol would not be prosecuted. Indians would be charged with alcohol related offenses under the *Criminal Code of Canada* (like everyone else). On reserves, Indians were not allowed to possess alcohol unless the reserve's Band Council specifically voted to allow it. *Section 97(b)* of the *Indian Act* had stated that it was illegal for an Indian to be intoxicated on a reserve. However, this clause was challenged in the courts as a violation of the Canadian *Charter of Rights and Freedoms* (as a result the clause was repealed).

Since 1985, changes in the law have reversed the situation, so that Indian reserves are all now automatically "wet"(alcohol possession permitted), unless the Band Council specifically votes to make it "dry"(alcohol possession forbidden). Of six hundred local governments across the country, almost two hundred have voted themselves dry since 1985.

Dependence on mild altering substances provides a coping strategy to offset the effects of powerlessness, isolation, and loss of cultural identity. Alcohol related offenses introduce aboriginal people into a judicial system that magnifies the cultural differences that already exist. For example, a more fluid approach to time management, associated with some aboriginal peoples, often conflicts with the rigid schedules of the judicial system, leading to "no-shows" by offenders, which then results in additional charges being laid.

Aboriginal Policing

One approach to solving the problem of cultural differences has been the creation of distinct aboriginal police services in partnership with traditional law enforcement agencies like the federal RCMP and provincial police. Federal, provincial and reserve authorities are involved in tripartite arrangements to design and provide the services to meet community needs. Funding is split about evenly between the federal and provincial governments.

The Mohawk Peacekeepers

Until the late 1960s, policing on the Kahnawake Mohawk Reserve (then known as Caughnawaga—an anglicized version of the Mohawk name), on Montreal's south shore was carried out under the guidance of the Royal Canadian Mounted Police (RCMP). Special constables from the reserve were sworn in under the *RCMP Act* and were accountable to the federal government. In 1968, the Caughnawaga Iroquois Police (CIP) was formed and later became part of a larger organization called the Amerindian Police. It was accountable to the Quebec government and sworn in under the *Quebec Police Act*. This became increasingly unacceptable in the late 1970s as the renewal in aboriginal pride gained momentum. In 1979, the Mohawk contingent withdrew from the Amerindian Police and formed an independent law enforcement body, the Kahnawake Peacekeepers. They were accountable to the civilian Peacekeeper Accountability Board (PAB), which must answer to the people of Kahnawake. In 1995, the federal and provincial government signed a tripartite Policing Agreement outlining the responsibilities of each level of government with regard to police services. For example, the federal jurisdiction includes Drugs, Custom and Excise, and Immigration. Provincial responsibilities include the *Criminal Code*, provincial highways, and training and supervising native forces. In 1996 there was a swearing-in ceremony to uphold the Kahnawake Peacekeeper Law. In serving the 8000 people on the reserve, Peacekeepers perform a full range of police functions and activities such as law enforcement, criminal investigation, laying of charges, court duty, radar patrols, spot checks and breathalyzer, and crime prevention. They also provide programs and services to the community such as bicycle safety, child injury protection, CPR and first aid • courses, ride along programs, designated drivers, rabies prevention and vaccination, Alcohol and Beverages Control Board, and Justice Commission. Inscribed on the badge of every Peacekeeper is the Mohawk word "Rotinatanonhnha," which means "he who minds the village."

The "Just Sanction"

In an attempt to deal with the high rate of aboriginal imprisonment, and a high rate of recidivism, the Parliament of Canada amended the sentencing provisions of the *Criminal Code* in 1996, stating that "all available sanctions other than imprisonment that are reasonable in the circumstances should be considered for offenders, with particular attention to the circumstances of aboriginal offenders" (*Section 718.2(e)*, *Criminal Code of Canada*). In the case of aboriginal offenders, the fundamental purpose of sentencing was "to contribute to respect for the law and the maintenance of a just, peaceful and safe society by imposing just sanctions." There are six objectives, according to the amendment, one or more of which must be part of a "just sanction": denunciation, deterrence, separation (incarceration of offenders), rehabilitation, reparation, promotion of responsibility and the acknowledgement of harm.

The idea was to direct aboriginal offenders away from prison and into community-based programs to help them overcome problems. Offenders would take responsibility for their criminal actions by offering restitution to their victims and reintegrating themselves as law-abiding members of their communities. They must ask forgiveness for their acts to the victim's family or clan. Only when amends have been made can harmony within the community be restored. This concept of "restorative justice" differs from the traditional Anglo-Canadian approach of "punitive justice" where the main goal is to protect other members of society by punishing and segregating offenders from the community. Under "restorative justice," offenders would serve their sentence in their own communities where the circumstances of the case were best understood and where the appropriate components of a "just sanction" could be applied. One form of "restorative justice" involves the use of "sentencing circles." This is an informal arrangement whereby offenders, victims, family, and respected members of the community assemble in a circle to determine by consensus the sentence to be carried out. The offender is usually required to make amends to the victim by some form of public apology, an act of community service, and by participating in a "healing" activity, which demonstrates they have learned something from the experience. Sentencing circles are usually reserved for minor offenses such as petty theft, vandalism, and common assault. Controversy has arisen when the concept of "restorative justice" has been applied to more serious offenses.

Opposition To The New *Criminal Code* Provisions

Within a short time, the concept of a "just sanction" came under attack when a Metis woman in British Columbia, Deanna Emard, killed her husband with a butcher knife during a drunken brawl. Instead of a jail term, Emard was sentenced to two years less a day of community service. Her lawyer argued that Emard suffered from a multitude of problems stemming from her aboriginal background, including alcohol and drug abuse, and an impoverished upbringing. The judge in the case cited Emard's aboriginal heritage as grounds for the lenient sentence.

The decision was immediately criticized in newspaper columns and editorials. According to Michele Mandel, of the *Toronto Sun*, "in Canada there is not justice for all. For, if you're a native, you have a better chance of getting away with murder" (*Toronto Sun*, January 21, 1999). In her view, *Section 718.2(e)* of the *Criminal Code* amounted to a "get out of jail free card for aboriginals." The *Globe and Mail* published an editorial titled "Aboriginals deserve equal, not special treatment" with the sub-title "Overplaying the race card is in no one's interest. (*Globe and Mail*, April 29, 1999).

In the view of the critics, treating one group differently in the guise of treating them equally was risky because it undermined time-honoured doctrines of individual responsibility and accountability. In the view of the *Globe and Mail* editors, "if we truly want the punishment to fit the crime, we must adhere to the principle that everybody is equal before the law—as individuals, not as members of "unique" groups. Judges should take account of all relevant and mitigating circumstances in handing down sentences and, in some cases, that may well include aboriginal status, but nativeness by and of itself should not be so decisive a factor that we lose a coherent standard of justice "(*Globe and Mail*, April 29, 1999). Once again, at the root of the controversy is the question of "individual rights" and "group rights." Do historical injustices create mitigating circumstances that trump the classical liberal arguments about "equality before the law?"

Aboriginal Women

Aboriginal women face special challenges in overcoming a legacy of cultural denigration and gender-based discrimination of the kind found in the *Indian Act*. Spousal abuse and other forms of family violence continue to plague many aboriginal communities. Many question how these patterns of violence and psychological abuse took root. Douglas Brownridge, a researcher at the University of Manitoba, analyzed a 1999 Statistics Canada survey in which 12.6% of aboriginal women reported domestic abuse compared to 3.5% of non-aboriginals. The study also found that aboriginal women were three times more likely than non-aboriginal women to report that they had been threatened, five times more likely to report sexual assault, and seven times more likely to admit that they had been beaten. Brownridge attributed some of the differences to the greater likelihood of risk factors such as alcohol and substance abuse, unemployment, the relative youth of the aboriginal population, large families, common-law marriages and inadequate education. However, according to Brownridge, "there's something else going on. Even after we controlled for all those factors, there was still a big difference. Historians have demonstrated that pre-colonial aboriginal society didn't have much domestic violence at all. This is a community, a culture that has been devastated, most recently with the residential schools. What we're seeing here is the lingering effect of cultural domination" (*The Globe and Mail*, Feb.14, 2003).

The conclusions of Brownridge's study enraged some traditional aboriginal spokespeople. According to Ken Young, Manitoba's vice-chief for the Assembly of First Nations,

> I've seen first nations women abusing their husbands more than the other way around...I would be very skeptical about these results. If they're not based on economic factors or unemployment why would aboriginal people be different (*The Globe and Mail*, Feb.14, 2003).

The issue of domestic abuse is part of a larger debate about gender inequality as the drive towards aboriginal self-government intensifies. Many aboriginal women are beginning to speak out about what they consider to be their subservient role in the family, the community, and in political life. This was illustrated in July of 2003 when Chief Roberta Jamieson ran in an unsuccessful bid to become head of the Assembly of First Nations. According to Linda Otway, who teaches courses on the role of aboriginal women in aboriginal societies, "any women who would dare to do that needs to be supported and encouraged. These organizations are pretty much male-dominated from the elected positions on down" (*CBC News*, July 8, 2003).

It wasn't always this way according to students of aboriginal history and culture who characterize the traditional relations between the sexes as being based on mutual respect. For example, in the pre-colonial aboriginal communities that existed in eastern Canada women played an important role in political decision-making. In the Iroquoian culture, in particular, women selected and named male leaders (sachems) and had the right and the power to remove them if they failed to live up to their leadership responsibilities. Women were considered to be partners in the annual cycle of work and were responsible for establishing the cultural and social norms of the community. This began to change after contact with European fur traders who insisted on doing business with other males rather than the females who prepared the furs for market. Women's subservient position was reinforced by legislation such as the *Indian Act* that essentially defined an Indian as a male. The only way that a female could be considered an Indian was if her father or husband was an Indian. An Indian woman who married a non-Indian male lost her status while a non-Indian woman who married an Indian male gained status. It wasn't until the *Bill C-31* amendment to the *Indian Act* in 1985 that women and children who lost their Indian status through marriage regained it. Up until revisions to the *Indian Act* in 1951, women weren't allowed to run for chief or council positions and couldn't vote in Band Council elections.

Opportunities for aboriginal women are beginning to improve as they are increasingly taking advantage of post-secondary education. According to teacher Linda Otway, "there's going to be a tidal wave of them taking over significant positions. Right now, male dominated organizations are still getting away with hiring aboriginal males that don't even have a Grade 12, for example, and they'll hire them in high-up positions, and that's why you have all the problems with funding and what-not, because these people aren't qualified" (CBC News, July 8, 2003).

Otway believes women chiefs would tend to focus more on social issues like child welfare, housing, and health care rather than the traditional male oriented concerns over land treaties, resources, and hunting and fishing rights.

Chapter Eight
ETHNICITY, "RACE" AND CRIME

In Canada a disproportionate number of aboriginal people are jailed compared to their proportion of the overall population. According to Corrections Canada, of the approximately 13,000 offenders incarcerated in federal prisons in 1998, 16% or 2,100 were aboriginal. In the following year, 1999-2000, the figure rose to 17%. At the time, the aboriginal population comprised just 2.8% of the total Canadian population. In Alberta, Manitoba, and Saskatchewan, aboriginal offenders make up approximately 45% of the federal inmate population and over 50% in some penitentiaries. Aboriginal people are jailed at a rate 35 times higher than the non-aboriginal population in Saskatchewan (Corrections Canada, August, 2001).

There are also significant differences when it comes to the conviction rates, sentencing, and parole rates between aboriginal and non-aboriginal offenders. For example, aboriginal offenders are more likely to be jailed than non-aboriginal offenders (67.6% versus 56.7%). They are more likely to be convicted of sexual and other violent crimes (67% compared to 51.7% of non-aboriginals charged). Although they accounted for roughly 17% of the federal inmate population in 1999/2000, aboriginals comprised only 11% of the conditional release program. The full parole grant rate for aboriginal offenders in 1999/2000 was 8.9% below that of non-aboriginal offenders. Also, between 1998/99 and 1999/2000, 20.7 % of aboriginals had their full parole revoked compared to 13.7 % of non-aboriginals (Corrections Canada, August, 2001).

Legacies Of History

Like the African American population of the United States, a disproportionate percentage of the aboriginal population of Canada is poor compared to other groups in the society. Although they were never slaves, the Canadian aboriginal population was subjected to deliberate government policies that attempted to undermine their traditional culture and values. The legacy is a wide range of intractable social problems such as loss of identity, unemployment, substance abuse, and violence. The resulting high rates of incarceration and recidivism (re-offending) for a variety of offences are one of the most important challenges that face Canadian society. However, in Canada, an attempt is being made to seek alternatives to jail as a solution to these problems. Corrections Services Canada (CSC) has developed a National Aboriginal Strategy to establish partnerships with aboriginal communities to become involved in the care, custody and release of aboriginal offenders. This involves developing a number of aboriginal specific policies, programs and services such as "healing lodges," "Elder Services," halfway houses, "native brotherhood and sisterhood groups" that attempt to re-integrate offenders without resorting to incarceration. *Sections 81* and *84* of the *Corrections and Conditional Release Act* permits the transfer of correctional services to the aboriginal communities themselves.

It is part of a new and sometimes controversial approach called "restorative justice." Proponents of this approach prefer to see many offences committed by aboriginal persons as a violation of people and relationships rather than a violation of the law. In this view, punitive measures (such as incarceration) alone do not really solve problems and only contribute to new problems when the offender is released. Restorative justice obligates the offender to make things right for the victim or their families. It could be some form of service or financial compensation, or some other commitment to make amends. If this occurs, a "releasing circle," comprised of the offender and his/her family members, the victim, and community leaders, is convened to plan and manage the release and re-integration of the offender into the community. The hope is that this new approach will break the cycle of despair and repeated imprisonment experienced by aboriginal offenders.

Canada And The World

Although Canada's incarceration rate is lower than the United States (In 2001, 123 individuals per 100,000 population), it is higher than most European countries (Norway 57, France 88, Germany 96 per 100,000 population—1998 figures). Lower rates of imprisonment tend to be associated with countries that are more committed to reducing economic disparities within their societies. Canada falls somewhere in between the European countries and the United States in this regard. Imprisonment as a solution to social problems is quite costly. In 1999-2000 the total bill for operating the adult federal and provincial correctional system in Canada was $2.4 billion. It cost approximately $67,700 in that same year for the upkeep of an offender in a penitentiary compared to $29,900 for their upkeep in a halfway house, or $14,500 to supervise an inmate on parole (Corrections Canada, 2001). The cost for incarceration in the United States exceeds $40 billion annually (Human Right Watch, Annual Report, 2002).

Corrections Canada reports that 48% of federal inmates and 83% of provincial inmates are incarcerated for non-violent offences. Twenty per cent of admissions to provincial jails are for not paying fines. Does the punishment fit the crime? Does more and longer imprisonment make the society safer and discourage further crime? A recent Canadian study cited by Corrections Canada compared the recidivism rate between offenders who were imprisoned and those serving their sentence in the community, and found no difference. The same study found that longer sentences were not associated with a decrease in the recidivism rate but rather a 3% increase in recidivism.

Similar findings emerge from studies in other jurisdictions, according to Corrections Canada. An American study found no difference in the recidivism rate of offenders sentenced to probation instead of imprisonment. A British study found young people who were held in custody more likely to re-offend than those who remained in the community under specific conditions (Corrections Canada, August, 2001).

Accuracy Of Recidivism Data

According to American data about one-third of released prisoners are rearrested within three years (The Economist, August 23, 2003, p.26). The National Parole Board and the Corrections Service of Canada claim that recidivism, the rate at which freed prisoners break the law again, hovers at roughly 10%, rising to at most 15%. However, a study released on June 27, 2003 by then Solicitor General Wayne Easter, who was responsible for the federal prison system, found that the reconviction rate for federal offenders was 44% in 1994, 43% in 1995, and 41% in 1996. The study noted that nonviolent offenses accounted for the bulk of the new crimes. According to the report, "more than half the reconvictions occurred after the sentence was completed, when the offender was no longer under supervision" (Kingston Whig Standard, June, 28, 2003). The parole and correctional boards typically track reoffence *only while a freed prisoner is under some form of supervision and has not yet completed his or her sentence.*

The number of federal inmates in Canada increased significantly during the 1990s because of longer sentences, declining parole rates, more offenders being detained until the end of their sentences, and an accumulation of offenders known as "lifers." However, since the beginning of the new millennium the number of federal inmates has actually been dropping.

The American approach of building more prisons as a solution to their social problems is clearly not working. Canadians have been moving toward the idea that alternatives to imprisonment may be more effective in reducing the likelihood of recidivism and actually preventing crime in the first place. The Canadian approach now sees the best public protection results from offenders being successfully rehabilitated and returned to the community as law-abiding citizens. However, neither response alters the fact that less egalitarian societies impose harsher penalties on their less advantaged citizens and any long-term solution requires overcoming the barriers to mainstream opportunity and participation they face.

Growth Of The American Prison Population

The U.S prison population has tripled since 1980, growing thirty times faster than the overall population growth. In 2002, over 2 million Americans languished in prison. Between 1996 and 2002, the imprisoned population grew an average 3.8% annually (U.S Bureau of Justice Statistics, June, 2002). One in every 143 Americans was incarcerated in 2000 (Human Rights Watch, Annual Report, 2002). At year end, 2001, the number of adults under the supervision of the criminal justice system, behind bars, on parole, or on probation, reached a record 6.6 million people, or one in every 32 adults in the United States (U.S Bureau of Justice Statistics, June 30, 2002). Six American states spend more than $1 billion each year on corrections (Corrections Canada, August, 2001). In some American states (California), the proportion of the annual budget spent on prisons is now the same as the proportion spent on education. New prison construction is so brisk that over a thousand new beds per week are being added to accommodate the growing prison population. It is estimated that the prison population will grow to about 3 million in the next fifteen years.

The American Exception

Why is the prison population growing so fast in the United States compared to Canada and the countries of Western Europe? Crime levels are about the same for most offenses (per capita property crime, break and enters, and arson are actually higher in Canada) with the dramatic exception of aggravated assault and homicide where American rates are two to three times higher due mostly to the ready availability of guns.

The increase can be traced back some thirty-five years when public concerns over drug use caused politicians to launch a "War on Drugs." Starting with President Richard Nixon, election campaigns by Republicans and Democrats alike were waged with promises to get drug dealers off of the street. In the 1990s, President Bill Clinton signed an anticrime bill that called for more prisons and increases in mandatory sentencing as well as endorsing the death penalty. This "law and order" approach affected police, prosecutors, judges, and probation officers who were encouraged to "get tough" with offenders. Under reelection pressures, Governors in many states signed "three strikes and you're out" legislation, which greatly increased the length of prison sentences for repeat offenders. As a consequence of more punitive measures, the number of people in municipal, state, and federal jails increased fivefold between 1972 and 2002 to more than 2 million prisoners. The vast majority of those incarcerated were perpetrators of non-violent crime, usually simple drug possession, who would not be subjected to lengthy prison terms in either Canada or the countries of Western Europe. In 1980 there were 19,000 people *serving time* in prison in the United States for drug related offences (all kinds combined). By 2000, the number of people serving time in prison for the same offences was 251,100 (U.S Bureau of Justice Statistics, June 30, 2002). Since 1980, the American *arrest rate* for drug possession, trafficking and production has doubled, whereas the Canadian rate has declined 29%. In 2000, police in the United States arrested 454 people for every 100,000 compared to 100 for very 100,000 population in Canada (Statistics Canada, *the Daily*, Dec. 19, 2001).

Even more significant was the effect of the harsher legislation on young men in the black community, particularly in sentencing for drug possession. Although only 13% of drug users in the United States are black, they account for 74% of all those sentenced to prison for drug offences. Ten per cent of African-American males aged 25-29 were in prison in 2000 compared to 1.1% of white men in the same age category (Human Rights Watch Annual Report, 2002). In 1999/2000 there were 791,600 African American men in jail compared to 603,000 in college and university (Justice Policy Institute, August, 2003). One in seven adult black males has lost his voting rights because of a felony conviction (*Scientific American*, August, 1999, p.25). At year end, 2001, there were 3,535 sentenced black prisoners in the United States per 100,000 black males, compared to 1,177 sentenced Hispanic inmates per 100,000 Hispanic males, and 462 white male inmates per 100,000 white males (U.S Bureau of Justice Statistics, June 30, 2002). According to Justice Department projections 11.3% of boys born in 2001 will go to jail in their lifetimes. For black men, it will be one in three, if present policies are continued (*The Economist*, August 23, 2003, p.26).

The increase in incarceration rates in the United States also parallels an increase in income disparities that began in the 1970s when a large number of young black men could not take on the responsibilities of raising a family because of a lack of jobs. Income inequality is significantly greater in the United States than in Canada or Western Europe with a disproportionate number of poor people concentrated in black communities. In such a situation people may come to see criminal behaviour as the only solution to their problems. Therefore, crime and imprisonment rates become a reflection of the degree to which a society is willing to tolerate social inequality.

"Race," Ethnicity, Social Class, And Crime

According to the U.S Justice Department, American "blacks" are seven times more likely to end up in jail than American "whites" (Bureau of Justice Statistics, June 3, 2002). Approximately half the prison population in the United States is "black" even though African-Americans comprise only 13% of the total population of the United States. Does this mean that "blacks" are "genetically predisposed" to criminal behaviour as some racists have argued? Or does it mean that the American criminal justice system is simply more "racist" than other countries? Many African-Americans believe the latter explanation. For example, despite a mountain of evidence, including DNA tests, that former football star O.J Simpson was guilty of a brutal double murder of his wife and her male friend, a mostly black jury acquitted him in the belief that he was the victim of a racist conspiracy cooked up by the Los Angeles Police Department (LAPD).

The fact is that, in this case, both camps have it wrong. Overt white racism is certainly nowhere near as bad as it was thirty or forty years ago. As for the "biological argument" that "blacks" are genetically predisposed to criminal behaviour, the racists might be surprised to learn that Americans of any colour who earn more than the median income (incomes midpoint between the highest and the lowest incomes) are about equally likely to land in jail. The issue is money (or rather the lack of it) not "race." "Blacks" make up a higher *proportion* of the poor in the United States than "whites" and *the poor of all "races" are more likely to be incarcerated than the more affluent.*

Labour Market Changes

Why are "blacks" more likely to be poor? People often blame the lingering effects of slavery but there is a more subtle explanation based upon the changing nature of the labour market over the past fifty years. In the 1940s and early 1950s there was a huge internal migration of black Americans from the South to the northern cities to take advantage of jobs which were opening up in the automobile factories and steel mills that were the foundation of a prosperous postwar economy. Despite endemic racism, the position of black Americans started to improve dramatically until the industries that employed them began to automate their production processes. Almost 2 million blue collar jobs were wiped out between 1953 and 1963 because of automation, resulting in the layoffs of hundreds of thousands of the most recently hired who happened to be mostly blacks and "poor whites" (now referred to disparagingly as "white trash") from the South. As a consequence, unemployment rose dramatically and within one generation the inner cities of the north were transformed into the ghetto cultures that today are the source of so many social problems and criminal activities. The same problems affected poor whites but their *proportion* of the total population of American whites is much smaller. The point is that the crime problem in the United States has more to do with economics than "race" but because a proportionately larger number of poor people happen to be "black" it is easy to whip up racially motivated hysteria to justify new prison construction and tougher sentencing rules. This is exactly what has occurred over the past twenty-five years.

Chapter Nine
ORIGINS OF ENGLISH/FRENCH CONFLICT

T he colonization of Canada began with the exploration and settlement of New France or what we now call the Province of Quebec. Newcomers worked the land or engaged in fishing, trapping or fur trading, which became the basis for a social structure comprised of merchants, government officials, seigneurs (landowners), tenant farmers who worked the land, and the Roman Catholic clergy. New France was an integral part of France's North American empire, which extended all the way from Hudson's Bay through the Ohio Valley and the Louisiana territory to New Orleans. This period was dominated by territorial disputes that involved the indigenous population as well the rapidly expanding English and Spanish colonies.

The Conquest Of 1759 And The *Royal Proclamation Of 1763*
Throughout the 17th and 18th century disputes over territory continued between New France and the more heavily populated English speaking colonies to the south, resulting in a series of wars that culminated in 1759 with the Battle of the Plains of Abraham, where General Wolfe's victory over General Montcalm secured New France for the British. Four years after the Conquest, in 1763, the British issued a Royal Proclamation that gave the newly named Province of Quebec (reduced in size to the area comprising the St.Lawrence Valley) its first constitution and civil government. French civil and criminal law was abolished and Roman Catholics were barred from participation in government. The policy was designed to attract British colonists to the province and to eventually assimilate the French speaking population. The Proclamation also restricted Quebecois from entering territory west of the province's borders unless they obtained a special permit. To end a rebellion (the Pontiac Rebellion) by the Indian population of the Great Lakes region, who were fearful of British control of the entire western half of the North American continent, the Proclamation guaranteed Indians control of their territory by barring incursions by white settlers, including the French.

The *Quebec Act*

The effect of the *Royal Proclamation of 1763* was to undermine two crucial components of the French-speaking colony, namely the Roman Catholic clergy and the Seigneurs (the traditional land-holding elite). As relations between Britain and its American colonies to the south became more strained the importance of not alienating this elite leadership element increased. The British government feared that the French-speaking colony might join the Americans in their revolt against the Crown. To forestall this possibility it passed the *Quebec Act of 1774*, which reversed the *Royal Proclamation of 1763* and restored the powers of the Church and the Seigneurs, including their participation in the political governance of the province. A legal system consisting of a mixture of French civil law and English criminal law was instituted, which continues right to the present day. The territory of Quebec was also enlarged to include part of the Ohio Valley.

Role Of The Church

The political and social evolution of Quebec society was profoundly affected by the power of a conservative Roman Catholic Church hierarchy determined to resist the forces of assimilation on the North American continent. For example, it was given administrative control over all French language education in Quebec, a situation that continued until the Quiet Revolution of the 1960s. The church also exercised enormous leverage in the political system with parish priests openly supporting candidates and parties who promoted "traditional" values of loyalty to the homeland ("Le Patrie"), the family, and the Roman Catholic faith.

United Empire Loyalists

A few British settlers, mostly small businessmen from New England, migrated to Quebec in the wake of the conquest. However, it was not until the American Revolution in 1776 that thousands of United Empire Loyalists fled to Quebec. This large influx of English-speaking immigrants posed a threat to the continued dominance of the established French-speaking elite. Descendants of the Loyalists can still be found in the Eastern Townships and Chateauguay Valley areas of Quebec close to the U.S border. The fear of being overcome by this flood of English-speaking immigrants required a strategy to maintain the numerical dominance of the French-speaking population.

The Revenge Of The Cradle

The French Canadians attempted to increase their numbers through an extremely high birth rate (the *"Revenge of the Cradle"*) which was motivated by the labour requirements of an agriculturally based economy but was also encouraged by the clergy and political leaders as a strategy to resist assimilation. However, French Canada was subject to a high rate of emigration; up to one-quarter of the young people of Quebec moved away (roughly 900,000 people according to 1980 American Census data), mostly to the United States, especially to Maine, New Hampshire and Massachusetts, where they took employment in lumber and textile mills and quickly assimilated into American society. The famous American novelist Jack Kerouac (*"On the Road"*) was a descendant of one such family. New England phone books are filled with French Canadian surnames. However, the power of assimilation is so strong in the United States that very few descendants of these emigres can speak any French at all.

The Threat Of Assimilation

The underlying issue that is at the core of English/French conflict is the French Canadian fear of assimilation. This fear now manifests itself in discussions over the declining birth rate among Francophones (French speaking people) in Quebec (now the lowest in North America), the language and origins of new immigrants to Quebec, the language of work in Quebec, and the highly symbolic issue of "signs." Many Francophones feel that their language and culture is threatened or continually under siege by the overwhelming dominance of English in Canada and the rest of North America. This fear of assimilation has been a constant factor driving the politics of Quebec society since the conquest of 1759.

Strategies Used To Resist Assimilation

Several strategies have been used by French Canada to resist assimilation. When the Roman Catholic Church dominated social and political life (up until 1960), the French Canadian elite favoured a form of right-wing nationalism (sometimes called Ultramontane Nationalism because it advocated supreme papal authority in matters of faith and discipline) that has come to be known as *"La Survivance."* French Canadians were urged to remain devoutly loyal to the Roman Catholic Church, have large families, stay close to the land, and avoid the greed and materialism of the anglo-dominated business world. The consequence of this strategy was economic stagnation and retarded social development within the larger context of rapid North American development and "modern-ization."

This strategy to resist assimilation is most closely identified, in the modern era, with Maurice Duplessis, Quebec premier from 1936-40 and 1945-59. Duplessis, in a tacit alliance with the Roman Catholic Church hierarchy, used au-thoritarian methods of coercion (including improper use of the Quebec Provincial Police) to rig votes and oppose any groups that he thought to be a threat to tradi-tional Quebec society. The list of his enemies included trade unionists, socialists, communists, liberals, civil libertarians, homosexuals, Jehovah's Witnesses, and any political opponents. This period of Quebec life is sometimes referred to as "Le Grand Noirceur" (The Great Darkness). There was also a racist and anti-Semitic component associated with this strategy that is reflected in the writings of promi-nent intellectuals of the period such as the cleric Abbe Lionel Groulx.

Roots Of Modern Quebec Nationalism

Modern French Canadian nationalism arose out of drastic changes to the nature of the labour market at the end of the 19th century in Quebec. The rapid rate of growth of the French Canadian population had always made it difficult for young people to find work in agriculture and logging, the traditional sources of employment in the province. The result was a significant loss of people to Maine and other New England states.

However, the advent of hydroelectric power and a government policy that encouraged American owned businesses to locate in Quebec created a host of new jobs in the manufacturing sector at the beginning of the 20th century. Que-bec workers flocked to the cities, particularly Montreal, to seek their fortune. The jobs were hard and low paying, in companies owned and managed by Eng-lish speaking people.

The old virtues of living close to the land guided by the wisdom of the par-ish priests seemed increasingly antiquated and irrelevant to the daily lives of many workers. They began to organize unions to fight for better wages and working conditions. The Roman Catholic Church attempted to counter this threat by promoting their own labour organizations but they were often viewed by workers as ineffectual and too close to the owners.

The election of Maurice Duplessis in 1936, in the midst of the Great Depres-sion, represented an attempt to reconcile the continued need for foreign invest-ment and jobs, with the desire to maintain a conservative and agrarian society, dominated by the values of the Roman Catholic Church.

However, the old values were no longer tenable in the aftermath of World War II as the pace of change rapidly accelerated. An increasingly industrial and resource based economy produced labour conflict, such as the famous Asbestos Strike of 1949. The workers took on the combined might of the multinational asbestos industry, the Quebec government under Duplessis, and the Roman Catholic Church, in a bitter four month struggle to demand basic trade union rights. Joining them were idealistic, middle class journalists and university students like Gerard Pelletier and Pierre Elliott Trudeau who were fed up with the repressive nature of the old order. Pierre Trudeau would say later "it was a violent announcement that a new era had begun."

Rattrapage

Opposition to Duplessis gained strength in the late 1940s and early 1950s because of the activities of trade union leaders and intellectuals who wanted Quebec to "catch up" ("*rattrapage*") with the rest of North America and become a modern secular society rather than a traditional Church dominated one. Many of the reformers were associated with a Montreal based magazine called *Cite Libre*, including the famous "*Three Wise Men*" ("*Les Trois Columbes*"), trade union leader Jean Marchand, journalist Gerard Pelletier, and law professor Pierre Trudeau. Throughout the 1950s they continually challenged what they perceived as the retrograde nationalism and tribalism of the Duplessis regime. They would later become influential in federal politics as cabinet ministers, and Prime Minister, promoting the interests of Quebec society within the federal system.

The Trudeau Vision

The rise of modern Quebec nationalism produced two distinct visions among Quebec's intellectual elite. One vision, best articulated by Rene Levesque (who started his career as a Liberal but later became leader of the independence oriented Parti Quebecois), sought greater provincial autonomy or even independence from the Canadian federation as the best way to ensure the continued existence of the French language and distinct culture of Quebec. The other vision, associated with Pierre Trudeau, was to increase the influence of Quebec within the Canadian federation by promoting official bilingualism and greater representation of French speaking Quebecois in the federal civil service, in the media, and in business. The Trudeau Liberals were able to pass the *Official Languages Act* (1969) that enabled Canadian citizens to deal with the federal government in either official language and made bilingualism an almost essential prerequisite for employment in the federal civil service. Trudeau viewed "special status" or independence for Quebec as being a parochial and possibly dangerous expression of ethnic nationalism. In his view, the solution to the problem of English/French relations was the creation of a bilingual country, internationalist and cosmopolitan in orientation. The federal government would ensure the protection of the French culture in all of Canada.

Trudeau's vision did not endear him to the ultra-nationalist groups in Quebec and he soon became the focus of much of their anger. During the Ste. Jean de Baptiste parade on June 24, 1968, demonstrators protested his presence on the reviewing stand by pelting the gathered dignitaries with stones and bottles. They all fled except Trudeau who gained much support across Canada for his display of physical courage. Many people attributed his subsequent election later that year to his willingness to stand up to the demonstrators that night. Trudeau dedicated much of his term in office to constitutional matters culminating in the *Constitution Act* of 1982, which incorporated the Canadian *Charter of Rights and Freedoms* that put English and French on an equal footing in the eyes of the law.

The Liberal Period

After the death of Maurice Duplessis, in 1959, the demands for reform of Quebec society became more vocal and persistent. The Liberal government of Jean Lesage was elected in 1960 on a platform that promised the modernization of the Quebec educational system and an increase in jobs for francophones in the civil service. This marked the beginning of the so-called *Quiet Revolution* under the slogan of "Maitres chez nous" (Masters in our own house), meaning that the power of the state would be used to advance the economic interests of Quebecers while also protecting the continued existence of the French language and culture.

The Radical Strategy

The changes brought about by the Liberal government did not go far enough for some of the reformers. They wanted more power for the Quebec government or even outright independence from the rest of Canada. Some, like the writer Pierre Vallieres, likened Quebec to a Third World country whose inhabitants had developed a subservient, colonized attitude, which could only be changed through some form of revolution. Many of the ideas in his book, *White Niggers of America*, became the inspiration for the *Front de Liberation du Quebec* (FLQ), a terrorist group which became active in the early 1960s with a series of violent actions (mail box bombings, etc.) that finally ended in the October Crisis of 1970.

Electoral Nationalism

The more moderate Quebec nationalists rallied around a former Liberal cabinet minister, Rene Levesque (who had been responsible for the nationalization of several private electrical power companies and the creation of Hydro Quebec in 1962). Levesque broke with the Liberals and in 1968 organized the numerous separatist parties and organizations of the time into a new political party called the Parti Quebecois. It promised to protect the French language and culture, and work toward a negotiated independence with the rest of Canada. This party gained influence during the *October Crisis* of 1970 when the federal government invoked the *War Measures Act* to suspend the civil liberties of many Quebecois. They were thought to be sympathetic to the terrorist FLQ, which had kidnapped a provincial Labour Minister, Pierre Laporte (later to die in a botched escape attempt). About 500 innocent people were rounded up and jailed without due process, many of them P.Q sympathizers, but not terrorists. Much of English Canada supported the federal government (led by Pierre Trudeau) and its actions and this further alienated francophones in Quebec. Although most opposed the violent tactics of the FLQ, especially after the kidnapping and death of Laporte, many became increasingly sympathetic to the idea of gaining Quebec independence peacefully through the P.Q and the ballot box.

Language Wars

The Liberal government of Robert Bourassa tried to neutralize the threat of independence by implementing legislation that would respond to the demands of Quebec nationalists to promote the French language but also protect minority language rights and allow Quebec to remain in the federal system. For example, in 1974 the Bourassa government was responsible for the passage of *Bill 22*, which regulated the education of children in Quebec whose mother tongue was not English. At that time about 90% of the new immigrants to Quebec chose to educate their children in English. *Bill 22* forced children to switch to French schools unless they could pass a test that demonstrated a knowledge of English before age six. This outraged many in the immigrant community, particularly in the Italian community of St. Leonard where riots had occurred five years earlier to protest a similar attempt. More than 600,000 people, almost the entire English speaking population of the province at the time, signed a petition opposing the new legislation, and refused to support the Liberals in the following election, thereby allowing the more hard-line Parti Quebecois to come to power. The law was designed to encourage newcomers to assimilate to the French culture rather than to the English culture by promoting French as the preferred language in education, work, government services and businesses. In education, the result was a drastic fall-off in English language schooling between 1970 and 1993. Enrolment declined from about 248,000 students to about 99,000, a loss of 60%, compared to a loss in French enrolment of only 13% (*The Toronto Star*, January 29, 1993: D29). The percentage of "allophones" (Quebecois whose mother tongue is neither English nor French) attending French-speaking elementary schools increased from 15% in 1971 to 80% by 1996. For colleges it went from 16% in 1981 to 43% in 1996 (Secretariat, a la politique linguistique, Gouvernement de Quebec).

Election Of The Parti Quebecois

Bill 22 was not enough to satisfy the more ardent Quebec nationalists who wanted legislation that would require English businesses to use French as their working language, as well as make French the official language of Quebec. These aspirations were realized with the election of the Parti Quebecois in 1976 and the passage, one year later, of *Bill 101*, the *Charter of the French Language*. This legislation profoundly changed the nature of English/French relations in the province. From then onwards bilingualism would be the exception in the Quebec civil service, the legislature, the courts, in commerce, labour relations and education. Unilingual, French speaking Quebecois would no longer face discrimination in the job market. English commercial establishments would be required to provide fair and adequate services to French-speaking customers. Everyone would have to learn how to speak French. Public signs would be French only. The main architect of the legislation, Dr. Camille Laurin, a psychiatrist, saw the language legislation as a nation-building process, as essential as breathing to the nature of a distinct Quebec culture and society. For many people of the English-speaking minority in Quebec it represented the beginning of their marginalization in the province. They viewed the legislation as punitive, and a violation of their basic human rights, particularly after the establishment of a bureaucracy (Office de Le Langue Francais), which quickly became known as the "language police" (or the "tongue troopers") because of its sometimes petty and overzealous application of the law directed mainly at small businesses in the province. Led by the Sun Life Insurance Company, many businesses moved their head offices out of Quebec to protest the new legislation. It sparked an exodus of some 400,000 people over the next twenty years.

The First Referendum

During the election campaign of 1976, the P.Q. had also promised to hold a referendum on the issue of independence at some time during their term in office. They delivered on this promise in the fall of 1980, when they asked the people of Quebec for a mandate to negotiate the terms of independence ("sovereignty-association") with Ottawa. Both the federal government under Prime Minister Pierre Trudeau, and the provincial Liberal party under Claude Ryan urged Quebecers to reject this mandate and promised to "renew federalism" in a way which would take into consideration the legitimate demands of Quebecois for constitutional protection of Quebec's unique language and culture in the Canadian context. On this basis the PQ's demand for a mandate to negotiate Sovereignty/Association with Canada was rejected (60% against—40% for such a mandate, of those who voted).

The Canadian Constitution And The *Charter Of Rights And Freedoms*

Two years later the Trudeau government succeeded in gaining agreement among the provinces for acceptance of a new constitution to replace the old *British North America Act* (BNA), which still required British consent for any legislation to pass. All provinces accepted the new constitution except Quebec, which argued that the new *Charter of Rights and Freedoms* guaranteed freedom of linguistic choice in areas where the Quebec government had legislated restrictions (in 1984, the Supreme Court of Canada ruled against Quebec's schooling restrictions contained in *Bill 101*). Quebec also demanded a veto over any proposed constitutional changes.

The Meech Lake Accord

In the federal election of 1984, a Conservative government, led by Brian Mulroney, was elected with strong support from Quebec. The support was based on promises made by Mulroney to fashion an agreement that would respond to some of Quebec's concerns about the protection of its language and culture, and make it possible for the province to be brought back into the constitutional fold.

In the following year, a Liberal government, led again by Robert Bourassa, was elected in Quebec. It was open to negotiating Quebec's adherence to the *Constitution Act* of 1982 if five conditions were met: (1) recognition of Quebec as a distinct society (2) increased powers over the selection and settling of immigrants (3) participation in appointing Quebec judges to the Supreme Court of Canada (4) limitation of the federal government's spending power (5) recognition of a veto right for Quebec over constitutional amendments.

On April 30, 1987, the provincial and federal leaders agreed to these conditions at a meeting convened at Meech Lake in Quebec. In June, the 10 provincial premiers and the Prime Minister adopted the wording of the Meech Lake accord in Ottawa. The agreement had to be ratified (passed with a majority of votes) by all provincial legislatures and the House of Commons within three years.

The "Sign Law"

In 1988, the Quebec government passed a very controversial piece of legislation (*Bill 178*). The bill was introduced to respond to a Quebec Superior Court and Supreme Court of Canada decision that had ruled that the banning of English on storefronts was unconstitutional and a violation of both the *Quebec Charter of Rights* and the Canadian *Charter of Rights and Freedoms*. *Bill 101* (*The Charter of the French language*) prohibited the use of English or bilingual signs on the outside of any business establishment in the province. The Courts acknowledged that the Quebec government could promote the use of the French language but could not prohibit the use of other languages without infringing on the protections of individual rights outlined in the *Charter*. The Quebec government enraged the English minority in Quebec, and the English majority in the rest of Canada, by invoking the "notwithstanding clause" (*Section 33*) in the Canadian Constitution, which permitted it to override the *Charter* rights for a period of five years. In passing a new piece of legislation, *Bill 178*, Quebec continued the prohibition of outdoor bilingual signs but permitted them inside an establishment. The Quebec government justified this action on the grounds that it had to take extraordinary measures to resist the trends toward assimilation on a continent of 300 million English-speaking people. To protest the legislation some dissident Liberal members of the National Assembly broke away and helped form a new party, the Equality Party, which gained four seats in the following election.

In 1993, a United Nations human rights committee released a report that called *Bill 178* a violation of the *International Covenant on Civil and Political Rights*. Three months later, the Liberal government in Quebec introduced new legislation, *Bill 86*, allowing bilingual signs both inside and outside of businesses as long as the French was predominant. It was an attempt to comply with the law after the five year expiry date for the use of the "notwithstanding clause." Both French and English federalists in the province viewed the new law as a step in the right direction. However, the opposition Parti Quebecois vowed to revoke the law if they were elected. In 1994, the party was elected on the promise to abolish *Bill 86* and restore unilingual, French-only signs. But they postponed their decision until after the referendum of 1995, and then decided to keep the law and work to toughen up other language laws instead. One year after their narrow defeat in the referendum, the Parti Quebecois re-introduced the dreaded "language police," to the chagrin of Montreal storeowners who periodically had to confront government officials armed with measuring tapes to determine if the size of French lettering on signs was no less than twice the size of English lettering. Violations brought fines and warnings that drove the wedge between the two communities even further.

The Death Of The Meech Lake Accord

Support for the Meech Lake Accord began to erode in English Canada. Manitoba was the first province to oppose the agreement after the "notwithstanding clause" was invoked by Quebec and the introduction of the new "Sign Law" (*Bill 178*). Later, Newfoundland Premier Clyde Wells opposed the accord on the same grounds. On April 5, 1990, he was able to get the Newfoundland Provincial Legislature to nullify his predecessor's signature on the Meech Lake Accord.

In May of 1990, a report was tabled by a commission headed by a federal Conservative party member, Jean Charest (now Liberal Premier of Quebec), which was established in the wake of the sign law legislation. It recommended that the federal government be made responsible for recognizing Quebec's linguistic duality. It was an attempt to placate the anger felt by the English minority in Quebec and the ripples felt throughout the rest of Canada. It instead inflamed a Conservative Member of Parliament from Quebec, Lucien Bouchard, who resigned his position and denounced the "Charest Report" as an attempt to water down the five conditions for Quebec's acceptance of the Meech Lake Accord. This was a major blow to Prime Minister Mulroney who had relied on Bouchard's support in Quebec to gain a landslide election victory in both 1984 and 1988.

On June 9, 1990, Prime Minister Mulroney convened a meeting in Ottawa attended by all the provincial premiers. It was one last effort to salvage the Meech Lake Accord. The premiers made a commitment to ensure that the agreement would be put to a vote in their provincial legislatures before the June 23 expiry date. However, opposition to granting any special recognition for Quebec had been growing across Canada, as opinion polls indicated.

The growing disillusionment with the accord in English Canada caused resentment in Quebec that was demonstrated by the enthusiastic reception breakaway Conservatives received in the province when they announced the creation of a new party, the Bloc Quebecois, led by Lucien Bouchard. The party promised to defend the interests of Quebec in the face of what was perceived as English Canada's rejection of the Meech Lake agreement. They would unabashedly promote the idea of sovereignty.

On June 12, 1990, an aboriginal member of the Manitoba legislature, Elijah Harper, blocked the ratification vote for the Accord in that province on the grounds that it ignored similar concerns about special recognition for aboriginal people's claims. On June 22, two days before the accord's expiry date, Newfoundland Premier Clyde Wells recanted his approval for the agreement but agreed to bring the matter to the Newfoundland provincial legislature for debate.

With the rejection of the accord by Harper and Wells, the reaction in Quebec was bitter among both sovereignists and federalists alike. Upon hearing Well's position the same day, Quebec Liberal Premier Robert Bourassa rose in the Quebec National Assembly and passionately proclaimed that "English Canada must understand in a very clear manner that whatever is said or done, Quebec is today and for all times a distinct society, free and capable of assuming its destiny and its development"(*Journal de Debats*, June 22, 1990).

The leader of the opposition Parti Quebecois, Jacques Parizeau, crossed the floor of the National Assembly to shake Bourassa's hand, accompanied by spontaneous and prolonged applause from all parties present. The following day, June 23, the Meech Lake Accord was officially dead with the refusal of Manitoba and Newfoundland to sign the agreement. Premier Bourassa declared at that time that any future negotiations would be between Quebec and Ottawa alone, and no longer among the eleven leaders.

Quebec's traditional Ste.Jean Baptiste Day parade (now called the Fetes National) was held a day after the death of the Meech Lake Accord. A half million Quebecois poured on to the streets of Montreal carrying the blue and white provincial flag (the Fleurs de Lys) that over the years had become a potent symbol of Quebec nationalism. Among them was Lucien Bouchard of the newly formed Bloc Quebecois and several other federal Members of Parliament who would announce their resignations from the Conservative Party the following day. Polls indicated that 60% of the Quebec population would have voted for independence in the immediate aftermath of the Meech Lake failure (McRoberts, Kenneth [1991]) *English Canada and Quebec: Avoiding the Issue*, Robarts Centre for Canadian Studies, Toronto, p.10). Many Quebecois interpreted the failure to ratify the Accord as a rejection of their legitimate concerns by the rest of Canada rather than simply a rejection by one provincial Premier and an aboriginal leader.

The Charlottetown Accord

The rejection of the Meech Lake Accord engulfed the country in a profound soul-searching exercise. In the two years that followed the death of the accord, a parliamentary committee undertook the most extensive consultations in Canadian history on the issue of the constitution, soliciting the views of politicians, academics, business leaders, aboriginal leaders, women's groups, and labour leaders. The result was a new set of constitutional proposals that called for decentralization of federal powers, an elected senate, recognition of concerns raised by aboriginal leaders and women's groups, and special recognition of Quebec as a distinct society. The agreement was reached on July 7, 1992. Liberal Premier Robert Bourassa joined the other provincial premiers on August 4, after deciding that the "essence" of the Meech Lake Accord was covered by the agreement. After final consultations in Ottawa and Charlottetown, the text of the Consensus Report on the Constitution was unanimously agreed upon on August 28,1992.

The provincial premiers agreed to hold two referendums on October 26, 1992, one in Quebec—under Quebec legislation to comply with the province's *Bill 150* (a controversial bill governing the modalities of referendums in the province) and the other in the rest of Canada under the provisions of the new federal referendum legislation. All the parties agreed that the question should be: "Do you agree that the constitution of Canada should be renewed on the basis of the agreement reached on August 28, 1992?"

On October 26, 1992, the Charlottetown Accord was rejected by a majority of Canadians who voted, in a majority of provinces, including a majority of Quebecois and a majority of aboriginals living on reserves. The only significant support came from the Maritime Provinces. The defeat represented a stunning and decisive repudiation of elite opinion by the Canadian people. Five years of constitutional wrangling had resulted in increased polarization in Quebec between federalists and sovereignists, and the rise of a new federal party, the Bloc Quebecois, devoted to taking Quebec out of confederation. In the next federal election the Conservative Party was virtually wiped off the electoral map and a new regional political party (The Reform Party—later called the Canadian Alliance Party and the Conservative Party) gained strength because of western Canada's disillusionment about the continued federal preoccupation with the "problems" of Quebec.

Canadian Unity At The Crossroads, The 1995 Referendum

In 1994, the Parti Quebecois was again in power in Quebec under the leadership of longtime sovereignist Jacques Parizeau. The P.Q put forward a draft bill on sovereignty in June of 1995, which called for a referendum later in the year. The referendum was held On October 30. 1995. A record 94% of registered voters in Quebec headed for the polls. Contrary to popular belief the referendum question did not ask for outright separation from Canada. The question asked was "do you agree that Quebec should become sovereign, after having made a formal offer to Canada for a new economic and political partnership, within the scope of the bill respecting the future of Quebec and of the agreement signed on June 12, 1995?" If, after one year, Quebec couldn't negotiate a new "partnership," then it would declare itself an independent country.

During the referendum campaign, the leader of the "No" side, Quebec liberal leader Daniel Johnson, argued that the P.Q could not win a campaign on outright separation so it was trying to deceive Quebecois by telling them they could make a new arrangement with Canada. If they won, according to Johnson, the result would be the loss of 100,000 jobs, cuts to social program spending, and massive government deficits as capital fled the province.

In the early run-up to the referendum it appeared as if the Sovereignists would suffer a major defeat. The early polling showed the "No side" ahead by 10%. However, on the Thanksgiving holiday weekend just before the vote, Lucien Bouchard, the charismatic leader of the federal Bloc Quebecois, and a major player in the Meech Lake drama, replaced the imperious Jacques Parizeau as leader of the "Yes" side. The effect was electric. In a series of fiery, emotion generating speeches across the province Bouchard appealed to the pride of Quebecois in their distinct culture and language. He spoke of their "humiliation" at the hands of the English who had refused to accommodate their demands for more powers within Canada so they could protect their culture. Bouchard's impassioned pleas struck a chord with the Quebec electorate resulting in a dramatic surge in support for the "Yes" side by referendum day.

The fear that the "Yes" side would win generated large rallies across Canada that expressed support for Quebecois and national unity. One hundred thousand Canadians from all across the country flocked to Montreal a few days before the referendum to participate in a huge rally to call for national unity and to urge Quebecois not to break up the country. Emotions ran high on both sides of the debate.

The Referendum Result And The Aftermath

The tension was palpable on referendum night, Oct 30, 1995 as both sides anxiously awaited the results of the vote. Canadians were glued to their television sets as the first results poured in. All evening the vote swung back and forth between the "Yes" and the "No" side, with each side either temporarily elated or despondent. In the late evening the final swing was to the "No" side by a razor thin margin. Of 4,700,000 votes cast 50.6% voted "No" and 49.4% voted "Yes," a difference of 53,498 votes separating the two sides. Ninety per cent of English speaking and immigrant Quebecois voted "No," most of them concentrated in the Montreal area. Sixty percent of French speaking Quebecois voted "Yes" (French is the first language of 82% of the Quebec population).

When the final results were announced Premier Parizeau addressed a late night gathering of "Yes" supporters at the Paul Sauve arena. He complained bitterly about the outcome, noting that 60% of French speaking Quebecois, of "who we are" in his words, had voted for sovereignty. He went on to blame the loss on "money and ethnic votes." The remarks drew an audible gasp and even scattered boos from those assembled in the hall. Later, supporters claimed that the Premier had too much to drink over the course of a very tense evening. However, many people, including people who supported the independence movement, were outraged by the remarks calling Parizeau a "racist" for causing friction among language groups and implying that not everyone who lived in the province was a true Quebecois. One day later Parizeau announced his resignation as leader of the party.

The leader of the sovereignist Bloc Quebecois, Lucien Bouchard, took the podium after Parizeau's controversial remarks on referendum night and promised those gathered in the hall that there would be a "next time" for a referendum and "soon." Shortly thereafter, he left Ottawa to assume the leadership of the Parti Quebecois. His government was elected in October 1998, on a platform that included a promise to hold another referendum but only under "winning conditions."

Canada's "Near Death" Experience And The *Clarity Act*

The close victory for the "No" side in the referendum shook federalists to the core, particularly after they learned that Jacques Parizeau had an elaborate plan in place to declare a unilateral declaration of independence (UDI) should Ottawa fail to negotiate the terms of independence after a "Yes" vote in the referendum. Billions of dollars in the Quebec Pension Fund had been set aside to prop up the Canadian dollar in the event of this outcome. To counter the possibility of a unilateral declaration of independence in the wake of some future referendum the federal government embarked on a risky strategy that led to the creation of *Bill 20* (known as *The Clarity Act*). On September 26, 1996, the then Minister of Justice, Allan Rock, asked the Supreme Court of Canada to give an opinion as to whether or not Quebec possessed the legal right under the Constitution, or international law, to secede from Canada by a unilateral declaration of independence.

On August 20, 1998, the Supreme Court of Canada rendered a lengthy opinion that stated that Quebec could not legally separate from Canada unless there was a "clear majority" of votes to a "clear question." The Court concluded that secession would require a constitutional amendment that would have to be negotiated by the federal government and the provinces.

The following year the federal government adopted much of the language of the Supreme Court opinion to introduce a bill (*C-20*) that would establish the rules under which a province could secede from Canada. The bill proposed that the Canadian House of Commons would determine if a referendum question was "clear," and if a "clear majority" in any vote actually represented a genuine expression of the will of the people. The bill did not define what constituted a "clear majority," but a simple 50% plus 1 would not be a sufficient basis for negotiation. It also stated that the government of Canada would be under no obligation to negotiate if the House of Commons decided that either the question asked or the majority obtained was unclear. Furthermore, no constitutional amendment for secession would be considered unless there were agreements dealing with issues such as the national debt, the rights of aboriginals and the protection of minorities.

Bill 99

The Parti Quebecois government of Lucien Bouchard was incensed by the *Clarity Act* and launched an expensive ad campaign in Quebec trying to arouse public outrage against the federal bill. It presented its own bill in the National Assembly to oppose the *Clarity Act*. However, when the Liberal opposition opposed the bill as written, the P.Q took it off the table with a promise it would be redrafted. They then held public hearings in an attempt to generate support for *Bill 99*, which claimed that Quebec had a right to secede from the Canadian federation, with all its territory intact, on the sole strength of a majority vote in a referendum set by Quebec. In essence, the legislation would amount to a repudiation of the Supreme Court advisory opinion on Quebec's right to secede. However, the campaign failed to convince the public and polls taken at the time instead showed that a majority of Quebecois supported the *Clarity Act* (*Montreal Gazette*, Dec.7, 2000).

In the federal election of Nov.27, 2000, the federal Liberals under Jean Chretien captured 44% of the popular vote in Quebec despite a strong anti-clarity campaign by the Bloc Quebecois and its sovereignist allies in Quebec. The legislation was passed in the National Assembly in Quebec on December 6, 2000. However, Lucien Bouchard, the tempestuous leader of the Parti Quebecois, resigned as Premier shortly thereafter, disappointed by the failure to generate more enthusiasm for the independence project. Bouchard's successor, Bernard Landry, also failed to rekindle any passion for the cause. In the election of April 14, 2003, the provincial Liberal Party, under the leadership of a lifelong federalist, Jean Charest, was elected on a platform of health care reform and a pledge to seek changes to federalism while steering clear of constitutional debates.

The Future

The history of English/French relations in Canada have been characterized by seemingly endless jurisdictional and constitutional squabbles that have attempted to reconcile the linguistic and cultural aspirations of French speaking Canadians with the overwhelmingly English dominance in the rest of Canada and on the North American continent. The intensity of the debate waxes and wanes with each successive generation yet, miraculously, a certain peaceful coexistence between the two dominant linguistic groups in Canada has been maintained. Quebec is still part of the Canadian federation. Why? It can't be because of the past thirty years of constitutional debate. Sovereignty sentiment in Quebec increased dramatically after the entrenchment of the *Charter of Rights and Freedoms*, after the failure of the Meech Lake Accord, and after the failure of the Charlottetown Accord. The answer is that *French-speaking Quebecois have been remarkably successful over the past thirty years in attaining their goals and aspirations without resorting to outright separation from the rest of Canada*. By the late 1980s, education in Quebec was conducted overwhelmingly in French, not only among those with French as their mother tongue (whose education was almost 100% in French by 1989), but also allophones (Quebecois whose mother tongue is neither English or French), 80 % of whom attended French language primary and secondary schools by 1996 compared to 43% in 1980 (Secretariat, a la politique linguistique, Gouvernement de Quebec).

Between 1970 and 1985 the income gap between Anglophones and bilingual francophones closed completely, although unilingual French speakers in Quebec still trailed behind even unilingual English speakers. By the early 1990s, there was a dramatic increase in both the ownership of businesses and management positions held by Francophones in Quebec (Vaillancourt, Francois [1992]) English and Anglophones: An Economic Perspective. In *Survival: Official Language Rights in Canada*, ed. by John McCallum, Toronto: C.D Howe Institute, p.85–88).

According to Statistics Canada, the percentage of persons working in French 90% or more of the time increased from 84% in 1971 to 89% in 1989, and, in Montreal from 42% to 56% over the same period. In 1995 consumers received service 95–100% of the time in French in the businesses surveyed and 66% of commercial signs were unilingual French. The 2001 Canadian census found that in Montreal, the province's largest city and main linguistic battleground, Quebecois whose mother tongue was French grew for the first time in three decades by 14,500 from 1996. The proportion of people *speaking French* in the city increased from 1996–2001, reversing a fifty-year trend. On the island of Montreal slightly over 20% of allophones spoke French most often at home in 2001 compared with 16% in 1996.

The Decline Of French Outside Of Quebec

Quebec nationalists see their efforts to maintain the dominance of the French language in Quebec vindicated as French-speaking communities outside the province are increasingly threatened by assimilation. For example, home use of French outside of Quebec has shown a persistent downward trend for over thirty years from 4.4% in 1971 to 3.6% in 1981 to 3.2 % in 1991 to 2.7% in 2001 (Census of Canada, 2001).

A 1994 report from Statistics Canada also showed French speakers outside of Quebec falling further behind English speakers in income levels. Even as the median family income gap between English and French in Quebec closed, it increased in Canada as a whole from 9.9% in 1977 to 14.1% in 1992 (*The Globe and Mail*, March 23, 1994: A1).

The Decline Of English Inside Quebec

The 2001 Census showed a continued exodus of English speaking Quebecois from the province. The number of Quebecois with English as their mother tongue declined by 30,500 to 591,400 from the previous census in 1996. However, Anglophones who could speak French was up 4% to 66% from 1996. Half of Quebec Allophones said they could speak both English and French, an increase of 3% from the previous Census. Ironically, Pierre Trudeau's dream of a bilingual Canada only finds resonance in Quebec where 41% of Census respondents say they speak both French and English, up from 38% in 1996.

Chapter Ten
ECONOMIC DIMENSIONS OF INEQUALITY IN CANADA

Differences between various regions, established and recently arrived Canadians, rich and poor, workers and bosses, employed and unemployed, skilled and unskilled, young and old, male and female, are the fuel for most of the important public policy debates of our time. Social programs and policies like welfare, employment insurance, old age pensions, student loans and bursaries, medicare, affirmative action, and employment equity are all attempts to bridge, or compensate for, the differences that exist among identifiable groups in Canadian society.

Measuring Social Inequality
Wealth, income, education and occupation are the "objective" measures of social inequality in an industrialized society along with such "subjective" measures as status or prestige. "Objective" inequalities are crucially important because, rightly or wrongly, they determine the degree of acceptance or "success" of individuals or groups in relationship to the larger society. By any objective measure there are significant differences between rich and poor, young and old, aboriginal and non-aboriginal, recently arrived and long established Canadians.

Wealth
Roughly 53% of the total estimated wealth (wealth refers to accumulated wealth or net worth rather than current income and is defined here as all personal assets minus all personal debts) of Canadians is owned or controlled by only 10% of the population.

At the very top of the wealth pyramid are five Canadian family dynasties (Thomson, Weston, Irving, Desmarais, and Bombardier-Beaudoin) that own or control over 700 medium and large sized companies in all the major sectors of the Canadian economy. Another 1000 families (including McCain, Reichmann, Molson, etc.) own or control many other major enterprises. Ranked by revenues the proportion of family owned firms represents about one-quarter of the 100 largest companies in Canada (*Globe and Mail*, June 29, 2001).

This small group of Canadian families constitutes an extraordinarily influential economic elite. Through their contributions to political parties, they can shape the agenda of the public policy debates that have an enormous impact on other Canadians. Not surprisingly, most contributions flow to the Liberals, and the Conservatives but only rarely to the New Democratic Party, which promotes policies that the financial elite finds disagreeable such as increasing capital gains or inheritance taxes. Canada has had no inheritance tax since 1972.

Inequality Of Wealth

According to Steven Kerstetter, in an analysis of data from Statistics Canada's Survey of Financial Security, and previous surveys, the wealthiest 50% of families in Canada held 94.4% of the wealth in 1999, leaving only 5.6% for the bottom 50%. Average wealth for the richest 10% of family units increased from $442,468 in 1970 to $980,903 (adjusted for inflation) in 1999, an increase of 122%. The poorest 10% of family units have negative average wealth, or more debts than assets. The poorest 20% of family units had financial assets of only $1,974, on average, in 1999, and their average income in 1998 was only $18,698. If their current income suddenly disappeared, their financial assets alone would be barely enough to keep the family going for five weeks. The richest 20% of family units had average financial assets of $262,186 in 1999 and average income of $62,518 in 1998. The financial assets were enough to replace income for four years. Families with incomes of $75,000 or more in 1999 (after federal and provincial taxes) had average wealth of $583,517. Registered savings plans, capital gains, and stock dividends all get preferred income tax treatment in Canada. In 1999, 72% of the $42 billion in registered savings plans was held by the richest 20% of families. The richest 20% also owned 94% of the $92 billion in stocks outside registered savings plans and 81% of the $80 billion in other mutual and investment funds (Kerstetter, Steven (2002) *Rags to Riches: Wealth Inequality in Canada*, Canadian Centre for Policy Alternatives).

Income Distribution

Another "objective" measure of differences between economic classes in Canadian society is how much of the total share of all income in society is earned by the more affluent and the less affluent, and those who fit somewhere in between the two extremes. One way of calculating the difference is by dividing the total population of income earners from lowest to highest income into five equal groups (quintiles) and then determining the percentage of the total income earned by everybody each quintile receives. Using this method it is possible to compare the "relative share" the lowest group of income earners receives with the highest group of income earners. Typically, the top 20% of income earners receive about 7- 9 times the income of the lowest 20% of income earners in Canada. The gap would be even larger were it not for the effects of certain social programs.

Growing Income Inequality

Over the past decade the gap between the two groups has been growing leading to concerns about the level of inequality between the "haves" and "have-nots" in Canadian society. For example, the number of earners in high-income brackets—those earning more than $100,000 (in inflation adjusted figures) increased dramatically in the 1990s. In 2000, roughly 447,000 people earned $100,000 or more, up from 264,500 a decade earlier. They represented 2.7% of all earners in Canadian society in 2000, compared with 1.8% in 1990. By contrast some 6.7 million Canadians (up 316,000 people or 5% in the 90s) have annual average incomes of less than$20,000.

The total income of families in the top 10% of income earners increased by over 14.6% in real dollars from 1990 to 2000 whereas the total income for the bottom 10% of income earners increased by less than 1% (see Figure 10.1). The 10% of families with the highest incomes in 2000 received $18 for every $1 of income for families with the lowest 10% of income. In the city of Toronto the gap was $27 to $1 (Statistics Canada, Census of Canada, 2001).

Strengths And Weaknesses Of Income Distribution As A Measure Of Inequality

While income distribution is a good way to measure the "gap" between high and low income groups in society there are certain weaknesses in this approach. For example, there is a tendency to assume that people in either the low or high- income groups remain in the same categories all their lives. In fact, there is significant mobility in and out of each income group depending on such factors as age or, for recently arrived immigrants, the length of time in Canada. Younger people, old people, and recently arrived immigrants tend to be in the lowest 20% of income earners. However, in the case of young people or recently arrived immigrants, they usually don't remain in this income category for very long. With increased education and experience they tend to earn more money as time goes on and soon move out of the lowest income group. Similarly, when older people leave the labour force their income tends to drop moving them out of the highest earning income group. For this reason income distribution statistics have to be examined carefully when claims about increased inequality are made.

Figure 10.1:Change in Average Income, by Income Deciles, Census Families, Canada, 1990–2000

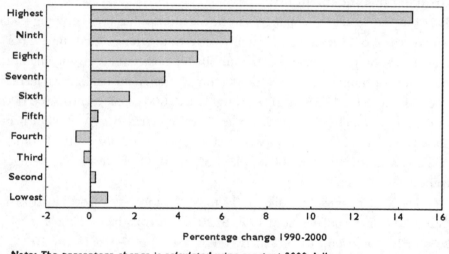

Income decile, census families

Percentage change 1990-2000

Note: The percentage change is calculated using constant 2000 dollars.

Social Mobility

Income distribution statistics present a "static" snapshot of income inequality in Canadian society at any particular time. This is misleading because of the age and other factors discussed above. The more important issue is the extent to which opportunities exist, on either an individual or collective level, to improve one's position. This is what is meant by the expression "*social mobility.*" Different types of social mobility have been identified as a way of determining and measuring the extent to which opportunity exists in any society. For example, the expression "*intergenerational mobility*" has been created to gauge how well children do in relationship to their parents over the course of their working lives. Up until recently, it was taken for granted that children would always do better than their parents through increased educational opportunities and improving job prospects. However, in the 1990s, a significant number of young people seemed to be "stuck" in low wage jobs with little chance for advancement. It appeared that these "Gen-X'ers" would be the first generation to experience "downward intergenerational mobility." Up until now Canadian society has had very little experience with a generation of children that has had poorer job prospects than their parents. If this trend were to persist it would have profound consequences on social policy issues such as the continuation of pension entitlements.

Figure 10.2: Men Younger Than 40 Experienced Little or No Gains in Average Earnings During the 1990s and Make Less Then They Did Two Decades Ago

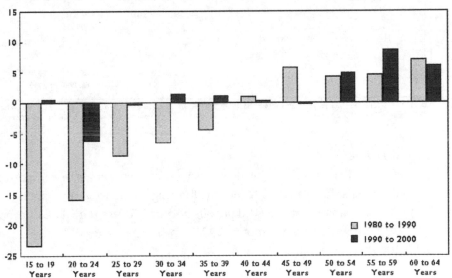

Canadian census data in 2001 revealed that workers under age forty experienced earnings losses over the past two decades (see Figures 10.2 and 10.3). Total average earnings only increased because those over age fifty experienced gains. For employees' aged 35-39 working full year, full time, average earnings in 2000 stood at $50,390, about $1,740 less than in 1980 in inflation adjusted dollars. The pattern was worse for all younger groups, with those people in their 20's experiencing back to back declines in each of the past two decades (Statistics Canada, Census of Canada, 2001).

Figure 10.3: Women Less Than 30 Earn Less Than They Did Two Decades Ago

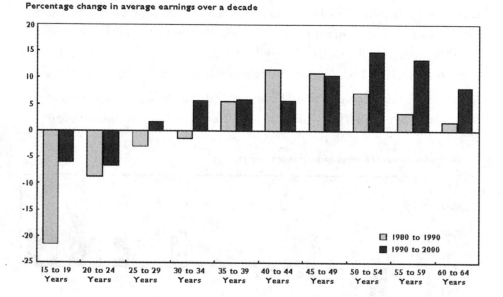

Percentage change in average earnings over a decade

Living At Home
According to Statistics Canada, this decline for young workers is one important factor that explains the increasing tendency of young adults to return or continue to live with their parents for extended periods of time. No less than 41% of people aged 20-29 lived with their parents in 2001, up from 27% in 1981 (Census of Canada, 2001).

Intragenerational Mobility
Another measure of the opportunities that exist to improve one's position is the extent of *"intragenerational mobility."* Many people start out in the labour market working at low paying, unskilled jobs but through increased experience or education eventually move on to higher paying, more demanding jobs. This improvement within a person's own lifetime is referred to as "intragenerational mobility." When people simply move from one job to another with the same pay and skill level it is referred to as *"horizontal mobility."* An example would be leaving a job flipping hamburghers at Macdonalds to flip hamburghers at Wendy's. The effect of two major recessions in the 1980s and the 1990s was to increase the amount of "horizontal mobility" and reduce the rate of intragenerational mobility. Young people remained longer in jobs that used to be considered "entry level," "seasonal," or "part-time temporary."

Structural Mobility

An increasingly important aspect of social mobility is the extent to which new technologies and services open up job opportunities for people who wish to improve their position. This is referred to as *"structural mobility."* For example, the past twenty-five years has seen the creation of entirely new industries and jobs spawned by the electronics and computer revolution. However, this rapid technological change also had destructive consequences. Many workers in previously secure, high paying jobs with benefits were displaced because of technological innovations and didn't find new jobs at the same pay or benefit levels. About half of all new jobs added to the economy in Canada in the 1980s were in the lower paying service sector (fast food, retail sales, etc.), which is characterized by high employee turnover, part-time work, and few, if any, health or pension benefits. One consequence was the decline in the proportion of Canadians with middle level incomes and an increase in the number of people who are classified as *"working poor."* These changes in the labour market had profound consequences on the level of inequality in Canadian society. There is a huge gap between those who have the right training and education for the "new economy" and those who are too old, lack skills, or are computer illiterate.

Education And Social Mobility

Education is one of the keys to social mobility. The more advanced the level of education the greater the likelihood of social distinction and accompanying material rewards. This is one of the most consistent findings of the social sciences and therefore explains why educational opportunity is so important in any discussion of social inequality. More than 60% of people in the lowest earnings category did not have more than a high school education in 2000, while more than 60% of those in the top category had a university degree. However, it is important to note that higher education is not a *guarantee* of a living wage. Sixteen per cent of those earning less than $20,000 a year in full time employment in 2000 were university graduates and 11% were community college graduates (Statistics Canada, Census of Canada, 2001).

Educational Controversies

There are a number of controversies that arise in connection with educational opportunity. For example, the original purpose of student loans and bursaries, free tuition at CEGEP (CEGEP refers to the junior college system which exists in

the province of Quebec), and low tuitions at universities, was to provide opportunities for students from low income backgrounds to gain knowledge and skills
that would enable them to adapt more readily to the changing labour market.
However, the debt crisis, the persistence of high unemployment, an increase in
student loan defaults, and changing attitudes about the benefits of education,
appear to be undermining the commitment to low cost accessibility to educational opportunities.

Questions are also being raised about who gets financial assistance and for
what purpose. For example, does the existence of student loans and bursaries
simply encourage mediocre students to remain in the educational system rather
than face the reality of no jobs or low-paid jobs when they leave? Is the dramatic
increase in student loan defaults (see Statistics Canada, *The Daily*, July 30, 1999)
a consequence of the proliferation of programs and courses with no discernible
connection to the labour market? Is the original purpose of loans and bursaries
being undermined if they are, in fact, more likely to be used by middle class students who find ways to disguise the fact that they have enough money to finance their own education without such programs? Are more affluent students
better able to obtain information on the availability of loans and bursaries and
how to become eligible for them? Instead of providing opportunities for students
from low income circumstances to improve their position, the expansion of the
education system is now seen by some critics as a potential barrier ("paper barrier") to mobility because jobs which previously could be filled by high school
drop-outs now require a college diploma or university degree and professional
jobs which formerly required a university degree now require a graduate degree.
The inflation of educational credentials isn't necessary for effective job performance and, in fact, works to exclude large numbers of people from jobs they are
quite capable of doing. Students from low-income circumstances often cannot
afford the additional time they must now spend in educational institutions chas-
ing paper credentials. The extent to which these problems exist is debatable. The
fact that they do exist is seen by some people as an unintended consequence of a
well-meaning attempt to expand educational opportunities.

Tuition Fees
Another concern has been the effect of rising tuition fees in limiting low-income
students' access to a university education. However, a recent study by Statistics
Canada indicates that the gap between students from high income and
low-income families attending university has actually narrowed in the past de-

cade. The number of students attending university with family incomes of $25,000 or less has doubled over the past two decades. The participation rate of such students is slowly catching up to that of students whose parents make more than $100,000 a year. But over the past two decades the percentage of students from middle-income families attending university has not changed and may have even slipped. This may be because tuition fees are high enough to represent a real financial challenge for some middle class students, particularly if their family income is too high to allow them more access to loans (*Globe and Mail*, October 4, 2003).

Poverty Controversies

There is a very precise but controversial method of measuring the degree of inequality in Canadian sociedy. Statistics Canada tries to calculate the share of the median (midpoint between the highest and lowest family income in the society) family's income that is spent on food, clothing and shelter. Right now, it's about 35% of weekly income. If a family spends 20 points more than the median family, meaning 55% of weekly income, on food, clothing and shelter, they are considered to be living in low-income circumstances. This "low income cutoff line" (LICO) is the basis on which most poverty statistics in Canada are constructed. For example, the income level at which an urban family of four spends about 55% of their income on food, clothing and shelter is said to be about $34,572 gross income (2000, LICO). People in this situation who fall below the low-income cutoff point are considered to be living in "*relative poverty*" by comparison to other Canadians. Using the LICO figures, pre-tax poverty levels in Canada remained at 16.2% in 2000, about the same as a decade earlier. The overall number of Canadians living below the low-income cut-off line increased to 4.72 million in 2000 from 4.28 million in 1990 and 4.09 million in 1980. *Although Statistics Canada doesn't consider these low-income cut-offs to be poverty lines and they have no official status as such, this is the way they are interpreted by the media and others when determining the poverty rate in Canada.*

As a measure of inequality between lower and average income earners in Canadian society the Statistics Canada low-income cutoff lines serve a useful purpose. However, there are several problems with using the low-income cutoff lines as a measure of poverty in Canada. At the beginning of the 20th century the average Canadian family spent about 70% of their yearly income on the basic necessities of food, clothing and shelter. So by the standards of today virtually all

Canadians at the beginning of the last century would fall below the low-income cutoffs and therefore be classified as poor. But as Canadians have become richer (GDP—Gross Domestic Product per person is now more than double what it was in the 1960s), the average Canadian family now spends only 35% of their yearly income on food, clothing and shelter leaving more money to spend on non-necessities or even luxuries. If the trend continues and the average Canadian family spends only 10% on the basic necessities 50 years from now, there would still be Canadians classified as "poor" because they spent 20 points more or 30% of their incomes on the necessities. The point is that by this arbitrary method of defining poverty there will always be a significant number of people who are classified as "poor" even though by today's standards they would be "rich."

Who Is "Poor?"

In spite of the conceptual problems associated with defining "poverty," the low-income cutoff lines are useful in determining how certain identifiable groups are doing in comparison to other groups in Canada. For example, people over the age of 65 or under the age of 25, the aboriginal population, women of all ages, lone parent families, people living in Quebec and Atlantic Canada, people with less than 9 years of education, and recently arrived immigrants are more likely to be living in low income circumstances than other groups of Canadians.

Immigrant Earnings Fall In The 1990s

Statistics Canada reports that the average earnings in 2000 of male immigrants aged 25-54 who arrived in Canada between 1990 and 1999 was $33,900, almost 25% lower than the Canadian-born. More importantly, this level was well below the average $40,100 among male immigrants who arrived in Canada two decades earlier.

The situation is particularly grim for children of recently arrived immigrants. Thirty-nine per cent of children from two parent families of immigrants who have arrived within the last ten years (1990-2000) are living in low-income circumstances, up from 33% in 1990 and 22% in 1980. For children from families where one parent is an immigrant who arrived from 1990-2000, the figures are only slightly lower with 33% living in low-income circumstances, up from 27% in 1990 and 20% in 1980. In actual numbers about 231,000 children of immigrants arriving from 1990-2000 were living in low-income circumstances by the end of the decade (Statistics Canada, Census of Canada, 2001).

People Of Colour

According to recent research done by Grace Edwards-Galabuzi, white immigrants to Canada do better economically than people of colour. During the post-1986 period when non-white immigration was relatively high, compared to other periods, non-white immigrants earned 28-31.5% less than white immigrants (Galabuzi, Grace Edward, (2002), *Canada's Creeping Economic Apartheid*, The Centre for Social Justice).

"Racialized Canadians" And Inequality

Galabuzi, a Political Science doctoral student at York University, has drawn attention to a disturbing and heretofore unexplored dimension of economic inequality in Canada, which is the gap between what she refers to as "racialized Canadians" and other Canadians. Galabuzi prefers the term "racialized groups" because the more commonly used term "visible minorities" categorizes people as a minority when in some urban areas like Toronto or Vancouver these minorities outnumber "whites." She also believes that the term "visible minorities" does not adequately convey the fact that racism acts as the dominant force setting people apart whereas the term "racialized groups" is more effective to that end.

In her study, Galabuzi uses a variety of data sources including a new specially designed run of Statistics Canada Survey of Labour and Income Dynamics (SLID) for 1996, 1997, and 1998. She also relies on previously unpublished data from the 1996 Canadian Census, Human Resources and Development Canada statistics, and the 1999 Employment Equity data.

According to Galabuzi's research, the individual pre-tax median earnings of "racialized Canadians" was $14,507 in 1998 compared to $20,517 for other Canadians. The gap translated into 28% less in median income and 25% less after taxes. Examining post-tax and post-transfers income, racialized groups earned 20% less in 1996 and 26% less in 1997, narrowing marginally to 25% in 1998.

Higher numbers from racialized groups are living in poverty. Individuals from racialized groups have poverty rates of 35.6% compared to 17.6% of the general population at the time of her study. Family poverty rates were 19% compared to 10.4% for other Canadians. In 1995, the rate for children under six living in low-income circumstances (below the LICO lines) was 45% compared to 26% for all Canadian children under six. While racialized groups comprise 21.6% of the population of urban centers they account for 33% of the poor in these cities.

Census data from 1996 showed that men in racialized groups had a 13.2 % unemployment rate compared to 9.9% for men in the general population. The unemployment rate for women in racialized groups was 15.3% compared to 9.4% for other women.

The gaps in employment income, unemployment rates and poverty rates are difficult to explain based on educational qualifications. According to Galabuzi's research, 22% of racialized men and 16.9% of racialized women had university degrees compared to 13.4 % of other men and 11.6% of other women.

One factor that significantly reduced the income disparities between racialized and other groups was membership in a union. The income difference fell to 8% in the unionized, full-time, full year work sector (using 1999-2000 data). However, of 2,905,100 unionized workers in Canada, only 203,100 are racialized group members, representing 7% of the population.

Aboriginal Poverty

According to an analysis of 1996 census data by the Canadian Council on Social Development, aboriginal people were more than twice as likely to live in low-income circumstances as non-aboriginal people. Although aboriginal people accounted for about 1.5%, on average, of the populations of the cities included in the study they represented 3.4% of the poor population. They accounted for 24% of the poor in the city of Regina, which was three times their proportion of the population of that city (*Urban Poverty in Canada: a Statistical Profile*, Canadian Council on Social Development, 2000).

In 2001, aboriginal children were twice as likely to live with one parent as non-aboriginal children. Aboriginal youth age 15-24 were twice as likely to be unemployed as non-aboriginal Canadians. Only 8% of aboriginal peoples in the 15-34 age category had a completed university degree, while 28% of all Canadians did (Canadian Council on Social Development, June, 2003).

Family Structure And Low Income

There has been a marked increase in the number of children living in low-income families since 1980 (18.4% in 2001 versus 15% in 1980). This is a consequence of two painful economic recessions and a significant increase in the number of single parent families. Lone parent families with at least one child under 18 have increased from 361,520 in 1980 or 5.7% of all census families in that year to 619,005 in 2000 or 7.4% of all census families in that year. This represents a 70% *cumulative* increase in lone parent families over a two-decade period, mostly headed by women. In the same period the number of two-parent families declined from 43.7% of all census families in 1980 to 33% of all census families in 2000. Only 11.2 % of married couples with at least one child under 18 fell below the low-income cutoff lines in 2000 compared to 45.8% of lone parent families (Census of Canada, 2001). It is clear that recent changes in family structure have contributed to the increase in the number of children living in low-income circumstances. Losing a breadwinner through divorce or separation can be enough to push a family below the low-income line.

In 2000, the percentage of poor children in lone parent families was 39% compared to 33% in 1980, but down from 42% in 1993. There is some more positive news from the 2001 census. The poverty rate of lone-parent families with children has dropped below the 50% mark for the first time in 20 years. Roughly forty-six per cent of lone-parent families are living in low-income circumstances as of 2001, compared to 54% in 1990 and 55% in 1980. Lone parent families with children aged 18 and under made important gains between 1990 and 2000, the result, according to Statistics Canada, of greater labour market activity (jobs) and increased government transfers (social programs). In 2000, the median income of these lone parent families was $26,000, up 19% from $21,800 in 1990 (Statistics Canada, Census of Canada, 2001).

The "Working Poor" And The "Welfare Poor"

The "poverty rate" in Canada, though it is not officially recognized as such, is based upon the Statistics Canada low-income cutoff lines. Using the LICO lines as a basis for measuring poverty about 16.2% of the population or 4.72 million Canadians are classified as "poor." Since about half of those working age adults classified as "poor" derive most of their income from work they are often referred to as the *"working poor"* to distinguish them from children, the disabled, or the *"welfare poor"* who derive most of their income from social assistance (welfare). The "working poor" are disproportionately concentrated in service industries, farming, fishing, sales, or any minimum wage occupation.

Unemployment In Canada

Unemployment in Canada has always been the subject of much heated controversy and debate. The debate centers on issues such as how unemployment is measured, why Canada's unemployment rate is persistently higher than most other comparably industrialized countries, and the effects of unemployment insurance (now called Employment Insurance) on unemployment rates and worker motivation.

Measurement Issues

The unemployment rate is commonly believed to count the total number of job-less Canadians. This is incorrect. The monthly unemployment statistics are de-rived from a monthly survey questionnaire of approximately 58,000 households selected by Statistics Canada as a "representative sample" of the Canadian work-force over the age of fifteen. People living on First Nation reservations, prison in-mates, residents of mental institutions, and the elderly are not surveyed. Survey participants are visited personally for the first questionnaire.

In order to be "counted" as unemployed, people surveyed must have been actively seeking work in the previous four weeks, on temporary lay-off await-ing a recall to work, or have found a job but haven't yet started to work. If the people surveyed don't fit into one of these very precise categories, they are not considered to be unemployed. People who are unemployed but not "actively seeking work" are not included in the official unemployment rate. These people are the so-called "discouraged workers." Although they are not part of the offi-cial unemployment rate Statistics Canada does track discouraged workers and estimates that they number about 100,000 to 400,000 in any given month, the size depending on the overall health of the labour market.

Hidden Unemployed

The official jobless rate also does not make allowances for part-time workers who want a full-time job (so-called "involuntary part-time workers") or people like students, housewives/househusbands who have dropped out of the labour force because of poor job prospects. While they are at school or at home they are part of the so-called "hidden unemployed." It is important to understand that even when the Canadian economy and the job market improves, the unemploy-ment rate may remain high because more of the so-called "discouraged work-ers" will rejoin the labour force "actively seeking work," and therefore will be counted as "officially unemployed."

Controversies

Some critics of Statistics Canada believe that the way unemployment is mea-sured in Canada minimizes the problem, particularly for young people and re-cently arrived immigrants, and undermines any political efforts to do something about it. However, there are other critics who argue that the problem of unem-ployment is exaggerated and does not take into account large numbers of people, including failed refugee claimants, who work "under the table" in the "underground economy." There are unofficial estimates that anywhere from 5 to 15% of Canadian Gross Domestic Product (GDP) may be produced in the underground economy, comprised of people who simply barter or exchange goods and services for cash as well as a more organized criminal element that engages in smuggling, drug dealing and other illicit activities.

Comparisons To Other Countries

Comparing unemployment rates for different countries is complicated because of variations in the way unemployment is measured. However, there is little doubt that in the 1990s Canada's unemployment rate rarely dipped below 10% (and even now stands at about 7%) and that this is relatively high compared to other industrialized countries of the Organization for Economic Cooperation and Development (OECD).

Effects Of Social Policy On Unemployment

In the past twenty years social programs such as employment insurance and welfare have come under attack as being a major cause of Canada's above average unemployment rate. Critics argue that the "generosity" of these programs encourages people to refuse available jobs and thereby artificially inflates the unemployment numbers. The existence of such programs is also seen as a magnet for attracting "bogus" refugee claimants.

In the early 1990s there was also heated debate about the abuse of social programs as a contributing factor to repeated yearly deficits and the rapidly accumulating national debt. However, many people were surprised when the main culprits responsible for the abuse were identified. In the fall of 1995, then Human Resources Minister Lloyd Axworthy stated that about 13% of companies in Canada were responsible for almost 40% of unemployment insurance benefits paid out by the federal government. He claimed that large companies in the construction, tourism, forestry, and auto industries sometimes adjust hiring and lay-offs so workers can collect employment insurance for part of the year. Axworthy charged that Canadians contributing "hard earned money" in employment insurance premiums end up subsidizing profitable businesses (*Montreal Gazette*, October 19, 1994).

In response to Axworthy's uncharacteristically blunt remarks, General Motors threatened to stop investing in Canada if Ottawa cut unemployment in-

surance benefits for temporarily laid off workers. According to a company representative, "if UI was not available then the union would be at the bargaining
table saying we need some kind of income protection program. That becomes a
direct cost to us as a manufacturer and puts us at a competitive disadvantage to
other jurisdictions" (*Montreal Gazette*, October 19, 1994).

The same rationale applies to other social programs which big business
tends to support such as Medicare and old age pensions, the costs of which are
paid through the tax system by all Canadians. Since the costs of these programs
are borne by the general public, large businesses avoid having to negotiate with
their workers over these benefits.

The other major example of employment insurance abuse was the east
coast fish plants where companies employed workers for 10 to 20 weeks every
year after which workers were eligible for 30 to 42 weeks of employment benefits. Once again, company hiring and lay-off patterns were adjusted to take advantage of the employment insurance benefits at the expense of the rest of
Canadian taxpayers.

Changes To Unemployment/Employment Insurance

A major revision of the federal government's Unemployment Insurance program occurred in 1971. Up until that time only 61-67% of the workforce was
covered and the eligibility requirements were quite stringent requiring at least
30 weeks of employment to qualify and a maximum of only 15 weeks of benefits for a minimally qualified applicant. The replacement rate for weekly income
was about 53%.

The early 1970s was the heyday of Pierre Trudeau's "Just Society" and the
liberalization of unemployment insurance eligibility and higher benefits were
viewed as an important component of the government's attack on social inequality. After the Act was revised in 1971, coverage was extended to about 87%
of all employees, the number of weeks required to be eligible for benefits was reduced from 30 to 8, and both the duration and amount of benefits received was
increased based on local and national unemployment rates. The replacement rate
for income rose to 66.7% of previous weekly income and by 1972 the average
duration of time on unemployment insurance had increased to 29.7 weeks.

A major economic slowdown occurred in 1973-74 resulting in a dramatic
increase in UI claimants. At the same time, the government began running up
yearly deficits to cover the costs of federal spending. Anecdotal evidence started

to emerge about the "abuse" of unemployment insurance by people who would work the minimum number of weeks and then quit to collect UI. By 1977, the government started to shift its position on unemployment insurance increasing the minimum number of weeks required to collect from 8 to 10-14 weeks. Two years later the replacement rate for lost weekly income was reduced to 60%. New labour market entrants and repeat claimants were required to have extra weeks of work to qualify for benefits. In 1990 the requirements for first–time claimants was increased to 10-20 weeks, depending on the local employment conditions, and benefits were reduced. Two years later, the replacement rate for lost weekly income was again reduced to 57% and people who quit their jobs were ineligible for benefits.

By 1997 a newly renamed Employment Insurance program required that first-time claimants have 910 hours (roughly 26 weeks at 35 hours a week) to qualify for benefits. The replacement rate for lost weekly income was reduced to 55% with a further 1% reduction for anyone who had collected more than 20 weeks in the past five years. Any additional 20 weeks claimed resulted in another 1% reduction to a maximum of 5%. The maximum benefit period was reduced to 45 weeks, down from 50 weeks under the old system. The maximum weekly benefit was reduced from $429 to $413 and a "clawback" was introduced for claimants who earned more than $39,000 and who had received more than 20 weeks of benefits during the previous five years. They were required to pay back 50 to 100% of their benefit, for every dollar of income earned above $39,000, 30 cents of insurance was taxed back up to the maximum.

Effects Of Changes To The Employment Insurance Program

While the "generosity" of the employment insurance program may have once contributed to the higher than average Canadian unemployment rate (about 1.1 to 1.3% according to Human Resources and Development Canada (HRDC) in a 1999 study) it became difficult to support this argument by the end of the 1990s. Beginning in January of 1997 eligibility requirements for collecting employment insurance tightened, and benefits were reduced. Since 1991 the number of employment insurance beneficiaries has actually dropped by 40-50% and the employment insurance fund now runs a large surplus. However, this change has had relatively little impact on the unemployment rate that still remains relatively high even during periods of economic recovery.

Changes To Employment Insurance

In January of 2004, the federal government introduced a new "compassionate-leave program" for Canadians with a close relative who is "at significant risk of death." If eligible, they will be allowed to take six weeks off work and collect employment insurance benefits to provide compassionate care for a dying relative. The six-week leave can be taken by a single member of the family or shared among various family members. As is the case with parental leaves, the program is only open to those who are eligible for EI benefits. According to government predictions 270,000 Canadians will use the program in 2004 to care for 160,000 gravely ill family members at a total estimated cost of $345 million. Self-employed or other Canadians who don't make EI contributions will not be eligible for the benefit (*Globe and Mail*, December 3, 2003).

The "Welfare Trap"

Critics who see social policy as a major contributor to higher than average Canadian unemployment rates also cite defects in the welfare system to make their case. For example, some studies have shown that it may be more economically advantageous for single mothers on social assistance (welfare) to remain there rather than working. At minimum wage levels, there is very little extra money to be gained and important benefits (free dental care, prescription drugs, eyeglasses, rental subsidies in some provinces, etc.) to be lost when a single mother moves from welfare to work. Critics charge that these disincentives to work have resulted in a dramatic increase in the number of "employable" people on welfare since 1980. However, there are problems with this type of explanation. It is difficult to determine whether or not the increase of "employable" people on welfare (45% in 1993 compared to 35% in 1980, for example) was the result of defects in the welfare system or the effects of the two major recessions (1983-84, 1989-91) since 1980. It is possible that the problem of work disincentives associated with the welfare system, while requiring reform, pale in comparison to the larger problem of recession-induced scarcity of jobs.

Deinstitutionalization And Homelessness

An important social problem that has emerged in the past fifteen years is the appearance of "homeless" people in the major Canadian urban centers. While their numbers are not nearly as large as in the United States, the increasing appearance of "street people," "panhandlers," "squeegee people," "runaway kids," "punks" and others has perplexed many Canadians.

In the United States, the problem of homelessness did not exist until the 1980s. It was a direct consequence of a change in attitude and public policy concerning the "mentally ill." Up until the late 1960s most of the mentally ill were housed in large institutions that were run by the individual states or the federal government. Conditions in these "snakepits" were often horrendous and many patients were subjected to lobotomies, electroshock therapy and excessive use of restraint devices in an attempt to control violent, delusional or "anti-social" behaviour. There was much criticism of the conditions in these institutions and the effects on people who had been "committed," particularly those who were considered to be only "borderline mentally ill."

The Donaldson Case

Kenneth Donaldson was a thirty-four year old married man with three children employed at a General Electric defense plant. In 1943 he experienced his first mental health episode. He was hospitalized at Marcy State hospital in New York and was subjected to 23 electro-shock treatments. Shortly thereafter he went back to normal life but in the mid-1950s he started to experience paranoid delusions, believing that he was being poisoned. During a visit to his parents' home in Florida in 1956, they had him "committed" involuntarily to Florida's Chattahoochee State hospital. He remained in the state hospital for fifteen years but refused all treatment and denied that he was ill. On many occasions he petitioned the courts to be released but was denied in spite of repeated offers from both a halfway house in Minneapolis and a friend in Syracuse, New York, to provide a home and supervision for him. Eventually the case made its way to the Supreme Court of the United States, which made its landmark decision in1975. In it, the Court declared "a finding of 'mental illness' cannot justify a State's locking a person up against his will and keeping him indefinitely in simple custodial confinement. In short, a state cannot confine a non-dangerous individual who is capable of surviving in freedom by himself or with the help of willing and responsible mentors or friends" (O'Connor vs. Donaldson, 422 U.S.563 [1975]).

In Donaldson's view the hospital's doctors would never agree to release him because he wasn't willing to play what he called "the game," which meant he gave no credit to the doctors for making him well but had insisted from the beginning that he was never ill.

The "Donaldson Decision," as the Supreme Court Decision was called, the discovery of drugs which could reduce violent or psychotic behaviour, and changes in public attitudes about the mentally ill because of movies like *"One Flew Over The Cuckoo's Nest*," led to a movement to "deinstitutionalize" mentally ill patients and reintegrate them into the larger community so they could live more "normal" lives. On Dec. 17, 1991, the United Nations' *Principles for the Protection of Persons with Mental Illness and for the Improvement of Mental Health Care* was adopted by resolution of the U.N General Assembly. The idea was that mentally ill people have rights and are entitled to certain protections from possible discrimination based upon their particular vulnerabilities.

By the early 1980s tens of thousands of former patients had been released. Adequate community support, alternative forms of housing, and monitoring of drugs were to be provided to make this a success. However, things didn't work out that way. Budgetary cutbacks in the late 1970s and early 1980s led to reduced funding of these support services. Consequently, many of those discharged from the mental institutions "fell between the cracks" and ended up in low rent neighbourhoods, or in "flophouses," without adequate community support or monitoring of their drug needs. About half of the "homeless" people in the United States fall into this category of deinstitutionalized persons who suffer from schizophrenia (a mental illness characterized by delusional behaviour) and other mental disorders. Areas where discharged mentally ill patients lived became magnets for others with "borderline mental disorders," or "anti-social" behaviour patterns, as well as runaway kids looking for cheap places to live. By the late 1980s this growing population was joined by some victims of corporate downsizing and others who could no longer afford skyrocketing rents in major urban areas.

The same process of deinstitutionalization occurred in Canada but funding for community support was never cut as drastically as in the United States. Consequently, the problem of homelessness did not occur to the same extent as in the United States. However, a similar pattern emerged whereby lower cost city areas favoured by discharged mentally ill persons also became a magnet for runaway kids and others who were down on their luck.

What Can Be Done About Inequality?

There are essentially two opposing visions that dominate contemporary thinking about social inequality and what should be done about it. They both share certain built-in assumptions about the virtues of private property and the limits of social change in a liberal democratic society. Although there is a wide range of opinion associated with each "vision" the label "neo-conservative" (a more accurate label would be "neo-liberalism") is attached to one and "liberal" ("social democrat" would be a more accurate label in this case) to the other. On any number of issues related to inequality each group has a decidedly different approach. What follows are some of the ways the two groups see things differently.

"Absolute Poverty"/"Relative Poverty"

"Neo-conservatives" define "poverty" differently from "liberals." In their view, poverty means a situation where people lack the basic necessities of food, clothing and shelter. They argue that if one uses this definition there is virtually no poverty in Canada. Even in the worst of situations people have access to homeless shelters and free food from the Salvation Army or some other charitable agency. From their standpoint, real poverty is what exists in the "Third World."

"Liberals," on the other hand, believe that poverty should not be defined this way. They argue that a person's situation in Canada should not be compared to that of a person in a Third World country. It should instead be compared with how other people in Canada are doing. When viewed this way, there are a significant number of people in Canada who are doing very poorly in comparison to their fellow Canadians. According to the liberals such people are experiencing "relative poverty," and this is the way that poverty should be defined in Canada. By this relative definition of poverty about 16.2% (LICO, 2001) of Canadians can be considered to be poor.

Culture Of Poverty/Structural Poverty

Why are some people poor? "Neo-conservatives" argue that to the extent that poverty actually exists it can be explained by the attitudes and values of the poor themselves. According to this view, the poor lack a sufficient "work ethic," are spenders rather than savers, and do not value or take advantage of educational opportunities. Adding to these factors are a desire for short-term gratification rather than long term planning and a weak attachment to families. These "cultural attributes" are perpetuated from generation to generation leading to a permanent underclass of underemployed or unemployable that end up relying on social services to survive.

"Liberals" see this explanation as reversing cause and effect. They see poverty as a consequence of the lack of well-paying jobs. People see no point in trying hard when most of the jobs available to them are dead-end and low paying. The self-defeating attitudes that people develop are a consequence of their labour market experience, which is reinforced by periodic recessions when there simply aren't enough jobs for everybody who wants one. This *"structural poverty"* is made worse by the elimination of well-paid factory jobs through automation and technological change. In addition, "free trade" and the "globalization" of the economy contribute to this "deindustrialization" as factory jobs previously occupied by North American workers are lost to low-paid workers in Third World countries.

Means Tested Programs/Universal Programs

What is the best type of social program? Many "neo-conservatives" favour *"means tested"* or "targeted" programs where only those who lack adequate "means" (income, property, etc.), the "genuinely poor," are eligible for benefits. In order to receive such benefits a person must prove they are poor enough to qualify. That's why they are referred to as "means tested." Many social programs in the United States, like Medicaid (basic medical services for low-income Americans), are means tested.

"Liberals" argue that means tested programs are demeaning and stigmatize the recipients as if they were social outcasts. They also believe that means-tested programs will always be poorly funded since it is not in the interest of more affluent groups to support programs they don't benefit from directly. Both of these criticisms are supported by tangible evidence from the United States where Medicaid patients receive inferior treatment in comparison to patients who are covered by private insurance. According to the research of two prominent physicians and health care reformers in the United States, about 55 million people lack insurance for at least a month in any given year, and over 28 months about 67 million are uninsured for at least one month, which means that one quarter of the American population has experienced a recent bout of "uninsurance" ("Bleeding the Patient" (2002), Common Courage Press, Himmelstein, David and Steffie Woolhandler, p.9).

Liberals tend to favour universal social programs such as Medicare (universal health insurance) whereby everyone, whether rich or poor, should have access to the same quality of services. The purpose of universal programs is to give all citizens a real sense of security in the face of possible injury, illness, unemployment, or old age. Programs such as Medicare and old age pensions enjoy a huge constituency of support in Canada because they benefit practically everyone. Therefore, it is easier to mobilize political support to adequately insure the quality and funding for these programs. The philosophy underlying universal programs is a commitment to equality where everyone, regardless of the size of their wallet, is to be included and has the right to certain basic public services. These ideas were very popular in Canada until the economic slowdown that engulfed Canada in the mid-1970s. Rising deficits between 1974 and 1993 led to an accumulated debt (The national debt) and the interest payments on that debt led governments to cut back on support for universal social programs. The resulting decline in quality services caused some people to question the principle of "universality." Negative attitudes about social programs became more common, particularly among those segments of Canadian society that could afford to pay for these services themselves.

Minimal State Intervention/Activist Social Policy

Differing opinions between neo-conservatives and liberals over social programs is part of a larger philosophical debate concerning the proper role of government in dealing with societal problems. For example, neo-conservatives favour a minimum of state intervention in areas of social welfare. They argue that people function best when the need to survive forces them to work hard, save, invest, and take advantage of educational opportunities. Anything that interferes with the discipline demanded by the "free market" will eventually have catastrophic effects. To bolster their case they cite examples of what they see as "abuse" of social programs like Medicare, employment insurance, welfare, and student bursaries. They believe that the "generosity" of such programs undermines people's ability to solve their own problems. Rather than eliminate social problems, the existence of social programs have contributed to these social problems and probably made them worse. Therefore, the role of government in these areas should be limited.

Liberals see government playing a more activist role in social policy. In their view, the experiences of the Great Depression and World War II proved that the operation of the "free marketplace" was inadequate to deal with the inequalities and social problems that exist in society. Only an institution as powerful as government can counteract or limit the built-in tendencies toward maldistribution of wealth and power associated with the capitalist marketplace. Society, through its government, has an obligation to ensure that the interests of the whole community are protected and not simply to be beholden to the desires of the wealthy few.

"Family Values"/"Humanist Values"

Neo-conservatives see social problems as the responsibility of the family rather than the state. When legislation and government policy makes divorce, unwed motherhood or same sex relationships more "socially acceptable" or financially more sustainable, the seeds of future problems are being sown, according to such critics. In their view, all of these situations create social problems such as abandonment, child poverty, teenage delinquency, alcohol and drug abuse, and indiscriminate sexual behaviour. If the state did not support these "choices" through legislation, social policy, or tax policies, the role of the family and "family values" would be strengthened. The family would be forced to take responsibility for any problems that arose rather than shifting responsibility to some government agency or social program.

Liberals, on the other hand, believe that the changing nature of the economy and the workplace, such as the increasing necessity of two income families, makes it impossible to lay the full burden of responsibility for social problems on the family. In this view, social programs such as universal high quality daycare make it possible for working women to contribute to family income while ensuring that their children are receiving adequate care and attention, thus avoiding later problems. In an increasingly mobile society people must often move far away from family kinship networks to find employment. It is unrealistic to assume that families hundreds or thousands of miles away can act as a support system in the case of sudden job loss or abandonment of a partner where children are involved. The government must provide services that enable people to cope in such situations.

The "humanistic values" which liberals tend to endorse are based on the idea that certain social problems are too complicated to be left solely to the responsibility of individual parents or families. They may not have the intellectual or material resources to deal with problems that are, to some extent, the responsibility of the larger community. In these situations, it is often better to deal with problems in a more dispassionate manner, through some state agency, on a case-by-case basis.

"Woodwork Effect"/"Social Investment"

Neo-conservatives believe that the provision of any type of "free" service will increase the demand for that service. They cite the example of food banks in Canada, which were almost non-existent before the recession of 1982, when unemployment reached its highest level in Canada since the Great Depression. Many well-intentioned people wanted to do something about the growing number of people who were falling through the holes in the "social safety net." As a consequence, a few food banks opened up so that people down on their luck could receive a free box of groceries. However, according to some neo-conservatives, the number and scale of operations of these food banks continued to increase dramatically even during the economic recovery of the mid-1980s. Some neo-conservatives see this growth as an example of the *"woodwork effect."* People who had previously found some way to provide for themselves were drawn "out of the woodwork" to take advantage of the free food offered at the food banks.

Liberals prefer to focus on the benefits of social programs rather than the perceived abuses. They see the provision of certain "free" services, particularly in the area of health and education, as an investment in the future. For example, by using tax money now to support programs that insure adequate nutrition, health care and educational opportunities for the children of the poor, society and the taxpayers will save money later in terms of fewer social problems and less crime. People who are healthy and well educated are better able to adapt to the changing nature of the labour market than those who lack these advantages. Society does not benefit from having a large number of people who lack the basic attributes that would enable them to "fit in" and succeed. The provision of certain social benefits to the poor is viewed as a form of "social investment" that benefits the donors (taxpayers) as much as the recipients

"Trickle Down Economics"/"Keynesian Economics"

The differences between liberals and neo-conservatives stem from a conflict of visions over the role of government in economic life. The breakdown of capitalism during the Great Depression led to the search for alternatives to the laissez-faire economic model, which was generating so much hardship. Some countries chose Fascism (Italy, Germany, Japan, Spain) or state socialism (Soviet Union) to deal with the massive unemployment problem. The United States, Great Britain and Canada tried a different approach based on the ideas of the British economist John Maynard Keynes. Keynes rejected Fascism and state socialism (complete government control of the economy) because they did not promote economic efficiency nor, more importantly, did they safeguard personal liberty. Keynes preferred a modified form of capitalism where the functions of government would be enlarged to compensate in the areas where the unrestricted laissez-faire economic model had failed. In particular, he favoured

greater governmental control over savings and investment (through low interest rates and public works programs) and deficit spending, if necessary, to stimulate consumer demand and employment. In his view, this would produce the
social justice and social stability that would allow capitalism to survive the periodic crises and depressions that are a built-in feature of this economic model.
Keynes ideas dominated economic thinking from the end of World War II until
the early 1970s. They are the basis of the liberal vision whereby the collective resources of society are pooled (through the tax system) to provide certain programs that attempt to promote greater equality and fairness in society. By the
end of the 1960s there was a general societal consensus that Keynesian policies
had been responsible for the incredible rate of postwar economic growth and resulting low unemployment. It appeared possible that the age-old problems of
poverty and economic struggle between the social classes could be resolved
through redistributionist social policies.

End Of The "Liberal" Consensus
The consensus over the value of Keynesian economics began to break down after
the oil crisis in 1973. A dramatic increase in oil prices worsened inflationary
pressures already building since the mid-1960s. At the same time attempts to
curb inflation through raising interest rates did not work, leading to a deadly
combination of unemployment and inflation known as "stagflation." Starting
in 1973, government expenditures began to outstrip incoming tax revenues. In
order to make up the difference (the deficit), the Canadian government began to
borrow heavily on world money markets. The interest payments on accumulated deficits (the national debt) started to eat away at tax dollars that were
needed to finance other services, including social programs. The government
was forced to borrow even more money just to cover interest payments on the
existing debt.

Neo-Conservative Influence On Social Policy
This situation provided the neo-conservatives with an opportunity to launch a
counterattack against the Keynesians. In their view, fighting inflation now had to
be the government's highest priority rather than reducing inequality or promoting social justice. Government spending was out of control and Canadians would
be forever mired in debt if social programs were not trimmed back or eliminated.

The neo-conservatives also argued that promoting social programs was not the best way to raise the income of the poor. Rather than focusing on the problems of the poor it would be better to provide greater incentives to the rich and the middle classes. Lower taxes, the elimination of bureaucratic rules and regulations, lower pollution and occupational health and safety standards, less restrictive labour legislation, and spending cutbacks in social programs would enable the rich and the middle classes to keep more of their money. By allowing them to increase their holdings they would be encouraged to buy more and invest more leading to a burst of economic growth and productive efficiency. The benefits of this rapid growth would eventually "trickle down" to the poor allowing them to improve their standard of living without reliance on social programs.

These ideas have strongly influenced social policy since the early 1980s. However, the experience of the past twenty years suggests that the primary beneficiaries of these policies have been the rich. The gap between rich and poor has increased rather than lessened, the unemployment problem is still with us, and there is widespread insecurity among many Canadians about a crumbling standard of living and the economic future of the country.

Debates Over Social Programs

Conventional debate over what can be done about inequality in society is often highly emotional because the proposed solutions often involve the creation of social programs that require the redistribution of money from those who have more to those who have less. This is usually done through the tax system.

More affluent taxpayers may support social programs as a kind of insurance policy in the event that, for one reason or another, they find themselves in need of help. In times of widespread lay-offs and unemployment, even among previously untouchable social groups (middle managers, public sector workers, engineers, etc.), it makes sense to support programs like Medicare and employment insurance which provide a safety net in the case of some personal calamity. For example, during recent recessions in the United States some affluent people lost their employer-sponsored health insurance when they lost their jobs and could not afford the high cost of private insurance while trying to get another job. They looked enviously to their counterparts in Canada who faced no such anxieties as Medicare is a publicly funded health insurance program that everyone, employed or unemployed, is entitled to by virtue of their Canadian citizenship.

More affluent groups in society can also benefit in indirect ways as a consequence of their willingness to give up more of their money in the form of taxes. For example, when poor children have access to good education they are more likely to acquire the skills and attitudes that will enable them to function and succeed in the modern labour market. By paying higher taxes now to insure this outcome, the more affluent might save later in terms of lower costs for welfare and prisons (It costs from about $60,000 to $100,000 a year to keep a person in prison). Taxes which improve the health and educational prospects for the poor are seen as an investment, rather than an onerous expense, which will pay dividends in the future in terms of fewer social problems and criminal activities.

Many middle class Canadians benefit from employment in jobs that depend on taxpayer support such as social workers, teachers, nurses, police officers, correctional officials and civil servants.

Business also benefits from the existence of social programs because the entire Canadian public, rich or poor, pays taxes to support Medicare, old age pensions, social assistance, and public education. This public subsidy of social programs reduces business costs because they might otherwise have to pay for some of these benefits themselves, as in the case of medical insurance in the United States. Another example is employment insurance where the cost of subsidizing the temporary lay-off of workers is shifted from the individual company to the general public.

The biggest beneficiaries of tax supported social programs are, of course, the poor and disabled, who would find it difficult to survive and live a decent life without some of the services that are available. However, the rich also benefit if their taxes provide them with more security from the discontent and social problems that often arise in societies where there is great inequality of wealth and little opportunity for advancement.

Riots, Rebellions And Revolutions

The inequalities that exist between rich and poor have often led to riots, rebellions and even revolutions. Paradoxically, many of these social disruptions occur when social conditions are actually improving. One way to avoid these outcomes is to "buy-off" ("co-opt" in the jargon of political scientists) the poor by directing some money to them to deal with their immediate concerns. For example, some critics of the Welfare State on the political Left argue that the real purpose of social programs such as employment insurance or welfare is to simply defuse dangerous social discontent. Affluent people are willing to pay higher taxes to support these programs if they will insure social peace. They may also be willing to pay higher taxes to try to moderate the demands of noisy and influential "special interest groups."

The Company Of Young Canadians

The children of the "baby boom" began to attend college and university in the late 1960s and early 1970s in Canada and the United States. This was a period of significant social turmoil in both countries. A powerful anti-war movement had developed among draft-aged young people in the United States in response to the increasingly unpopular Vietnam War. Much of the protest took place on college and university campuses where students were exposed to a wide variety of political groups, some espousing radical and even revolutionary viewpoints. Political demonstrations became increasingly confrontational and even violent as four students were shot dead by National Guardsman at Kent State University in Ohio. Race riots broke out in many American cities as many African Americans protested the lack of progress in dealing with the problems of the poor inner city ghettoes. There were assassinations of popular political leaders such as civil rights advocate Martin Luther King, Robert Kennedy and Malcolm X. A defiantly oppositional "counterculture" arose, comprised of students, political activists, and "hippies," which challenged the authority and legitimacy of existing institutions. Some people talked about "changing the system."

Canada was also undergoing social and political turmoil. The rise of separatist movements in Quebec threatened to explode into violence as one group, the Front de Liberation de Quebec (FLQ), inspired by Third World revolutionary movements, began using terror tactics (mail-box bombings, kidnapping, etc.) to advance the cause. Many young, idealistic students became interested in social justice issues like poverty, unemployment and racism. In response to the growing campus activism and the idealistic temper of the era the Canadian government created a number of special organizations and programs. Three of the most well known were "Opportunities for Youth"(OFY), the Local Initiatives Program (LIP), and the Company of Young Canadians (CYC). Although some taxpayers objected to these programs as a "boondoggle" (make-work projects), others believed that the programs served to channel the energy and idealism of young people into some very worthwhile community endeavours.

The strongest objections to these programs often came from critics on the Left of the political spectrum who argued that the government's real concern was that the anti-establishment attitudes of young people might lead to serious political challenges to the social order. The programs were perceived to be a classic example of the state using taxpayers' money to buy off or deflect the growing discontent of unemployed young "baby boomers" away from political "radicalism" and into more conventional community service programs. In the view of the critics, the government was "creaming off" (recruiting) the best and the brightest of the young idealists to channel their efforts into projects which did not fundamentally challenge the status quo, but instead served to reinforce it. The programs were eventually abandoned or modified as the economy improved and the political turmoil of the era abated.

Unintended Consequences Of Social Program Spending

One problem that both supporters and critics of social program spending are concerned about is the possibility that some social programs might end up benefiting the affluent more than those who really need help. For example, Medicare, and student loans and bursaries, were originally created so that lower income and poor people would have the same access to quality health care and educational opportunities as the more well to do. However, some analysts suggest that tax–supported programs like Medicare and student bursaries tend to be disproportionately utilized by the more affluent groups in the society rather than the less affluent groups. To put it simply, the people least in need of these social programs are the most likely to avail themselves of the services offered. More affluent groups seem better able to obtain information on the availability of these benefits and how to become eligible for them. They also seem better able to hide or disguise other sources of income they may have. The result of this phenomenon is that tax money that is originally targeted for more disadvantaged groups in society ends up in the pockets of those who least need it. Although higher income people pay more in taxes the money is essentially returned to them if they are more likely to take advantage of "free" health care or subsidized educational opportunities. Since statistics show that lower income people are less likely to avail themselves of these services, they may end up inadvertently subsidizing the more affluent because the poor also pay taxes, albeit at a lower rate, to help fund these programs. This was not the purpose of the programs when they were conceived (Lightman, Ernie (2003), *Social Policy in Canada*, Oxford University Press, Toronto, p.58–60).

One recent example of this phenomenon is the $5 dollar a day daycare policy which was introduced by the Parti Quebecois government in Quebec in 1997. The intent of the program was to provide quality daycare services at a low cost to reduce the financial burdens of low-income working mothers of young children. However, the demand for this service was so great that it was necessary to ration access with the result that fewer than half of the families who wanted this service could get it. In fact, by the fourth year of the program, there was a three-year waiting list for available daycare spots. That was because the estimated real cost of providing such a service was more like $40 a day. Even with the rationed access, the cost of the program to the Quebec government rose to $1.2 billion annually within four years of its implementation. This might be justified if the beneficiaries of the program were the lower income mothers who had to work to support their families.

However, a study of the $5 a day daycare program by the Montreal based Institute for Research on Social Policy discovered that poorer families, the intended beneficiaries of the subsidized day care policy, were less likely to be enrolled in the program than higher income families. Families making more than $60,000 a year are only 36% of all families in Quebec but represented more than 50% of $5-a-day daycare users. Poor families represent about 18% of the population but occupied only 9% of daycare places. The real beneficiaries of the program were two-parent families where both partners worked (*National Post*, September 2, 2003).

The Daycare Dilemma

Daycare is one of the most emotionally charged and controversial subjects of public policy debate in Canada today. In many provinces, women, who still bear the major burden of organizing childcare in most families and often pay exorbitant fees for daycare services, looked enviously when Quebec introduced a $5 dollar a day daycare program in 1997. However, by the summer of 2002, there was a province wide shortage of 60,000 spaces and irate parents were willing to do almost anything to get someone to look after their children while they worked. Reports surfaced of daycare directors who were either verbally abused or offered bribes by parents who desperately wanted a space for their children and didn't want to wait three years to get one.

In March of 2002, *Montreal Gazette* columnist, Sue Montgomery, expressed some of the ambiguity that many women felt about the issue. She wrote, "Paying five bucks a day is great, if you're lucky enough to get a spot. But at the same time I feel guilty because I know we could afford to pay more, and I know people who really need it, like single moms and parents with low incomes or on welfare aren't getting in. And then there are the wealthy parents who can afford not to work, have a full-time nanny at home, and yet still send their kids to daycare. It's as if once you offer something so cheaply, people automatically think that even though they don't need it, they might as well take advantage of it."

"Personally, I didn't see anything wrong with the old system, where we paid $25 bucks a day, and claimed it on our income tax. Low income families were actually better off under that system because they paid, with a subsidy, $4 a day and had a shot at getting a space."

According to Montgomery, "what this so-called affordable and universal system has done is re-create and allow an even healthier black market. As demand balloons, and choices disappear, anyone can care for kids in their home, ignore ratio limits, and charge whatever they want under the table, regardless of their qualifications" (*Montreal Gazette*, March 25, 2002).

Growth Of Bureaucracy And The National Debt

Some conservative critics argue that once social programs are established people develop a sense of entitlement and resent any attempt to end the programs if the circumstances demanded it. According to such critics, this problem arose in the mid-1970s as the ability to pay for social programs was undermined by repeated yearly deficits and a growing national debt. Solutions ranged from raising taxes to cutting back on social services. Some higher income earners felt that they were already paying too much in taxes and resisted attempts to raise them further. Therefore, governments were faced with the choice of financing the programs through yet more debt or cutting services.

The administration of social programs requires the creation of large bureaucracies that become entrenched and resistant to change, according to critics. They argue that that the increasing costs associated with maintaining these bureaucracies contribute to out-of-control government budgets, repeated deficits, and the "debt crisis."

The connection between social programs and the "debt crisis" has been challenged by defenders of the social safety net who argue that the amount spent on social programs has not been growing any faster than the growth of the overall economy. The Canadian government now spends roughly the same proportion of our Gross Domestic Product (GDP) on social programs as it did in the mid-1970s, when government deficits were small. While it is true that Canada's federal debt grew during the 1970's this resulted from the reduction in taxes during that decade.

The real driving force behind the "debt crisis," in the view of some economists, has been high interest rates rather than out of control spending. About 70% of debt growth can be attributed to the rising cost of interest payments in the late 1980s and early 1990s. The maintenance of high interest rates was a deliberate strategy of the Bank of Canada in its attempt to achieve a zero rate of inflation. The federal government actually collects more tax revenue than it spends – except for the money it has to pay to cover the interest payments on the national debt (Fortin, P. [1996]) "*The Great Canadian Slump,*" Presidential address to annual meeting of the Canadian Economics Association, *Canadian Journal of Economics*, 29, November, p761-787 but see also an alternative view by Richards, John [1997] "*Retooling the Welfare State: What's Right, What's Wrong, What's to be Done,* C.D Howe Institute, p149-152).

The "Globalization" Debate And Canadian Social Policies

The term "globalization" became popular in the late 1990s but it essentially describes a process with a lengthy history. Beginning in the 15th century, for example, colonialism produced worldwide trading empires that continue to the present day but in a different form. International markets fell out of favour for a short time between the first and second World War as open markets were seen by many nation states as a cause of world-wide depression and the associated widespread unemployment and poverty. This changed after World War II when many countries in the West began a concerted effort to create and strengthen ties through increased international trade and development. Agreements such the General Agreement on Tariffs and Trade (GATT) were created to determine codes of practice and rules governing fair trading practices in global commerce. Periodic negotiations at GATT took the form of "rounds." Since 1947 there were eight such "rounds," the last being the "Uruguay Round" from 1986-1994. Issues raised in these negotiations included rules concerning foreign investment, the extent to which "developed countries" should subsidize their domestic farmers and agricultural exports, and the relative willingness of more prosperous countries to "open up" their markets to goods and services from the "Third World." In 1994, the GATT was dissolved and became the World Trade Organization (WTO). The WTO is comprised of 141 member countries (as of 2001) with representatives from each country part of a general Council that meets annually. They help resolve disputes among member countries and can enforce their decisions by imposing penalties if necessary. The organization is also responsible for implementing and administering multilateral trade agreements, and regularly reviewing the trading policies of member nations.

The driving force of "globalization," as an *ideological* concept, is the belief that the removal of international trading barriers, the deregulation of national markets, and the elimination of government and labour market restrictions will result in greater growth and prosperity that will eventually benefit everyone affected. It is essentially an outgrowth of the thinking of a famous Scottish political economist named Adam Smith. Lowering or eliminating protectionist barriers will stimulate the free movement of capital and encourage companies to set up production facilities around the world. Vigourous, unrestricted trade will promote more choice for consumers at lower prices. Globalization will provide more information exchange, promote a greater understanding of different cultures, and allow democracy to triumph over autocracy. Such outcomes will be increasingly facilitated by the rise of the Internet and the latest advances in telecommunications.

For many consumers in western societies, and the businesses that have prospered, "globalization" is largely viewed positively as they have been the primary beneficiaries of rising living standards, greater consumer choice, and international trade and travel. They are the "winners."

Rhetoric Or Reality

However, critics of this process argue that "globalization" is just another euphemism for neo-colonialism as the rich countries of the "North" realize gains at the expense of developing countries and the income gap between the "haves" and the "have-nots" continues to widen. For example, in 1964, the leaders of many "Third World" countries felt that GATT served mainly to protect the trading advantages of the "Developed countries" of the North and so set up another forum for negotiation called the United Nations Conference On Trade and Development (UNCTAD).

Contemporary anti-globalization critics of both GATT and its successor the WTO see these organizations and their agenda of "liberalized trade" as a cover for the dismantling of trade unions, environmental standards, social services, or any type of protection for domestic industry or agricultural production. Any or all of these types of protections are seen as barriers to "free" and "open" trade in the rhetoric of the WTO.

Many people within the more prosperous countries also feel threatened and less secure in the workplace as deregulation allows companies to shift their production lines to low-wage countries. Multinational corporations are seen as having more power than democratically elected governments, putting shareholder interests above the interests of communities or even entire countries.

Environmentalists are concerned that the drive for marketplace supremacy will force national governments to lower water and air quality standards, and permit the exploitation of increasingly scarce natural resources. Critics' fear that entire national cultures and identities will be undermined as giant, international media conglomerates promote a consumption-oriented lifestyle driven by the profit concerns of the multinational corporations.

Rise Of A Worldwide Anti-Globalization Movement

As a result of these concerns a worldwide anti-globalization movement has arisen which has been spurred, rather ironically, by the ability of the Internet to provide communication and debate on these issues simultaneously across continents and countries. For example, a broad coalition of labour groups, environmentalists, anti-poverty activists, farmers, women's groups and indigenous people's came together to protest some of the activities of the WTO in Seattle, Washington, in 1999. The size and the impact of this demonstration, and subsequent ones (Quebec City, and Genoa), attracted a great deal of media attention but less publicized events had occurred previously. For example, in 1998, a grassroots campaign by the same coalition had succeeded in blocking a Multilateral Agreement on Investment (MAI) which would have set strongly enforced global rules limiting government's right and ability to regulate foreign investors and corporations.

At the core of the resistance is a demand for more transparency in the decision-making processes of transnational corporations and an open debate about the effects of such decisions on social inequality, social programs, human rights, and the natural environment. The positive aspects of this coordinated international activism has been an unprecedented increase in public awareness and discussion of human and civil rights issues, economic and social policy issues, and environmental concerns, which transcends mere national boundaries in a way that would not have been possible a generation before. This is one of the most hopeful byproducts of "globalization."

GLOSSARY

Affirmative Action Attempts by government or industry to introduce policies to overcome or compensate for past discrimination against particular ethnic or social groups. It can take the form of preferential hiring of certain historically disadvantaged groups in employment situations or lowered standards of admission to educational institutions in an attempt to provide greater access and representation for some groups.

Assimilation The process by which minority or marginalized groups in a society begin to lose or abandon their own cultural practices over time and come to adopt the behaviours and cultural practices of the dominant groups.

Asylum Shopping A term used by critics of Canada's refugee policies to describe a practice whereby allegedly "bogus" refugee claimants move around looking for the country that offers them the easiest entry and the best social benefits.

Band Councils The only elected political representatives of the Indian Population on reserves in Canada recognized by the federal government under the *Indian Act*.

Bill 22 Legislation passed in the province of Quebec in 1974 that regulated the education of children whose native tongue was not English. The idea was to get the children of new immigrants to attend French schools. Up until that time most immigrant parents had preferred to enroll their children in English speaking schools raising fears about the long-term survival of the French language in Quebec.

Bill C-31 An amendment to the federal *Indian Act* in 1985 that permitted women who had relinquished their "Indian status" by marrying a non-Indian to regain it if they applied. Because of this amendment some 76,000 women who had lost their status through marriage to a non-Indian were re-instated, resulting in 100,000 people being added to the registered Indian population of Canada.

Boat People An ethnic minority (Chinese) in Vietnam who were persecuted after the Communists came to power in 1975 and fled the country by boat to refugee camps in surrounding countries. Canada took in about 60,000 refugees from such camps in the late 1970s. In the years since they have become the model for successful refugee integration into Canadian society.

Caste System A hierarchical social structure in which status and occupation are fixed on a hereditary basis, thereby severely limiting social mobility. Marriage between members of different castes is discouraged or forbidden. It is a social structure most often associated with the Hindu community of India.

Chinese Exclusion Act (*Chinese Immigration Act*) A piece of legislation that prohibited any Chinese immigration to Canada from 1923 to 1947, when the Act was repealed.

Civil Disobedience The deliberate refusal on the part of individuals or groups to comply with certain laws or regulations as a form of political protest.

Continuous Journey Stipulation A piece of legislation passed in 1908 (federal legislation 1910) which excluded South Asians from immigrating to Canada by denying them entry to Canada unless they had made an uninterrupted journey to Canada with through-tickets purchased in their home country. The only company (Canadian Pacific) that offered such tickets was ordered by the Canadian government not to sell them for boat passage between India and Canada, thus serving the purpose of excluding South Asians without explicitly discriminating against them.

Cullen-Couture Agreement An agreement between the Canadian federal government and the province of Quebec that grants Quebec certain powers with regards to the selection of immigrants to the province.

Cultural Relativism The idea that the practices of different cultures have to be judged or evaluated on their own terms and not by the standards or values of the culture one happens to belong to.

Donaldson Decision In 1975, the Supreme Court of the United States ruled that it was unconstitutional to commit an individual (to a psychiatric institution) involuntarily who is not (imminently) dangerous to himself or others.

Employment Equity A Canadian approach to affirmative action whereby certain designated groups (Aboriginals, women, visible minorities, and handicapped persons) that are underrepresented in employment situations will be given preference when they apply for jobs, provided that they have the same qualifications as people from non-designated groups. Employment equity principles are incorporated in Canadian legislation such as the *Employment Equity Act of 1986*.

Eugenics   A pseudo-science, popular at the beginning of the 20th Century, which aimed to improve the human species by "selective breeding" or controlled reproduction to eliminate traits that were deemed to be undesirable. At its worst eugenics led to the genocidal, race based policies of Adolf Hitler who used the theory to justify the elimination of Gypsies, Jews, homosexuals, and the mentally and physically handicapped in Germany during the 1930s.

Family Class   An immigration category which enables relatives of Canadian citizens or landed immigrant to gain admission to Canada without having to accumulate points for specific job skills or educational and language requirements.

Front de Liberation de Quebec (FLQ)   A revolutionary group dedicated to gaining independence for Quebec by violent means if necessary. Left-wing anti-colonial movements in the Third World inspired the group. Throughout the 1960s the FLQ carried out dozens of mailbox bombings and other terror activities culminating with the kidnapping in 1970 of British Trade Commissioner James Cross and Quebec Labour Minister Pierre Laporte. This incident became known as the October Crisis.

Genotype   The genetic constitution of an individual organism that essentially determines its potential development. However, potential development can be affected by factors such as diet, environment, exposure to drugs or toxins, and social factors such as parenting or child rearing practices.

Gentlemen's Agreement   An agreement between the government of Canada and the government of Japan in 1907 to limit the number of Japanese immigrants to Canada to no more than 400 persons a year. The policy reflected the virulent anti-Asian sentiment that existed in Canada at the time.

Horizontal Mobility   The term refers to a movement from one type of job to another of equal status.

Hyphenated Canadianism   A term used to describe Canadians who continue to be identified by their ethnic origins such as Chinese-Canadians or Indo-Canadians. Critics believe it serves to "ghettoize" certain groups as second-class Canadians. Others see it as a way to celebrate the diverse ethnic origins of Canadians, which in no way detracts from their common identity as Canadians.

Identity Politics   An approach to political analysis and action that focuses on the concerns of social groups, identified primarily on the basis of ethnicity, gender and sexual orientation. For example, the early 1970s saw the rise of the

"Women's Liberation Movement," the "Black Power" movement, the "Red Power" movement and the "Gay Power" movement. The purpose was to draw attention to, and recognition of, the historic victimization of people like themselves and organize, as a group, to ensure that such victimization would not continue.

Immigration Act 1910   Legislation that contained an implicit "colour bar" based on an immigrant's country of origin, which had the effect of limiting non-white immigration to Canada.

Immigration Act 1962   Restrictions on immigration based on race, religion, or country of origin are removed.

Immigration Act 1967   The "point system" is established in an attempt to provide more "objective" criteria for entry to Canada. Immigrants can gain admission based on the accumulation of points for education and training, occupational demand, and ability to speak either of the two official languages, etc.

Immigration Act 1976   Revisions to the *Immigration Act* contain a formal commitment to the elimination of racial discrimination in immigration policy. Four basic categories for landed immigrant status are created: Independent class, family class, humanitarian class (refugees), and assisted relative class. The creation of the humanitarian class for the first time recognizes a separate selection and admission process for refugees.

Independent Category   Immigrants can gain admission to Canada based on the accumulation of "points" for education, age, occupational skills, and ability to speak the official languages of the country.

Indian Act   A piece of legislation enacted in 1876 by the Canadian government to assimilate the indigenous population of Canada by banning traditional cultural ceremonies and practices and by undermining traditional methods of self-governance.

Intergenerational Mobility   A term that refers to a change of economic or social status between parents and their children.

Internment   The forced detention of 26,000 Canadians of Japanese origin during World War II in camps in the interior of British Columbia. Internment was also used to forcibly detain Canadians of Italian and German origin in camps in Ontario and Quebec. Since Canada was at war with their countries of origin, government viewed the people detained as possible enemy sympathizers.

Intragenerational Mobility   The term refers to a change in economic or so-cial position that a person experiences within his or her own lifetime.

Just Sanction   An attempt to deal with the high rate of aboriginal imprison-ment in Canada by amending the sentencing provisions of the *Criminal Code of Canada* in 1996. According to *Section 718.2 (e)*, *Criminal Code of Canada*, "all available sanctions other than imprisonment that are reasonable in the circum-stances should be considered for offenders, with particular attention to the cir-cumstances of aboriginal offenders. There are six objectives, according to the amendment, one or more which must be part of a "just sanction": denuncia-tion, deterrence, separation (incarceration of offenders), rehabilitation, repara-tion, promotion of responsibility and the acknowledgement of harm.

Komagatu Maru   The name of a ship carrying South Asians attempting to get around the restrictive immigration requirements of the *Continuous Journey Stipulation*. The ship's passengers were never allowed to disembark on Cana-dian shores and eventually had to return to India.

Laissez-faire Capitalism   A type of economic arrangement based on the idea that the government should not interfere or intervene in the workings of busi-ness and the market through social policy or excessive regulatory legislation.

"Means Tested" Social Programs   Social programs where only those who lack adequate "means" (income, property, etc.) are eligible to receive benefits. In order to receive such benefits the recipients must prove they are "poor enough" to qualify. Many social programs in the United States such as "Medicaid"(basic medical services for low-income Americans) are "means tested.

Miscegenation   A term (no longer widely used) that refers to inter-ethnic mixing.

Multiculturalism   The idea that cultural differences in a society should be ac-knowledged and even celebrated. The Canadian *Multiculturalism Act* was pro-claimed in 1988, making Canada the first nation to establish multiculturalism as a national policy. *Section 27* of the Canadian *Charter of Rights and Freedoms* explicitly acknowledges the need to recognize and protect the multicultural character of Canadian society.

Natural Selection   An evolutionary process whereby organisms better adapted to their environment are more likely to survive and pass on their genes to the next generation. The theory is associated with the British Naturalist, Charles Darwin.

October Crisis An event precipitated by the kidnapping of British trade commissioner James Cross and Quebec Labour Minister Pierre Laporte in October of 1970. The federal government, led by Prime Minister Pierre Elliot Trudeau, responded to the kidnappings by invoking the *War Measures Act*, which suspended the civil liberties of several hundred Quebecois who were detained by the police on the suspicion that they were sympathizers with the Front de Liberation de Quebec (FLQ). The Canadian army was deployed on the streets of Montreal because of the fear of an "apprehended insurrection." This angered many moderate French Canadian nationalists who felt the federal government was overreacting to the threat and was using the crisis to undermine the independence movement. At the same time, the death of Pierre Laporte, while trying to escape his FLQ captors, caused widespread revulsion among Quebecois of all political sympathies and led to the rapid demise of the FLQ and its violent tactics.

Pogroms Massacres of the Jewish population in Russia who were made scapegoats by authorities for economic hardships the country was experiencing. Many Russian and European Jews fled to Canada to escape such persecution in the latter part of the Nineteenth Century.

Point System Immigrants to Canada under the Independent Category are admitted if they can accumulate a certain number of points based upon their age, educational and occupational skills, personal suitability, and ability to speak one or both of Canada's official languages.

Quebec Act of 1774 A piece of legislation that reversed the *Royal Proclamation of 1763* by restoring the power of the Roman Catholic Church and the Seigneurs (the land-owning class in Quebec society), including their participation in the political governance of the province. A legal system consisting of a mixture of French civil law and English criminal law was also instituted, which continues right to the present day.

Quiet Revolution The terms refers to policy changes instituted by the Liberal government of Jean Lesage in Quebec in the early 1960s in an attempt to bring about the modernization of Quebec society through reforms to the educational system and the civil service.

Quotas The term refers to the setting of a fixed number for members of certain social or ethnic groups when it comes to university admissions policies or hiring policies. Quotas may be used both proactively to overcome the historic disadvantages of particular groups and reactively to deny certain groups' access to desirable positions. The use of quotas is highly controversial. In the case of affirmative action programs, for example, proponents view the use of quotas positively as a necessary measure to increase the representation of underrepresented groups. However, opponents of such quotas argue that it is a form of "reverse discrimination" if qualified candidates are denied access to desired positions. The employment equity programs in Canada attempt to get around this problem by insisting that groups designated for employment preference must have similar qualifications to non-designated groups.

Racism The idea that "races" differ in the possession of certain important abilities and social traits, and thus justifies the ranking of people as inferior or superior with some entitled to special rights and privileges that are denied to others.

Racial Profiling The Ontario Human Rights Commission defines "racial profiling as any action undertaken for reasons of safety, security or public protection, that relies on stereotypes about race, ethnicity, ancestry, religion, or place of origin, or a combination of these, rather than on reasonable suspicion, to single out an individual for greater scrutiny or treatment."

Rattrapage It refers to a desire by trade union leaders and intellectual leaders in Quebec in the early 1950s to "catch up" with the rest of North America and become a modern secular society rather than the traditional, church dominated one that existed at the time.

Registered Indian A category of aboriginal persons recognized under the federal *Indian Act* by a status or treaty number They are entitled to certain rights and health and educational benefits associated with this status as well as exemption from federal taxes on income earned on a reserve.

Relative Poverty A measure of the inequality which exists between high income and lower income people in Canada. It refers to individuals and families in Canada who have to spend significantly more of their income on the basic necessities of food, clothing and shelter than do others in the society.

Reproductive Isolation Through migration, some human populations can become isolated from others for long periods of time. Genetic mutations may occur in an isolated group that do not occur in another group, which accounts for some of the differences that exist in human populations.

Residential Schools Institutions run by Christian clergy in Canada in a failed attempt to assimilate young aboriginal children to the dominant white culture.

Restorative Justice An attempt to break repeated cycles of imprisonment for aboriginal offenders in Canada through alternative sentencing procedures, which commit offenders to make amends for their actions by community work or some other form of extended public service.

Restrictionists Critics of Canadian immigration policy who would like to restrict or limit the entry of new immigrants to Canada.

Restrictive Covenants Discriminatory practices directed against ethnic and racial minorities who were prohibited from living, or owning property, or renting apartments in certain residential areas of Canada until the middle of the Twentieth Century.

Revenge of the Cradle The attempt by French Canadians in Quebec to resist assimilation by maintaining a very high birth rate.

Safe Country Provision A provision in the *Immigration Act* that would prevent refugee claimants from making a claim in Canada if they arrived from a "safe country," which meant a country that was democratic, respected human rights and the rule of law, and a signatory to international conventions (*Geneva Convention*, 1951) on the fair treatment of refugee claimants. It was a provision that proved difficult to implement because some countries deemed "safe" had friendly relations with countries whose governments had bad human rights records. As a result, they would not recognize the refugee claims of people fleeing from such countries whereas Canada might recognize that the claims were legitimate.

Scapegoat Singling out a particular individual or group and blaming them for all the misfortunes a society is experiencing. It is often used to direct criticism and blame away from the failed economic, social and political policies of dominant individuals and groups and toward more vulnerable or marginalized individuals or groups.

Seditious Libel Making false statements to incite rebellion against the authority of the state.

Self-fulfilling Prophecy A process whereby an individual or social group accepts a label or stereotype applied to them by dominant individuals or groups and come to act or behave in a manner that tends to support or confirms the original label or stereotype. For example, a teacher has labeled a certain student as being "dumb." The student accepts this as being true and doesn't bother to study anymore. If the student's grades fall, it serves to confirm the teacher's definition of the situation even though it may be incorrect. The same process can occur when applied to particular social or ethnic groups leading to statistics that appear to support existing stereotypes.

Sexual Selection   The idea that some differences that exist among certain identifiable groups in human populations can be attributed to varying "beauty standards" which, depending upon social and cultural influences, determine the desirability of prospective mates. People with the desired traits are more likely to attract partners, have children, and pass on the same "desirable" genetic traits to succeeding generations.

Singh Decision   A decision by the Supreme Court of Canada, which granted all refugee applicants on Canadian soil the right to a full oral hearing by the Immigration and Refugee Appeal Board before they could be removed from the country. While waiting for their hearing, refugee applicants are entitled to the same legal and social protections accorded to Canadian citizens under the *Charter of Rights and Freedoms*, except the right to vote.

Snakeheads   Organized crime groups located in the Fujian province of China who charge Asian migrants exorbitant amounts of money to smuggle them into North America.

Social Darwinism   An ideology, popular at the beginning of the 20th Century, which attempted to justify the inequalities between rich and poor, and between peoples of different colour, based on the idea that the differences were the result of evolutionary processes.

Social Mobility   A term used to describe a change in status or occupation.

Sponsorship Breakdown   Refers to the inability of a person to live up to a sponsorship agreement with the federal government that requires them to financially support a relative they have sponsored to immigrate to Canada for a period of three to ten years. The result being that one or both of the parties to the agreement requires social assistance.

Structural Mobility   The term refers to changes in the nature of the labour market that open up new opportunities for social mobility that didn't exist before. For example, the development of computer technology has revolutionized the job market over the past thirty years.

Structural Poverty The idea that poverty is a consequence of the structure of the labour market in a capitalist society, which can never produce enough well-paying jobs for everyone who want one.

Survivance A strategy developed by right-wing nationalists in Quebec which urged French Canadians to resist assimilation by remaining devoutly loyal to the Roman Catholic Church, having large families, staying close to the land, and avoiding the greed and materialism of the Anglo-dominated business world.

Survival of the Fittest A belief, popular at the beginning of the 20th Century and associated with Social Darwinism, that any attempts to help the poor or reduce inequalities between men and women, or between peoples of different colour, would weaken or undermine the ability of the human species to survive. The effect was to justify the inequality that existed.

Three Wise Men A label applied to three Quebec reformers, Pierre Trudeau, Gerard Pelletier, and Jean Marchand, who challenged what they perceived as the retrograde right-wing nationalism of Maurice Duplessis in Quebec in the 1940s and 1950s.

Underground Railroad A network of "safe houses" organized by opponents of slavery in the United States and Canada to help black refugees escape to Canada before the American Civil War.

United Empire Loyalists Americans who wished to remain loyal to the British crown during and after the American Revolution. Many of them fled to Canada and settled in Ontario, Southern Quebec, and Nova Scotia.

Universal Social Programs Social programs like old age pensions or Medicare to which everyone in Canada has access to regardless of income or social status.

Visible Minorities This term is applied to any group that is distinguishable by its skin colour in a predominantly white society. It may result in a vulnerability to prejudicial attitudes or discriminatory practices.

Voyage of the Damned An incident involving Jews attempting to escape the Nazi regime in Germany just before World War II. Nine hundred desperate people who made their way to North America by boat, the *St. Louis*, were denied entry as refugees by the Cuban, American, and Canadian government and were forced to return to Europe, many finally ending up in concentration camps. The incident revealed the pervasive anti-Semitism that existed in North America at that time.

War Measures Act Legislation enacted by the Canadian federal government on August 22, 1914, which gave the government the right to bypass the normal legislative process, suspend habeas corpus, and deport without trial. In both World War I and II, this legislation permitted the internment of Canadians deemed to be "enemy aliens" or potential threats to the war effort. During World War II, the legislation was used to intern Canadians of Japanese, German and Italian origins. It was also used in 1970 during the October crisis in Quebec when 453 suspected FLQ sympathizers were rounded up and detained without a hearing for several days. Only 20 were convicted of any charge. The rest were political activists who favoured political change through the electoral process. The *War Measures Act* was repealed in 1985 and replaced by the *Emergencies Act*, which subjects any governmental decision to parliamentary review. Any temporary laws enacted are also subjected to the *Charter of Rights and Freedoms*.

Welfare Poor The term refers to people who live below the Statistics Canada Low-Income Cut-off Lines (LICO) and derive most of their income from social assistance.

Woodwork Effect The idea that the provision of "free" social services, health services, food or other items will encourage more people to "come out of the woodwork" and take advantage of these services.

Working Poor People who live below the Statistics Canada Low-income Cut-off Lines (LICO) and derive most of their income from work.

Yellow Peril A term used to describe the fear of the white, Canadian-born population at the end of the Nineteenth Century that the willingness of Chinese and other Asian immigrants to work long hours for low wages would undermine their standard of living. It also can refer to the alleged threat of subversion of the war effort by Canadians of Japanese origins during World War II.

RESOURCE GUIDE

Chapter One: The Human Rights Revolution in Canada

Chapter Objectives: After completing this chapter you should be able to:

- Describe the nature and extent of human rights violations in Canada at the beginning of the 20th Century.
- Outline the social factors and legislative changes that promoted the advancement of human rights in Canada.
- Debate some of the controversies surrounding the application of the Canadian *Bill of Rights* and the Canadian *Charter of Rights and Freedom*.

Study Questions

- How did the courts justify the refusal of services and accommodations to black persons in Canada at the beginning of the 20th Century?
- Women were denied the right to run for or hold public office at the beginning of the 20th Century. Why?
- What factors promoted the change in attitudes towards human rights during and after World War II?
- Why was the effectiveness of the Canadian *Bill of Rights* limited?
- The development of provincial human rights codes and the establishment of human rights commissions added "teeth" to human rights legislation. Explain.
- Why did the Canadian *Charter of Rights and Freedoms* prove to be more effective than the older Canadian *Bill of Rights*?
- How did the Supreme Court justices determine that sexual harassment was a violation of the equality provisions of the *Charter* when there was no specific mention of it in the document?
- Explain why freedom of expression is one of the most important yet controversial guarantees in the *Charter of Rights and Freedoms*. Give examples. What is the connection between the creation of the *Charter* and several important cases involving freedom of religious expression in Quebec?
- Many people believe that the *Charter* is the crowning achievement of the human rights revolution in Canada? Others believe it gives to much power to "special interest" groups and even undermines democracy. Explain.

Recommended Reading:

Morton, F.L and Ranier Knopff. (1999) *The Charter Revolution and the Court Party*. Broadview Press, Peterborough, Canada.

Mandel, Michael. (1994) *The Charter of Rights and the Legalization of Politics in Canada*, Thompson Educational Publishing, Toronto, Canada.

Suggested Websites:

www.canlii.org/ Canadian Legal Information Institute provides all decisions rendered by the Supreme Court since 1985 and a wide range of federal and provincial. statutes and regulations, constitutional documents and much more.

www.llrx.com/features/canadian3.htm This site provides an overview of sources of Canadian law on the web.

Chapter Two: Perspectives on Human Diversity

Chapter Objectives: After completing this chapter you should be able to:

- Discuss the origins of the "race" concept and its effects on social structure and public policy from the 19th century to the present time.

- Identify the problems associated with trying to fit the human species into distinct categories called "races."

- Compare biological, anthropological, and sociological explanations for differences that exist among human populations.

Study Questions:

- Why were the ideas associated with the eugenics movement so popular at the beginning of the 20th century? Why did they fall into such disrepute at the end of World War II?

- How were naturalist Charles Darwin's ideas on "natural selection" in the plant and animal kingdom misrepresented to justify the existence of social classes and social differentiation in society?

- Why is it difficult to assign people to a specific and clear-cut category called race? Give examples.

- What biological and social factors account for the differences that exist in human populations? Give examples. How do environmental factors shape the appearance of populations in different regions of the world?

- Compare biological and sociological explanations that attempt to account for the differences in cognitive performance in human populations.

- Why do some forensic anthropologists continue to find the "race" concept useful in their line of work? What development would cause them to abandon this approach?

Suggested Videos:

(2003) *The Power of an Illusion*—excellent three-part documentary about race in society—produced and written by Jean Cheng, Creator/Executive Producer Larry Adelman, Ford Foundation. For ordering information: www.newsreel.org or 1-877-811-7495 or 1-802-846-1850.

Episode #1 *The Difference Between Us*—examines the contemporary science, including genetics—that challenges our common sense assumptions that human beings can be bundled into 3 or 4 fundamentally different groups according to their physical traits: 56 minutes.

Episode #2 *The Story We Tell*—uncovers the roots of the race concept in North America, the 19th century science that legitimated it, and how it came to be held so fiercely in the Western imagination. Shows how race served to rationalize, even justify, social inequalities as natural: 56 minutes.

Episode #3 *The House We Live In*— asks if race is not biology, what is it. This episode uncovers how race resides not in nature but in politics, economics and culture: 56 minutes.

(1999) Skin Deep (Quantum)—Discussion of the Human Genome Diversity Project—includes y chromosone data that compliments the nt. DNA data in supporting a recent African origin for our species, deals with blood groups, etc., debate for and against the human genome project.

(1998) *Skin Deep: The Science of Race*—Canadian Broadcasting Corporation—The Nature of Things with Dr. David Suzuki: 50 minutes—discussion of a wide range of issues including the "Out of Africa" hypothesis, natural selection, history of race "categories," and several current debates. The program can be shown in its entirely or broken up in parts to deal with specific topics. Students always find this video interesting and informative.

(1987) *Evolution and Human Equality* MA: Insight Video with Steven Jay Gould: 42 minutes—a discussion of the early evolution of man, human variation, the eugenics movement, and the idea that variation within groups is greater than variation between groups. A "talking head" video but the late Steven Jay Gould always brought humour and great insight to any topic he tackled.

Suggested Websites:

www.racesci.org/links—links to a wide range of sites dealing with human diversity.

www.diversityhotwire.com/diversity_resources.html—wide range of good links.

www.genome.gov/—National Human Genome Research Institute—latest research.

Recommended Reading:

Marks Jonathan. (1995) *Human Diversity: Genes, Race, and History*, New York, Aldine de Gruyter.

Chapter Three: From "White Canada" to the Multicultural Mosaic

Chapter Objectives: After completing this chapter you should be able to:

- Describe how the needs of the labour market influenced Canadian immigration history.
- Outline the role different ethnic groups have played in the development of Canadian society and the obstacles they faced when they first arrived.
- Describe how changes to immigration policy have changed the ethno-cultural composition of Canadian society.

Study questions:

- Why did the Canadian government introduce legislation to restrict Chinese immigration to Canada in 1885?
- How were immigrants from India indirectly restricted from settling in Canada in the early 1900s?
- How did anti-Semitism affect Canadian immigration policy until the end of World War II?
- How was the *War Measures Act* used against Canadians of Japanese origin during World War II?
- How did revisions to the *Immigration Act* of 1962, 1967, and 1976-78, change the nature of Canadian immigration policy?

Suggested Video:

A Scattering of Seeds: The Creation of Canada—a 52 part television series celebrating the contribution of immigrants to Canada—info@whitepinepictures.ca.

Suggested Websites:

www.cin.org/themes/immigration.html—immigration history and themes.

www.cic.ca—Canadian Department of Immigration.

Recommended Reading:

Knowles, Valerie. (1997) *Strangers at Our Gates: Canadian Immigration and Immigration Policy*, 1540-1997, Revised Edition, Toronto, Dundurn Press.

Avery, Donald H. (1995) *Reluctant Host: Canada's Response to Immigrant Workers*, 1896–1994, Toronto, McClelland and Stewart.

Chapter Four: Immigration Debates

Chapter Objectives: After completing this chapter, you should be able to:

- Discuss the problems associated with attempts to reform the refugee determination process.
- Identify differences in the admission criteria for refugees, family class and independent immigrants.
- Compare opposing viewpoints on the issue of immigration.

Study Questions:

- What was the purpose of the "Safe Country" provision? Why were some people so opposed to this provision?
- How did the "Singh Decision" affect the behaviour of "asylum seekers" and the refugee determination process?
- What arguments do those favouring an "open door" immigration policy and those opposed to such a policy use?
- Some people view immigration debates as a "hot potato" or potential "minefield." Explain.

Suggested Videos:

(2002) *"The Undefended Border"* by Peter Raymont and Lindalee Tracey, White Pine Pictures—info@whitepinepictures.ca—An examination of immigration policing and enforcement policy in Canada post 9/11. This fast-paced documentary shows how immigration officers and police are reacting to increased political pressures to toughen border entry requirements and deal with illegal immigrants already in Canada.

(2001) *"Dying to Get In"*—parts 1 and 2—Directed by Robin Benger for "Witness," Canadian Broadcasting Corporation, narrated by Ann Medina. This two-part documentary provides a forum for advocates of both the "open door" and "restrictionist" positions on Canadian immigration and refugee policies.

(1991)" *Who Gets In?"*—National Film Board of Canada—narrated by Ann Medina. A documentary dealing with the controversies surrounding the criteria for admission to Canada either as a landed immigrant or refugee, the "cash for visa" controversy, and the importation of women from the Philippines to work as nannies, under the domestic worker category.

Suggested Websites:

www.marcopolis.org/newcomers—immigration research and updates.

www.cic.ca—Immigration Canada website.

www.web.net/~ccr/state.html—Canadian Council For Refugees website.

Recommended Reading:

Li, Peter S. (2003) *Destination Canada: Immigration Debates and Issues*, Toronto, Oxford University Press.

Stoffman, Daniel. (2002) *Who Gets In: What's wrong with Canada's immigration program—and how to fix it*, Toronto, Macfarlane Walter &Ross.

Borjas George. (1999) *Heaven's Door: Immigration Policy and the American Economy*, New Jersey, Princeton University Press.

Chapter Five: The Challenge of Diversity

Chapter Objectives: After completing this chapter you should be able to:

- Identify conflicts and controversies arising from the changing ethnic make-up of Canadian society.

- Outline the strengths and weaknesses of multiculturalism, employment equity, and other government policies designed to respond to an increasingly diverse Canadian population.

Study questions:

- How does the issue of "racial profiling" illustrate the problem of the "self-fulfilling prophecy?"

- Why is the issue of "identity" so important in debates over multiculturalism?

- Why is multiculturalism less popular with many French Canadians, and the aboriginal population?

- What are the legal mechanisms that exist to protect society against racism and discrimination?

- Why are census questions about ethnicity and race the source of controversy?

Suggested Video:

(1994) *Hearts of Hate: The Battle for Young Minds*. This documentary deals with the rise of hate groups in the 1990s and the role of the media.

Info@whitepinepictures.com—Winner, Gold Apple Award, National Educational Media Competition, 1995—Tel: 1-416-703-5580: Address: White Pine Pictures, 822 Richmond Street West, Suite 200, Toronto, Ontario, M6J 1C9.

Suggested Websites:

www.crr.ca—Canada Race Relations Foundation.

www.diversitywatch.ryerson.ca/—good source of information on diversity issues.

www.hrdc-drhc.gc.ca/common/home.shtml—Human Resources Canada.

Further information on employment equity in Canada can be found here.

Recommended Reading:

Elliott, Jean Leonard, Fleras, Augie. (2003) *Unequal Relations: An Introduction to Race and Ethnic Dynamics in Canada*, Toronto, Prentice Hall.

Chapter Six: Cultures in Conflict: The Hijab and Kirpan Controversies

Chapter Objectives: After completing this chapter, you should be able to:

- Explain how changes in religious affiliations in Canada are related to recent immigration patterns.

- Describe the origins and key components of the four fastest growing religious affiliations in Canada

- Discuss the issues that have arisen and the challenges posed as a consequence of the growing religious diversity in Canadian society.

Study Questions:

- How does the increasing religious diversity of Canada relate to changes in immigration policy in the 1960s?

- How have events in the Middle East shaped popular perceptions about the nature of the Islamic faith? Give an example.

- Why does the wearing of the "Hijab" (head scarf) signify "liberation" for some Muslim women? Give an example.

- Does the issue of "female circumcision" pose a challenge to aspects of Canada's commitment to multiculturalism?

- How do controversies involving the Sikh community in Canada reflect the tensions between religious and cultural traditions and the secular nature of much of contemporary Canadian society? Give examples.

- How do social and political problems in their country of origin continue to plague many new immigrants once they have arrived in Canada? Give examples.

- Why are many immigrant women reluctant to report incidents of domestic abuse?

Suggested Videos:

(1999) *Religions of the World*, Schlessinger Media, narrated by academy award winner Ben Kingsley—Thirteen: 50-minute videos explore world cultures and history through the examination of religion. An in-depth look at the role played by religion in creating cultural diversity. A teacher's guide accompanies all titles. For more information call 800-843-3620.

(1999) *Under One Sky: Arab Women in North America Talk About the Hijab*, directed by Jennifer Kawaja, National Film Board of Canada, Montreal, 43 min, 30sec. Highly recommended.

(1998) *Hijab: An Act of Faith*, directed by Jawad Jafry, Soundvision, 60 min. Canadian women discuss the pros and cons of wearing the hijab.

(1998) *Some Kind of Arrangement*, directed by Ali Kazimi, Canadian Broadcasting Corporation and National Film Board of Canada, 43 min. 45 sec. Three women discuss the issue of arranged marriages. For more information and educational sales call 416-516-9775.

Suggested Website:

www.bbc.co.uk/worldservice/people/features/world_religions/index.shtml—short summaries of the attributes of major religious faiths.

Recommended Reading:

Demerath N.J. (2001) *Crossing the Gods: World Religions and World Politics*, New Jersey, Rutgers University Press. Examines the strained and often violent role that religion plays in some fourteen countries around the world from a sociological perspective.

Chapter Seven: Canada's Aboriginal Population

Chapter Objectives: After completing this chapter you should be able to:

- Identify differences among aboriginal groups in Canada in terms of their origins, cultures, demographic, and legal status.
- Understand the effects, both intended and real, of government policy towards the aboriginal population since Confederation.
- Describe how current policy has evolved to correct the injustices of the past and meet the challenges of the future.

Study Questions:

- What is the significance of the Band Councils, residential schools and reserves in relationship to the *Indian Act* of 1876?

- How was gender based discrimination used as a technique of assimilation in the *Indian Act* of 1876?
- Why do some Indian Bands oppose the *Bill C-31* amendments to the *Indian Act*?
- What techniques were used in the residential schools in an attempt to assimilate young Indian children?
- How did the residential schools affect the self-image of aboriginal children?
- Why was the aboriginal community so opposed to the "White Paper" proposals of the Liberal government of Pierre Elliot Trudeau?
- What are the arguments for and against the idea that aboriginal offenders should be treated differently by the criminal justice system in Canada?

Suggested Videos:

(2000) *First Nations, The Circle Unbroken*. Videos 5: 100 minutes, 42 seconds - 23 short programs about current issues, cultural identity, and relations between First Nations and Canada, National Film Board of Canada.

(1997) *Spudwrench—Kahnawake Man*, directed by Alanis Obomsawin, National Film Board of Canada, 57 min 50s.

(1996) *Power*, directed by Magnus Isacsson, National Film Board of Canada, 75min 31s. Conflict surrounding the James Bay hydroelectric project.

(1993) *Kanehsatake 270 Years of Resistance*, directed by Alanis Obomsawin, National Film Board of Canada, 119min 15s.

(1991) *The Learning Path*, directed by Loretta Todd, (National Film Board of Canada and Tamarack Productions), 56 min 50s. On overcoming the legacy of Residential Schools.

Suggested Websites:

www.aboriginalcanada gc.ca/—Aboriginal portal—good links to aboriginal issues.

www.ainc-inac.gc.ca/—Indian and Northern Affairs website.

www.indians.org/welker/canada.htm—links to a variety of other sites of interest.

Recommended Reading:

Miller, J.R (1991) *Skyscrapers Hide The Heavens: A History of Indian-White Relations in Canada*, revised edition, University of Toronto Press.

Chapter Eight: Ethnicity, "Race" and Crime

Chapter Objectives: After completing this chapter you should be able to:

- Discuss the factors associated with the high rate of incarceration in the United States compared to Canada, and its relationship to social and ethnic inequality.

- Contrast the American and Canadian approach to offenders in the criminal justice system.

Study Questions:

- What is the relationship between economic status and the likelihood of being imprisoned in the United States and Canada?

- What legislative changes help explain the dramatic increase in the American prison population in the past twenty-five years?

- How has the African-American population been affected by these changes?

Suggested videos:

(2002) *To Kill or to Cure*—a two-part CBC "Witness" documentary—directed by Josh Freed and Jon Kalina: 2 hrs—discusses the dramatic growth of the prison population in the United States with the implementation of "Three Strikes and You're Out" legislation. Compares the increasingly harsh treatment of offenders in the United States with approaches elsewhere, including Canada. A must see for Correctional Intervention Technology students and Police Technology students.

Suggested Websites:

www.csc-scc.gc.ca—Corrections Canada Website.

www.ojp.usdoj.gov/bjsl—Bureau of Justice Website in the United States.

Chapter Nine: Origins of English/French Conflict

Chapter Objectives: After completing this chapter you should be able to:

- Describe the social and political strategies used by Quebecois to resist assimilation.

- Outline the manner in which Quebec society made the transition from a traditional, church dominated culture to a modern, secular one.

Study Questions:

- What was Britain's motivation in passing the *Quebec Act* of 1774?

- What was the conservative or "traditional" strategy that Quebec's political elite used to resist assimilation? What factors led to the "Quiet Revolution" in Quebec?

- What events are associated with the "radical" strategy to gain independence? How did these events eventually lead to the eventual electoral success of the Parti Quebecois?

- How did the passage of *Bill 101*, the *Charter of the French Language*, fundamentally alter the nature of English/French relations in the province?

- How did failed attempts at constitutional reform lead to disillusionment in Quebec and the rise of the Bloc Quebecois?

- Describe how the evolution of language policy changed the social and political dynamics of the province.

- Despite thirty years of constitutional squabbles, Quebec remains in the Canadian federation. Why?

Suggested Videos:

(1997) *Never-endum Referendum*, National Film Board of Canada, directed by Paul Jay, 71min 03s, personal stories of lives affected by the referendum debates.

(1996) *Referendum —Take 2/Prix deux*—National Film Board of Canada—directed by Stephane Drolet, 75min 35s, events leading up to the 1995 referendum.

(1973) *Le Devoir, Part 2: 1945-1973, The Quiet Revolution*, National Film Board of Canada, directed by Hughes Poulin, Jean-V Dufresne ,26 min 50s, The Duplessis years, Jean Lesage, the rise of the Parti Quebecois and the October Crisis.

(1973) *Action: The October Crisis of 1970*, directed by Robin Spry, National Film Board of Canada, 87 min 09s.

Suggested Websites:

www.2.marianopolis.edu/quebechistory/index.htm—excellent site on Quebec history and social issues maintained by a college history professor.

www.gouv.qc.ca —Quebec provincial government website.

Recommended reading.

McRoberts, Kenneth (1993) *Quebec: Social Change and Political Crisis*, Third Edition, Toronto, McClelland and Stewart.

Chapter Ten: Economic Dimensions of Inequality in Canada

Chapter Objectives: After completing this chapter you should be able to:

- Describe the criteria by which inequality is measured in Canadian society.

- Understand the concept of social mobility and its relevance to any debate about reducing the level of inequality in Canadian society.

- Debate the controversies surrounding such issues as the definition of poverty, the "welfare trap" and Canada's high unemployment rate.

- Compare the strengths and weaknesses of the two main approaches to the issue of social inequality in the contemporary era.

- Identify the differences that exist between "liberals" and "neo-conservatives" on the issue of poverty, social programs and the role of government in dealing with social inequality.

- Debate the arguments for and against doing something about inequality through social programs.

Study Questions:

- How is social inequality measured? Explain "subjective" and "objective" measures.

- What are the strengths and weaknesses of income distribution as a measure of inequality?

- What is social mobility and why is it so important in any discussion of social inequality? Explain the types of social mobility. Why is education so important in any discussion of social mobility?

- How is poverty defined in Canada? What are the problems or controversies associated with defining poverty in this manner? What is the relationship between family structure and low income in Canada?

- Who are the "homeless?" What is the relationship between the public policy of "deinstitutionalization" and the development of this problem?

- How is unemployment measured in Canada? What are the problems associated with the way the unemployment rate is measured?

- Explain why the existence and extent of "poverty" in Canada depends on how it is defined?

- How do "liberals" and "neo-conservatives" differ as to the type of social program best suited to reduce inequality? Give an example.

- What approach did governments in Canada use from the Great Depression until the mid-1970s in dealing with social inequality? Why did this change and what ideas are associated with the changes?

- Provide four arguments for doing something to reduce social inequality through the tax system. Who might support these efforts and why?

- Why are social programs seen as a "problem" rather than a "solution" by some critics? Give an example.

Suggested Videos:

(2000) *For Man Must Work or The End of Work*, directed by Jean Claude Burger, National Film Board of Canada, 52 min 01s. The effects of technological change on the global economy, focusing on Canada, France, and Mexico.

(1995) *The Emperor's New Clothes*, directed by Magnus Isacsson, National Film Board of Canada, 53 min 05s. A provocative documentary on the effects of the North American Free Trade Agreement (NAFTA) on Canada, on the United States and on Mexico.

Suggested Websites:

www.hrdc.gc.ca/common/home.shtml—Human Resources Development Canada website provides information on employment insurance, pensions, student loans, job training, and issues of concern to children and youth, aboriginals, seniors, and persons with disabilities.

www.ccsd.ca/—The Canadian Council on Social Development is a non-profit research and advocacy organization focusing on research, commentary and statistics on social and economic inequality in Canada.

www.ncwcnbes.net/ —The National Council of Welfare (NCW) is a citizen's advisory body to the Minister of Human Resources on matters of concern to low-income Canadians.

www.policyalternatives.ca/—Canadian Center for Policy Alternatives is an independent, non-profit research organization that examines economic and social policy issues. Good source of research from the "liberal" standpoint on social and economic issues.

www.fraserinstitute.ca/—The Fraser Institute is an independent public policy organization which focuses on the role competitive markets play in providing for economic and social development. Good source of information about the "neo-conservative" standpoint on social and economic issues.

Recommended Reading:

Lightman, Ernie (2003) *Social Policy in Canada*, Toronto, Oxford University Press.

Graham, John, Karen Swift, and Roger Delaney (2000) *Canadian Social Policy: An Introduction*, Toronto, Prentice Hall.

Teeple, Gary, editor (2000) *Globalization and the Decline of Social Reform: Into the Twenty-first Century*, revised 2nd edition, Garamond Press, Aurora, Ontario.

Watson, William (1998) *Globalization and the Meaning of Canadian Life*, University of Toronto Press, Toronto, Ontario.

INDEX

Figure 4.3: "Labour Force Participation Rates for immigrants and non-immigrants (Percentage)," from the Statistics Canada publication "The changing profile of Canada's labour force, 2001 Census (Analysis series)," Catalogue 96F0030, February 2003, available at: <http://www12. statcan.ca/english/census01/products/analytic/companion/paid/canada.cfm>

Figure 5.1: "Singled Out," *Toronto Star*, October 20, 2002, online at: http://www.thestar.com>

Figure 5.2: "Who Gets Arrested," *Toronto Star*, October 20, 2002, online at: <http://www. thestar.com>

Figure 6.1: "Immigrants by major religious denominations and period of immigration, Canada, 2001," from the Statistics Canada publication "Religions in Canada, 2001 Census (Analysis series)," Catalogue 96F0030, May 2003, available at: <http://www12. Statcan.ca/english /census01/products/analytic/companion/rel/canada.cfm>

Figure 6.2: "More religions by median age, Canada, 2001 Census," from the Statistics Canada publication "Religions in Canada, 2001 Census (Analysis series)," Catalogue 96F0030, May 2003, available at: <http://www12.statcan.ca/english/census01/products/analytic /companion/rel/canada.cfm>

Figure 7.1: "Persons registered under the Indian Act, provinces and territories," from the Statistics Canada Website <http://www.statcan.ca/english/Pgdb/demo37.htm>

Figure 7.2. "Population reporting Aboriginal identity, by age groups, Canada, 1996 and 2001," from the Statistics Canada publication "Aboriginal Peoples of Canada: A Demographic Profile, 2001 Census (Analysis series)," Catalogue 96F0030, January 2003, available at: <http://www 12.statcan.ca/english/census01/products/analytic/companion/abor/canada.cfm>

Figure 10.1: "Change in average income, by income deciles, census families, Canada, 1990-2000," from the Statistics Canada publication "Income of Canadian Families, 2001 Census (Analysis series)," Catalogue 96F0030, May 2003, available at: <http://www12.statcan.ca /english/census01/products/analytic/companion/inc/canada.cfm>

Figure 10.2: "Men younger than 40 experienced little or no gains in average earnings during the 1990s and make less than they did two decades ago," from the Statistics Canada publication "Earnings of Canadians: Making a living in the new economy, 2001 Census (Analysis series)," Catalogue 96F0030, March 2003, available at: <http://www12.statcan.ca/english/census01 /products/analytic/companion/earn/canada.cfm#3>

Figure 10.3: "Women less than 30 earn less than they did two decades ago," from the Statistics Canada publication "Earnings of Canadians: Making a living in the new economy, 2001 Census (Analysis series)," Catalogue 96F0030, March 2003, available at: <http://www12.statcan.ca /english/census01/products/analytic/companion/eam/canada.cfm#3>

BOOKS of RELATED INTEREST

RESHAPING THE WORLD FOR THE 21st CENTURY: Society and Growth
Virginia R. Smith

Evaluates post–World War II economic development efforts in the United States, in Canada, in Brazil, and in Mexico, and argues that the plan of the more fortunate countries to bring prosperity to the less developed ones failed: the development effort did not stop the growth of poverty, did not protect the environment sufficiently, and did not promote human rights energetically.

> Goes beyond the customary litany of critiques to offer, and analyze, potential avenues for improvement. —Arturo Escobar, Anthropology, University of Massachusetts

> A well thought-out work that exposes the dangers of the present political and ideological *malaise*. —J. Nef, Political Science and International Development, University of Guelph

VIRGINIA R. SMITH's articles have appeared in many publications including *Maclean's*, and the *Toronto Star*. She is the co-author of *Perpetuating Poverty: The Political Economy of Canadian Foreign Aid*.

208 pages ✱ paper 1-55164-194-1 $19.99 ✱ cloth 1-55164-195-X $48.99

PLANET EARTH: The Latest Weapon of War
Rosalie Bertell

Though Bertell's findings run from terrifying (the strategy of U.S. Space Command to fight in space), to outright bizarre (the U.S. military tossed 350 billion copper needles into orbit to create a "telecommunications shield" in the early 1960s, and they're still rotating around the planet), her greatest concern is how the quest for military power has destabilized the delicate natural balance of the earth's ecosystem, causing widespread devastation in environmental, economic and social terms and she calls for a new approach to security, which rises above national agendas, to seek global solutions to a global problem.

> A wealth of disturbing, almost unbelievable information. A no-nonsense writer who presents stark facts in an accessible fashion, Bertell builds her compelling case with care and solid methodology. —*Quill & Quire*

Scientist Dr ROSALIE BERTELL is a respected activist and lecturer, founder of the International Institute of Concern for Public Health, in Toronto, and author of *No Immediate Danger: Prognosis for a Radioactive Earth*.

272 pages ✱ paper 1-55164-182-8 $24.99 ✱ cloth 1-55164-183-6 $53.99

BOOKS of RELATED INTEREST

REBEL MUSICS
Human Rights, Resistant Sounds, and the Politics of Music Making

Daniel Fischlin, Ajay Heble, editors

Original in concept and content, *Rebel Musics* examines how musical activism resonates in practical, political terms, how musical resistance brings together voices that might otherwise remain silent, and how political action through music increases the potential for people to determine their own fate. It is a fascinating journey into a rich, complex world, where music and politics unite, where rebel musicians are mobilizing movements for political change and social justice.

> A rich collection of ideas and information about music that inspires, delights, and educates at the same time. It is especially welcome at a time when people are called upon by world events to walk out on the stage and do the unexpected. —Howard Zinn, *A People's History of the United States*

> Casts a wide net with respect to musicians, span of years and nationalities. —*Small Press Review*

> Diverse and challenging, celebratory but refreshingly realistic, I strongly recommend *Rebel Musics* to all those interested in music and its political possibilities. —Chris Gibson, University of New South Wales

Apart from the editors, contributors include: cabaret artist, author and musician Norman Nawrocki; film makers Marie Boti and Malcolm Guy; musician Jesse Stewart; poet George Elliott Clarke; author Timothy Brennan; author Martha Nandorfy; radio host Ray Pratt; and music reviewer Ron Sakolsky.

DANIEL FISCHLIN is Professor of English at the University of Guelph and co-author with Martha Nandorfy of *Eduardo Galeano: Through the Looking Glass* (Black Rose Books). He has been active as a musician for most of his life.

AJAY HEBLE is Professor of English at the University of Guelph and Artistic Director and Founder of The Guelph Jazz Festival. He is the author of *Landing on the Wrong Note: Jazz, Dissonance, and Critical Practice*.

264 pages, photogrpahs, bibliography, index
Paperback ISBN: 1-55164-230-1 $24.99
Hardcover ISBN: 1-55164-231-X $53.99

BOOKS of RELATED INTEREST

PARTICIPATORY DEMOCRACY: Prospects for Democratizing Democracy
Dimitrios Roussopoulos, C.George Benello, editors

This wide-ranging collection probes the historical roots of participatory democracy in our political culture, analyzes its application to the problems of modern society, and explores the possible forms it might take on every level of society.

Apart from the editors, contributors include: George Woodcock, Murray Bookchin, Don Calhoun, Stewart Perry, Rosabeth Moss Kanter, James Gillespie, Gerry Hunnius, John McEwan, Arthur Chickering, Christian Bay, Martin Oppenheimer, Colin Ward, Sergio Baierle, Anne Latendresse, Bartha Rodin, and C.L.R. James.

DIMITRIOS ROUSSOPOULOS is an author, activist and political economist. C.GEORGE BENELLO taught at Goddard College until his untimely death.

380 pages ✳ paper 1-55164-224-7 $24.99 ✳ cloth 1-55164-225-5 $53.99

YEAR 501:The Conquest Continues
Noam Chomsky

From the brutality of Christopher Columbus upon his arrival in the Americas to the persecution of Indonesians in the 1960s, Chomsky appeals to the reader to review the evidence amassed over the last 500 years.

Offers a savage critique of the new world order. —*MacLean's Magazine*

Tough, didactic, [Chomsky] skins back the lies of those who make decisions. —*Globe and Mail*

A world renowned author, linguist, radical philosopher, and outspoken critic of the mass media and U.S. foreign policy, NOAM CHOMSKY is Institute Professor of the Department of Linguistics and Philosophy at MIT.

331 pages ✳ paper 1-895431-62-X $19.99 ✳ cloth 1-895431-63-8 $48.99

---

send for a free catalogue of all our titles

 BLACK ROSE BOOKS

C.P. 1258, Succ. Place du Parc
Montréal, Québec
H2X 4A7 Canada

or visit our website at http://www.web.net/blackrosebooks

Printed by the workers of
MARC VEILLEUX IMPRIMEUR INC.
Boucherville, Québec
for Black Rose Books